IMAGES
of America

AROUND RIPLEY

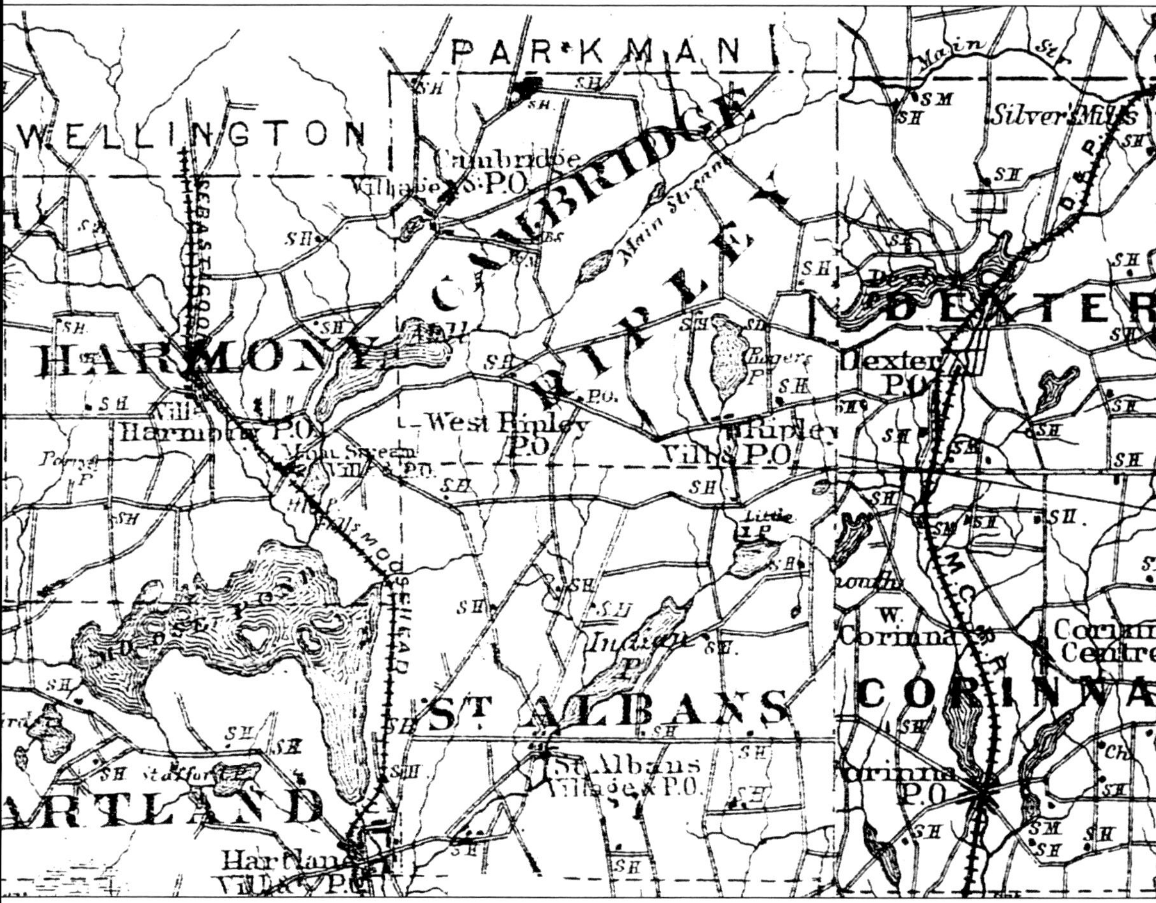

THE FIVE TOWNS AROUND RIPLEY, 1884. Known today as "the heart of Maine," this part of central Maine is a scenic area popular for its green rolling hills, uncrowded atmosphere, and pleasant people.

IMAGES
of America

AROUND RIPLEY

Frank E. Spizuoco

ARCADIA
PUBLISHING

ISBN 0-7385-1332-6
First printed in 2003.

Published by Arcadia Publishing
Charleston, South Carolina

Printed in the United States of America

Library of Congress Catalog Card Number: 2003109378

For all general information, contact Arcadia Publishing:
Telephone 843-853-2070
Fax 843-853-0044
E-mail sales@arcadiapublishing.com

For customer service and orders:
Toll-free 1-888-313-2665

Visit us on the Internet at www.arcadiapublishing.com.

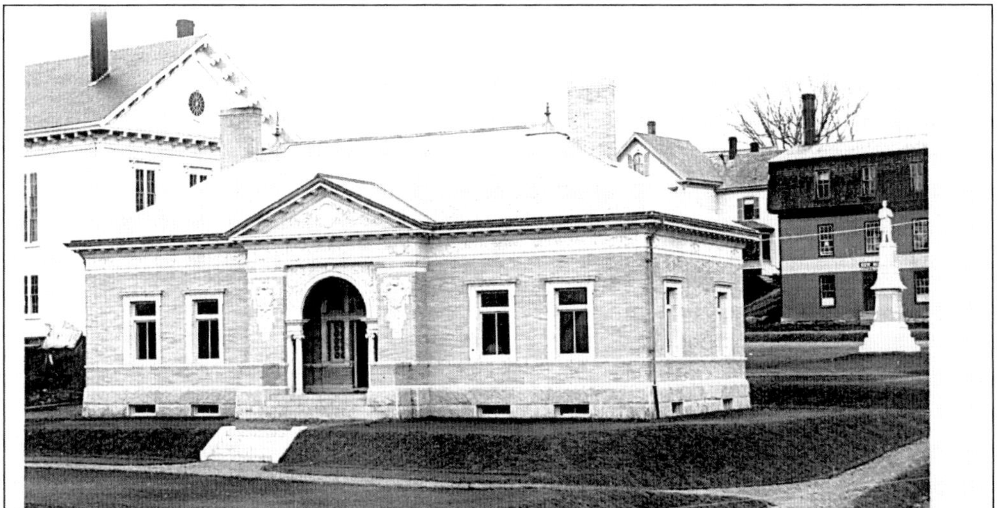

The Abbott Memorial Library, Dexter. This postcard was mailed from Dexter on December 13, 1905, to Ava Leach in South Paris, Maine.

Contents

ACKNOWLEDGMENTS

I approached each historical society in the six towns and asked for help to secure exciting, moving photographs that pictured their community. It involved many hours seated at kitchen tables, poring over personal photographs of families and viewing snapshots possibly ignored since they were taken many years ago. Slowly, the word spread in each town, and it became easier to get photographs to look at and to choose the ones appropriate for the book.

I must thank each historical society and key members who helped me locate photographs: Lloyd and Audrey Bolstridge and Carl Smith, from the Corinna Historical Society; Wendall Bubar, from the St. Albans Historical Society; Roland Herrick, Debbie Burdin, Evelyn and Ed Farrar, Carolyn Dubay, and Elmer Folsom, from the Cambridge Historical Society; Paul and Barbara Herrick and Robert Decker, from the Harmony Historical Society; Rita Farrar, Andy Sevey, and Ginny Ellms, from the Ripley Historical Society; and Rick Whitney and Carol Feurtado, from the Dexter Historical Society. Carol also helped with proofreading. Fred Wintle helped with captions and proofreading. Dave Breton, from Central Maine Drafting, printed maps, and the Dexter Print Shop made copies of those prints. The Advantage Gazette has an excellent technician in Duane Neverman, who skillfully scanned the photographs. Special thanks to Liz Breault, librarian at the Abbott Memorial Library, for providing inspiration and instant research about any topic.

INTRODUCTION

At one time 200 years ago, six tiny villages were settled no more than 15 miles apart, nestled in the rolling hills of central Maine. Their populations in 1810 were virtually identical. As waterpower technology advanced, those villages located on larger bodies of water with sufficient fall increased in population as industry and commerce developed. Three towns had the railroad, which greatly expanded their economic development for a time.

Electric power, the telephone, and the automobile were the great "eveners," and by the 20th century, waterpower made little difference for economic growth. The six towns soon accepted their fate and, after fluctuations in their populations, have become small hamlets that are bedroom communities for distant Bangor, Waterville, Skowhegan, and Dover-Foxcroft. Farming is almost extinct there today.

The area has mostly maintained its scenic beauty, with no large malls, condominiums, fast-food joints, or other markers of urban sprawl.

The fast-developing modern era has brought on a different kind of isolation unknown to the many small neighborhoods scattered about in each town that used to nurture, entertain, and care for each other. Each of the communities featured in this book of photographs taken over a 130-year period shows a vibrant rural way of life. Readers will notice many farm-related photographs. Everyone had ties to animals. If you did not know how to take care of a horse and drive it, you stayed home. If you did not know how to take care of other farm animals or dig your hands in the earth, you starved. Children grew up among many kinds of animals and an extended family that taught them valuable lessons of living. They learned to bond with animals and their grandparents at an early age. What a loss to our culture to eliminate from our lives direct contact with animals that we depended on for transportation, food, and spiritual enrichment, and to only see our grandparents occasionally.

The present-day residents of the communities featured in this book have taken the modern life in stride. They are proud of their towns and what they have accomplished in the past. All have historical societies to preserve and honor their previous citizens.

In "Ode to Ordinary People," Carl Sandburg wrote, "These are heroes then—among the plain people. They give all they've got and ask no questions and take what comes and what more do you want?"

—Frank E. Spizuoco

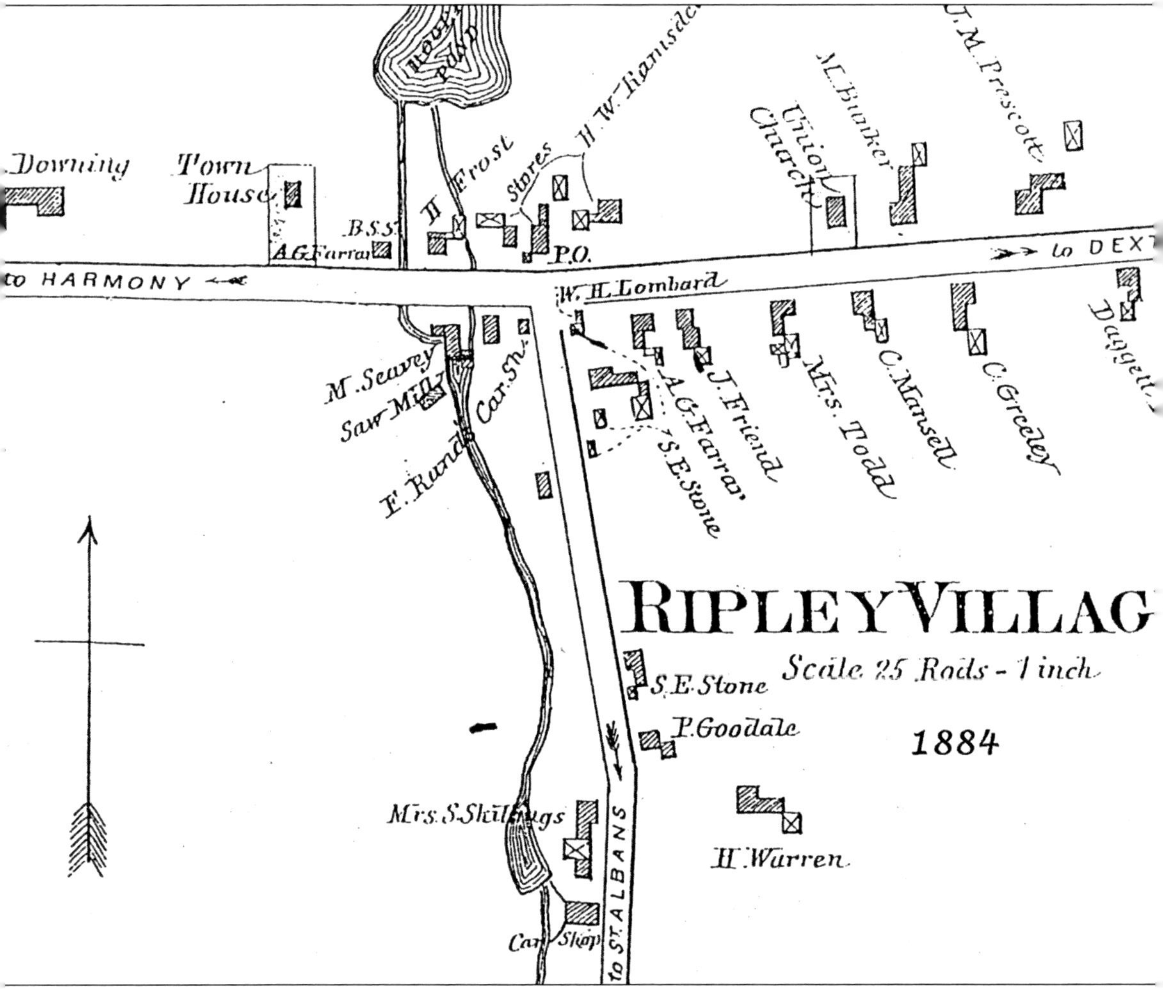

A Map of Intown Ripley, 1884. At the time this map was made, Ripley had one constable, one physician, three justices, two merchants, eight manufacturers, and one barber.

One

Ripley

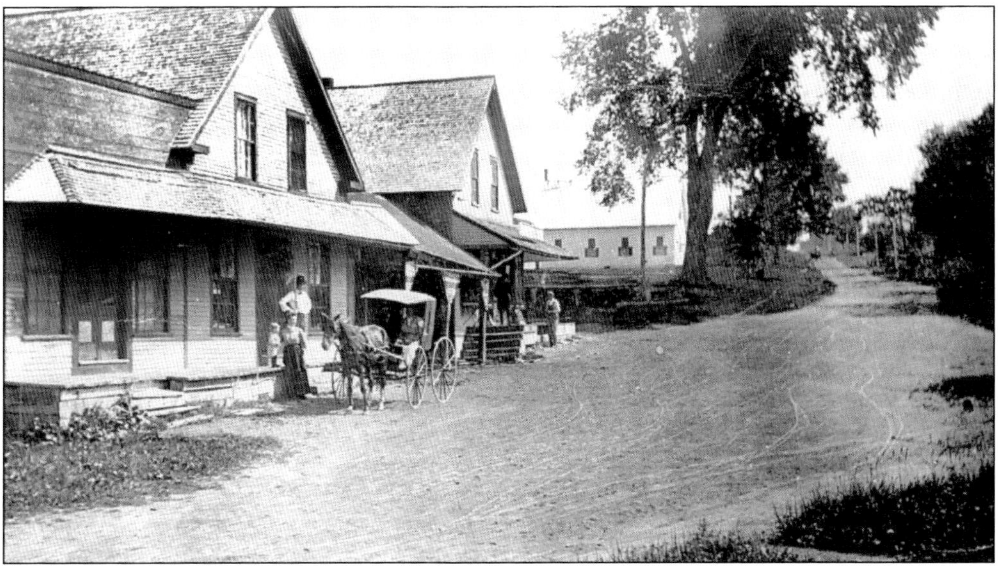

Main Street, Ripley, Maine. First settled in 1801 and incorporated in 1816, the town split off from Cambridge in 1834. The first settler was likely David Maloon (born in 1777), who was from Epping, New Hampshire. He moved to Todd's Corner in West Ripley in 1801. Ripley's population in 1820 was 325. Over the years, the population has fluctuated, with the highest at 655 in 1860 and the lowest at 297 in 1970. In 2000, Ripley was home to 452 people.

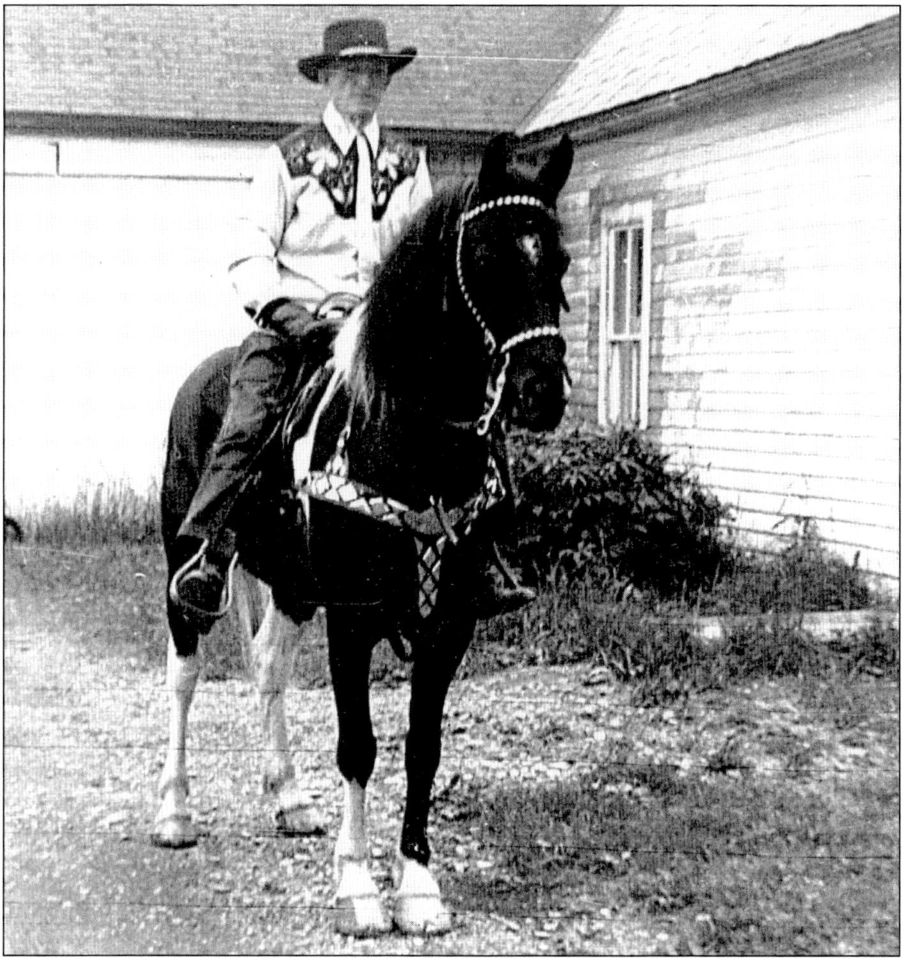

"**Myrtle, My Horse Has Come Home!**" With these few words, Les Rees was embroiled in a stolen horse escapade between Ripley and Dexter that is all but forgotten today. Camp Dexter had recently opened as a summer boys' camp on the shore of Lake Wassookeag, where I was employed. One morning, I discovered two horses and five ponies missing from the pasture. They ended up at Les Rees's farm in Ripley. Les had locked up Silver in his barn and chained him to the wall. The others were in his pasture. The police and sheriff were called. Les then collapsed in the excitement, and Hazel Rees Downing, his daughter, took the key out of his pocket and gave it to Don Holsapple to unchain the horse and "get out of Ripley," which he did immediately, using one of Les's bridles. I was chosen to return the bridle that evening, at which time Mr. Rees calmly related his story. It seemed a dealer by the name of Smith in Bangor sold a mule to Les that was no good. No one could ride him. Les said nothing to Smith but went back down to Bangor and bought a white horse for $100, paying $25 down and the rest on account. When Les got home, he called up Smith to come get his mule and considered the white horse as fully paid for. Smith was furious at getting beaten by Rees. Smith got a kid to rent the white horse, and when he was down the road, Smith picked up the horse with his truck. He sold the horse in Aroostook County. The next year, however, Clyde Harris of Corinna bought it and hauled it right back down and sold it to Camp Dexter, not three miles from Les's farm. Les Rees had hired a lawyer, who told him, "If you ever see that horse again, take him, he's yours." That is exactly what Les did on that June morning in 1957, when Silver was leading the pack back to Les's. Shown here is Les Rees on his favorite horse.

Hazel Rees Downing. The daughter of Les Rees, Hazel witnessed the stolen horse battle and helped Don Holsapple get away from her father with the horse. When Hazel turned 100 years old in the spring of 2003, she became the oldest living Ripley resident, beating Pauline Folsom by 11 days.

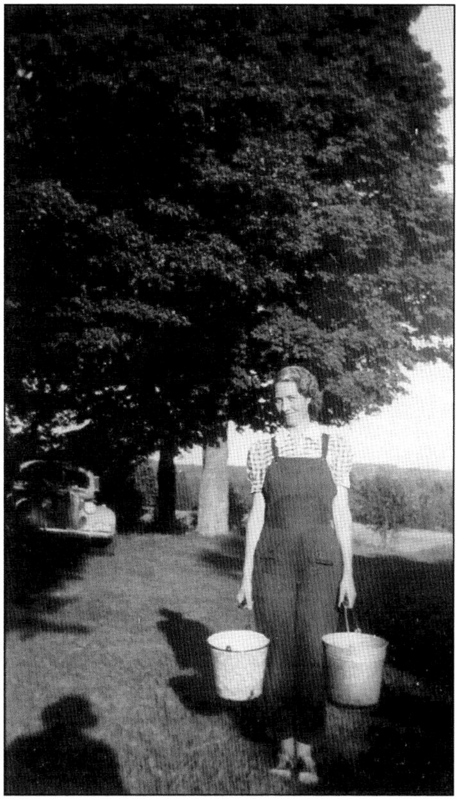

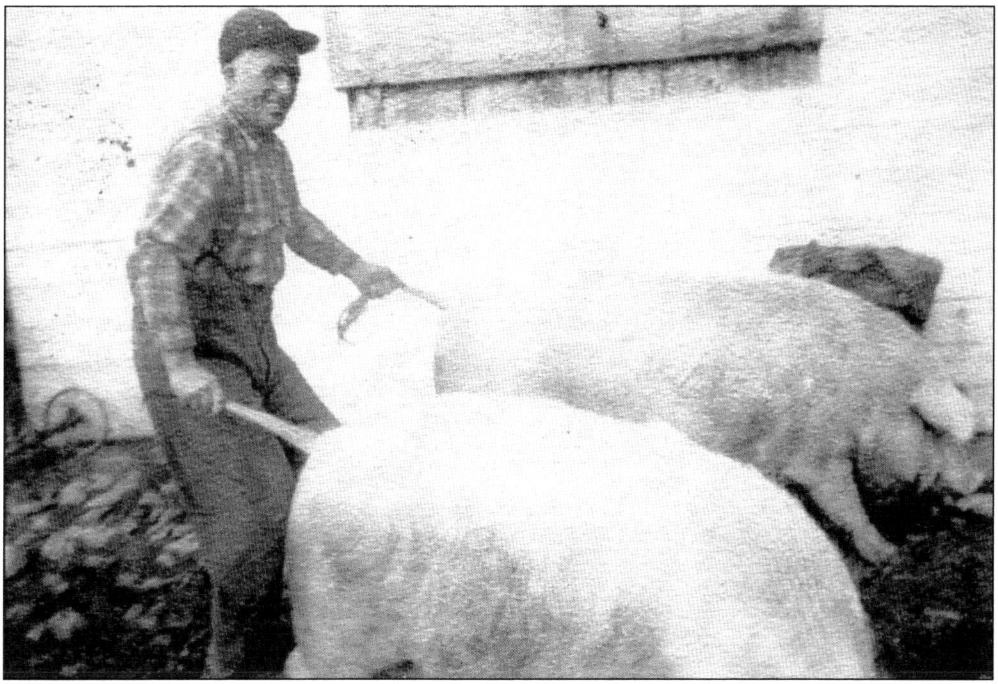

Les Rees Handling the Pigs. Gene Gould and others claimed they saw Les Rees jump in and out of 10 potato barrels in a row and then proceed to jump backward to the point he started from.

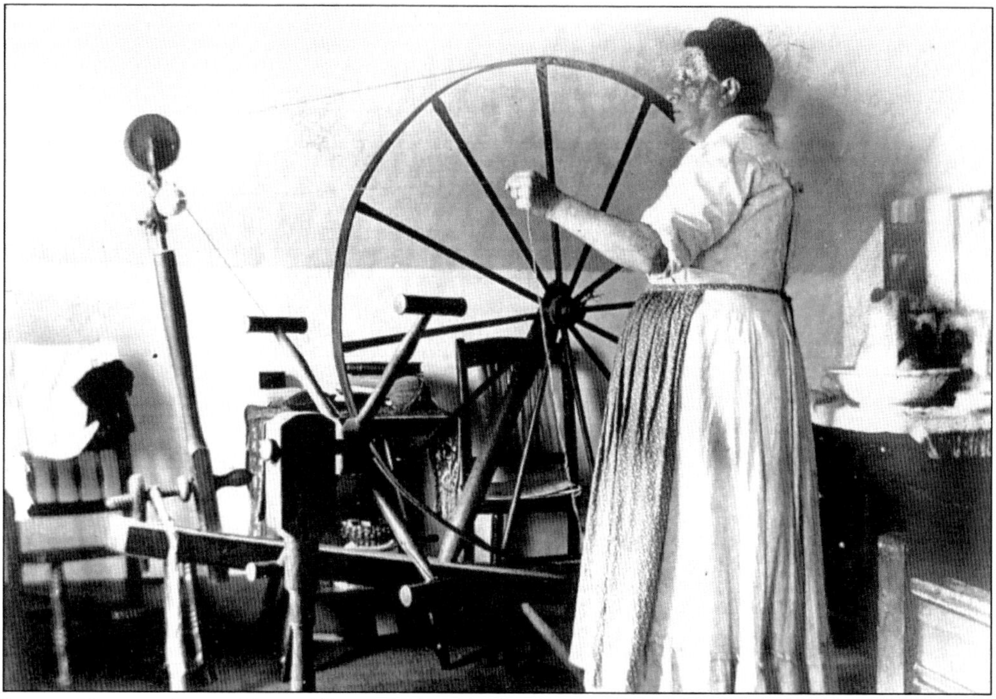

Lizzie Higgins Page Knew How to Spin. Ed Page's wife is seen at the spinning wheel in her Page Hill farm in the early 20th century. This upstairs sewing room was off-limits to the children and remained virtually unchanged into the 1970s. The farm burned in 1981. Everyone in the neighborhood remembered the family's pet crow, for it would supposedly drink milk from a dish on the kitchen table.

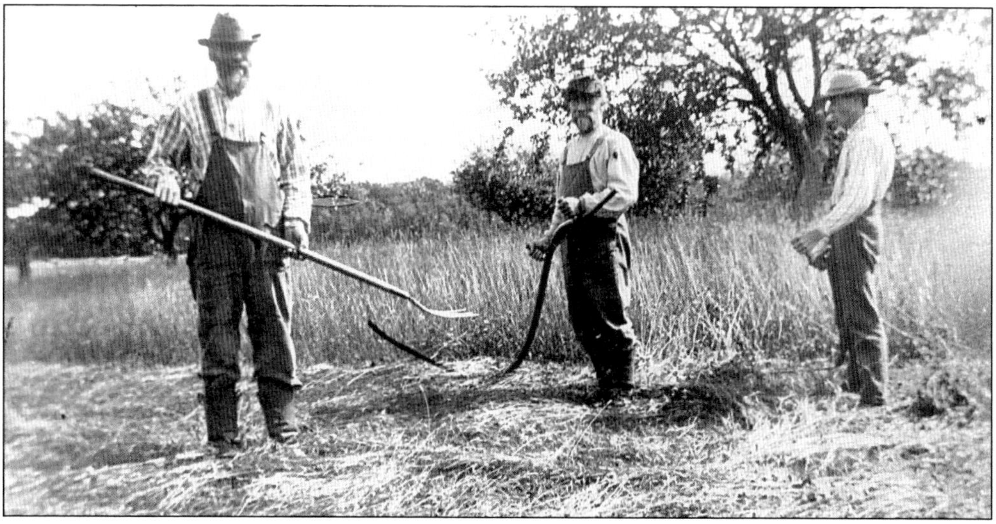

The Page Farm Boys Cutting Hay. The Pages were successful and prosperous farmers, and their ancestors were some of the earliest settlers of Ripley. Shown, from left to right, are Stanwood, Ardel, and Ed Page. It is said they frequently lent the Town of Ripley funds to help out until the necessary tax revenues were collected. The 1901 Ripley town report recorded a $200 loan to the town from J.A. Page. Early Ripley settler Josiah Page built a log house on the North Road *c.* 1804.

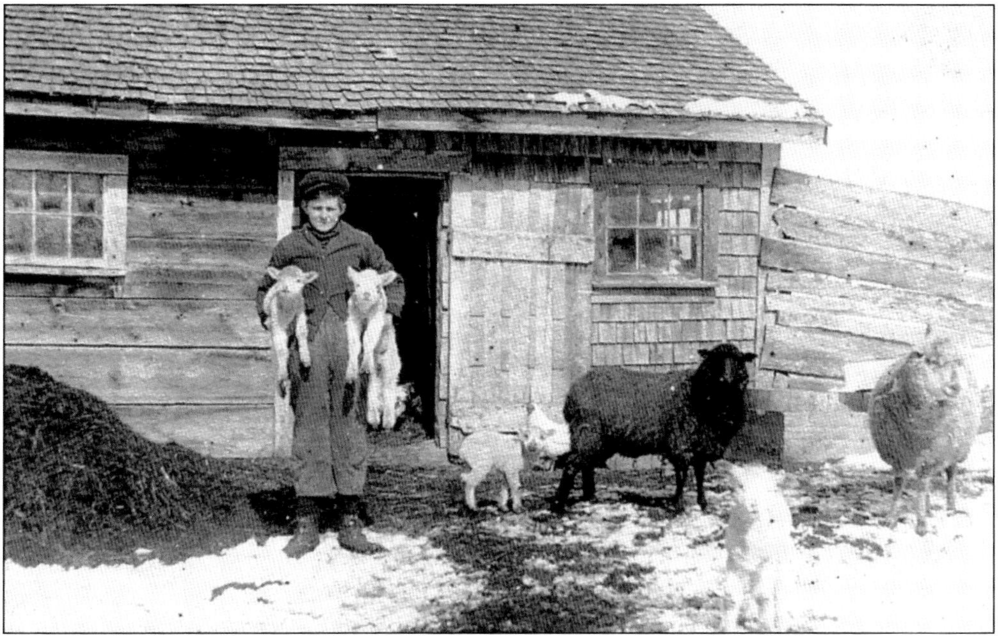

LAMBING TIME IN SPRING. On most Maine farms 100 years ago, this was a common and important scene. Every farm at one time had sheep. They provided vital food and clothing needs for the subsistence farms dotting the countryside all over New England. This photograph was taken c. 1910 by Jennie Perkins (Barbara Goulette's mother) at the Will Hurd farm on Chandler Hill. Ripley was home to 498 sheep in 1910.

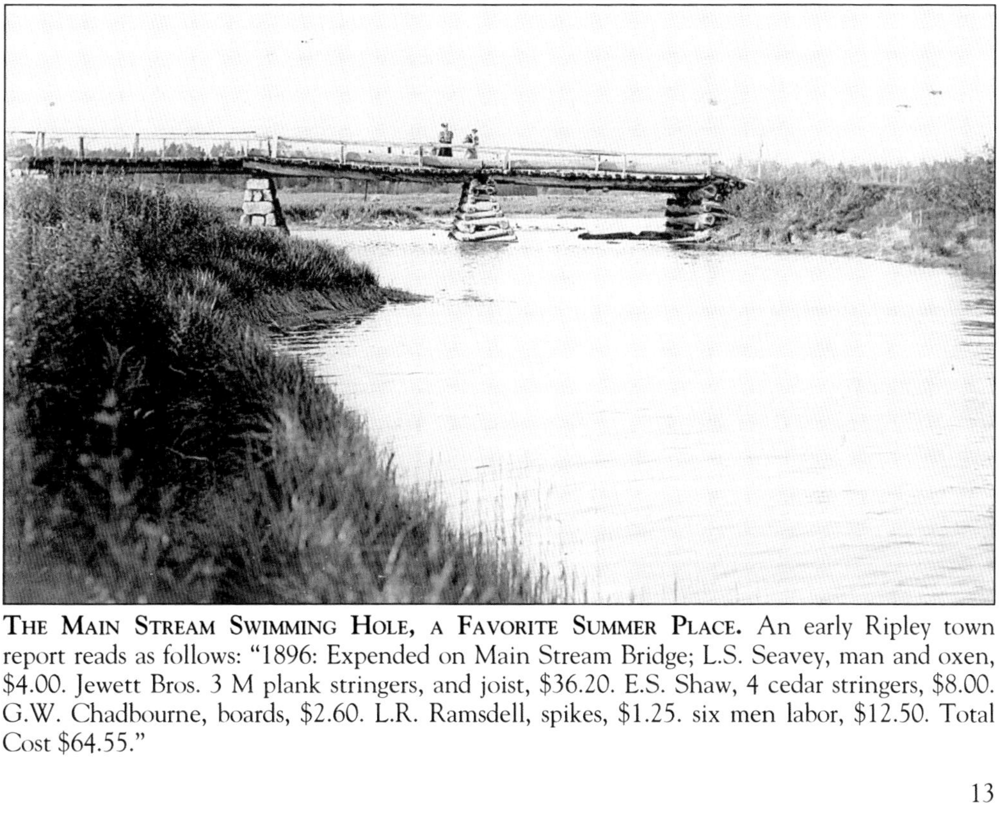

THE MAIN STREAM SWIMMING HOLE, A FAVORITE SUMMER PLACE. An early Ripley town report reads as follows: "1896: Expended on Main Stream Bridge; L.S. Seavey, man and oxen, $4.00. Jewett Bros. 3 M plank stringers, and joist, $36.20. E.S. Shaw, 4 cedar stringers, $8.00. G.W. Chadbourne, boards, $2.60. L.R. Ramsdell, spikes, $1.25. six men labor, $12.50. Total Cost $64.55."

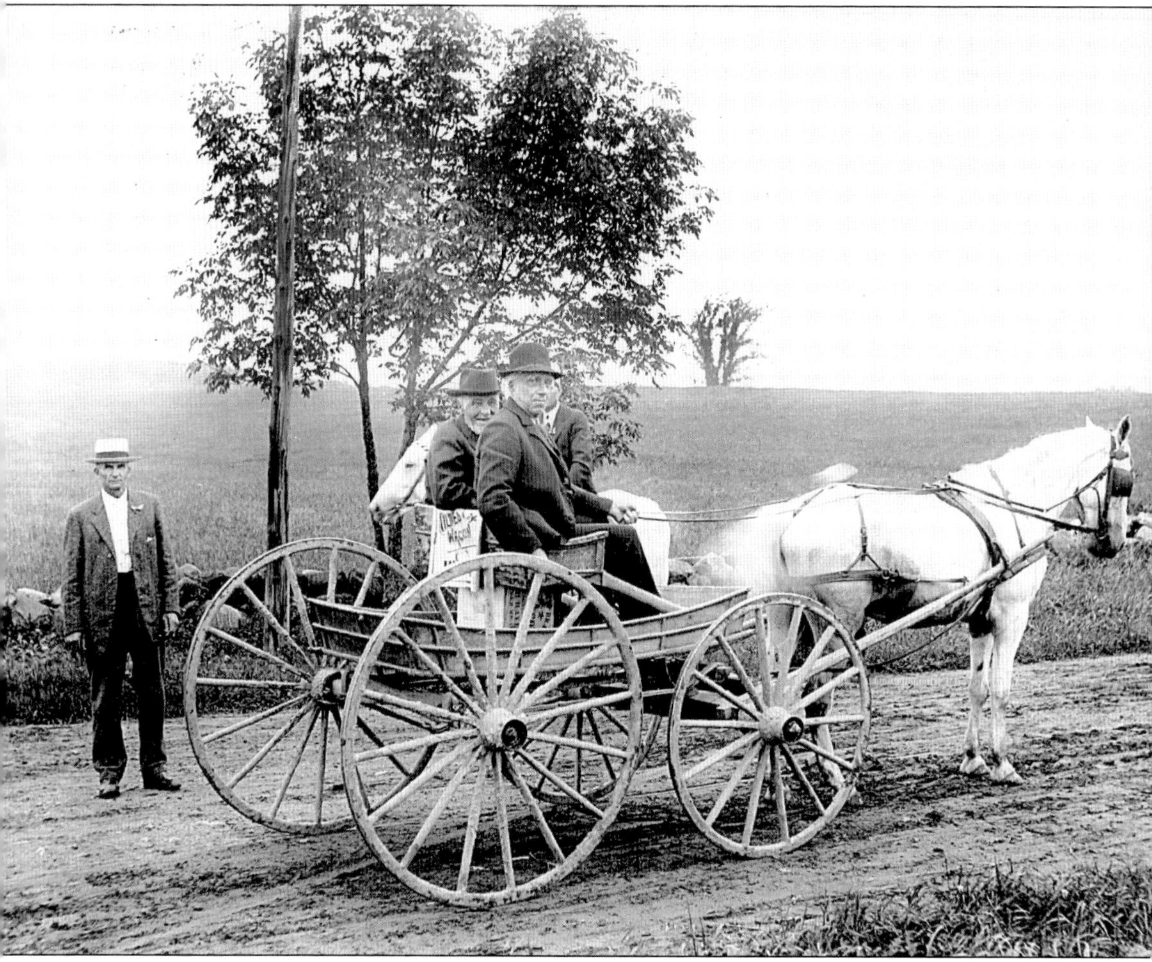

NEWLAND WOODCOCK, UNAWARE HIS STORE WILL BE ROBBED. Little did Newland Woodcock (standing behind the wagon) realize that as he celebrated the 1916 centennial of Ripley, his store on Main Street would soon be robbed. Joe Downing of Dexter was arrested and charged with breaking, entering, and larceny. Downing, called a "thief and midnight marauder" by the local newspaper, was nearly blind and was suspected of bringing his girlfriend's 12-year-old daughter along to assist him. Downing's farm was searched, and a large quantity of loot taken from Ripley was found as well as goods from Dexter stores. Deputy Levenseller believed that the Downing farm had been the headquarters for a gang of thieves who operated in the area for several years. This photograph shows Vic Hanson driving the oldest wagon in the 1916 celebration.

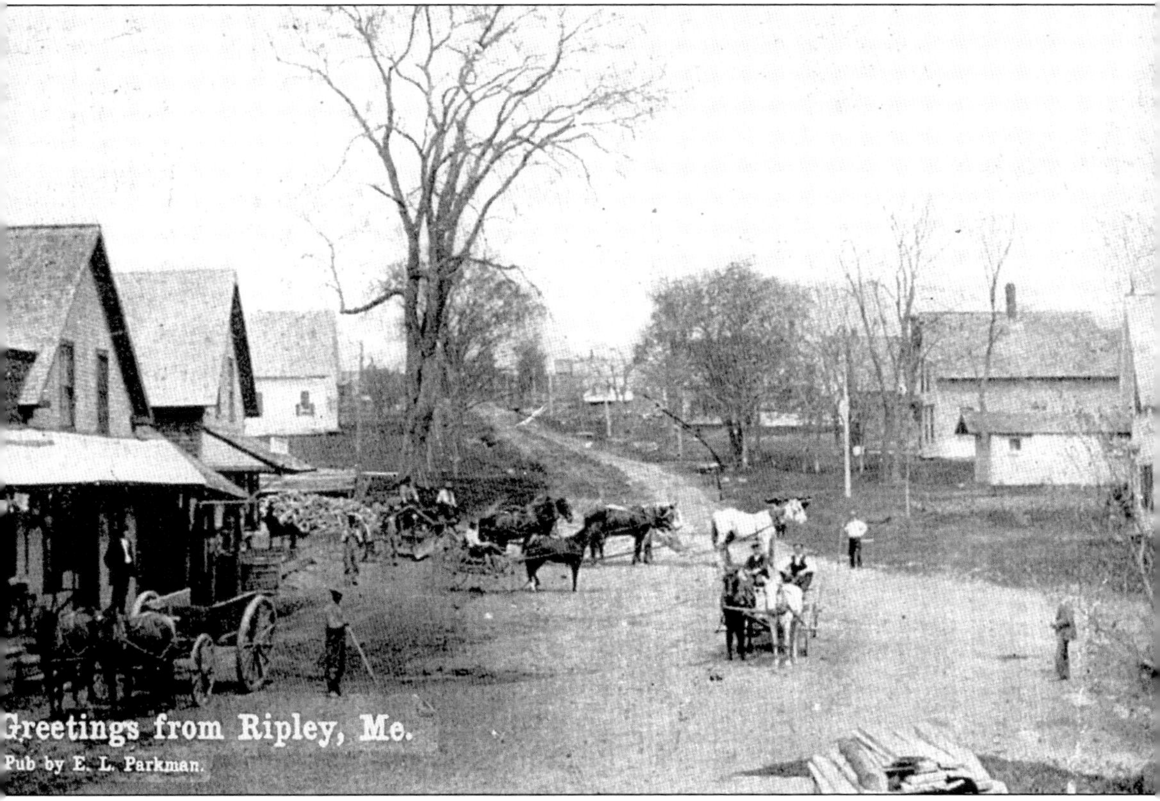

THE DOWNING GANG ROBS WOODCOCK'S RIPLEY STORE. Do not let this tranquil scene of Ripley Village fool you. When the people in this photograph went home at night, Joe Downing and his gang were roaming about, up to no good. While Downing was awaiting trial in Somerset County Jail, he sprung another surprise. His girlfriend, Mrs. Corson, originally from Solon, appeared at the Dexter Town Office and requested a marriage license. The selectman of Dexter refused to issue a license so as to prevent the marriage. "Mrs. Corson is a pauper with five children and Solon is reimbursing Dexter for her aid while she lives with Joe." If she married, she would become a charge of Dexter. We have no record of them ever marrying. We do know that Joe spent the winter of 1920 in Bangor Jail for illegally selling hard cider. When his time was up, he refused to leave jail, and Dexter was billed $5.25 monthly for room and board from Sheriff Orman P. Fernandez of Bangor. When the weather warmed, Joe came home.

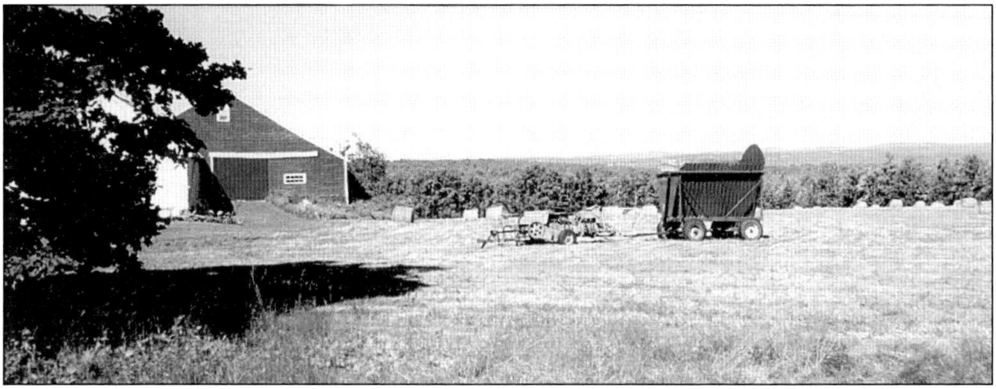

An Atheist Causes a Stir in Christian Ripley. On this scenic hillside at the corner of the North Road and Lane Road, John Langdon Jones (1811–1875) lived at one time. John stood out because of his refusal of a belief in God while living in a Christian community. He felt so strongly about it that he had a poem carved on his gravestone monument, espousing his disbelief in faith, resurrection, and life eternal. Jacob Hale also lived on this farm for a while before building an inn on Main Street. Since 1901, the Jones farm has been occupied by the Ellms family. Rufus Cooley's square hay baler is pictured, with large, round bales dotting the landscape in the background.

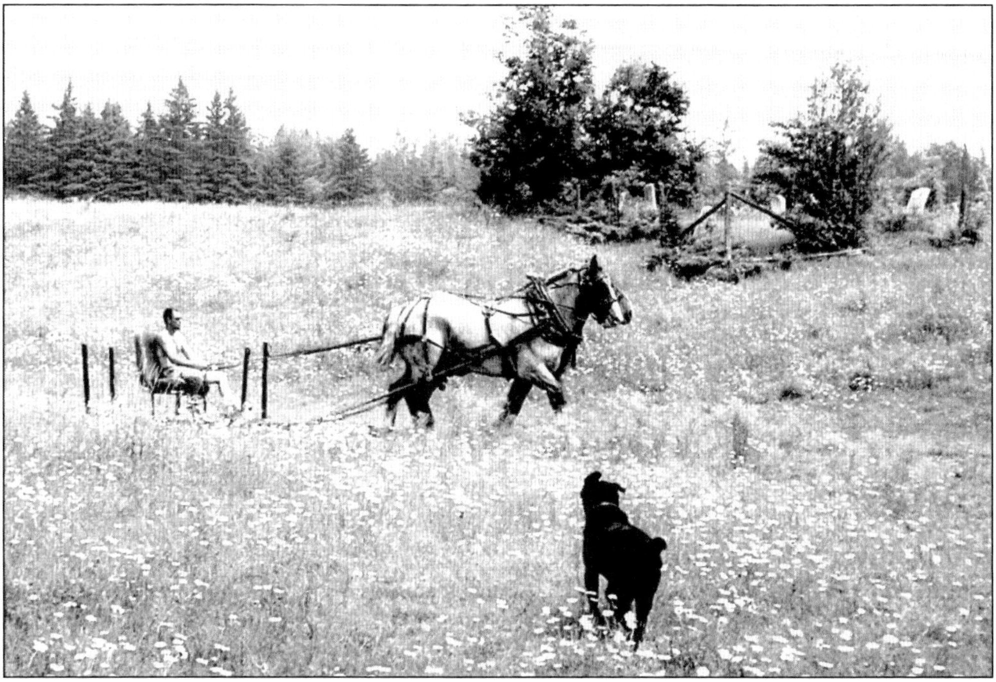

Teamsters, a Long Tradition in the Gould Family. Travis Gould trains Nip and King, preparing them for pulling at the fairs. Travis is the most recent Gould family member to be involved with horses. Travis's great-great-grandfather Freeland Gould had a livery stable on Spring Street in Dexter across from the Exchange Hotel. Freeland's brother Gershom was a local teamster and had a hay press business, selling hay all over New England. Travis's great-grandfather Harry raised and broke colts. Alton (Pat), Travis's grandfather and father Blaine had a team that went all over the state, winning horse-pulling events. Pat also broke and trained horses for the Mountain boys, "Nig" and "Nummie," at their farm on the Dover Road.

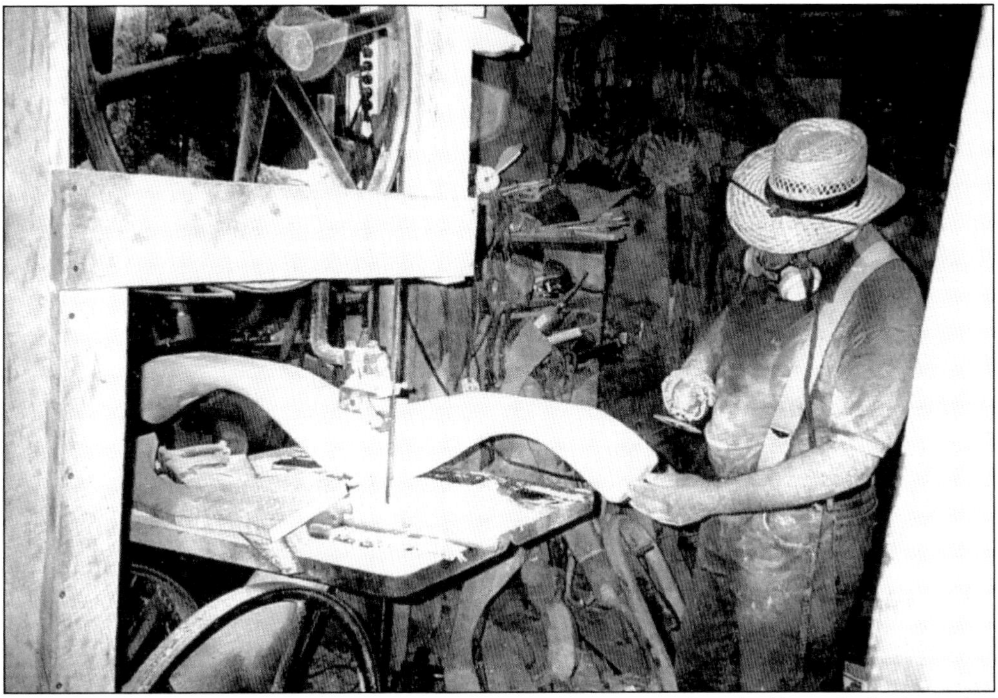

Bud Making an Ox Yoke for Delivery to California. Bud and Ellen Kluchnik settled on the North Road on the old Pat Gould place in 1994. From New Gloucester, they brought their skills in ox raising, training, showing, and dog grooming. Yoke orders come in from all over the United States. Head yokes are a specialty. Many times, Bud has to travel to the farm to personally fit the yoke, whether in Georgia, Michigan, or Arizona. Bud also has the sole dealership for horn knobs in the country and creates them in his shed, shipping them out by the dozen.

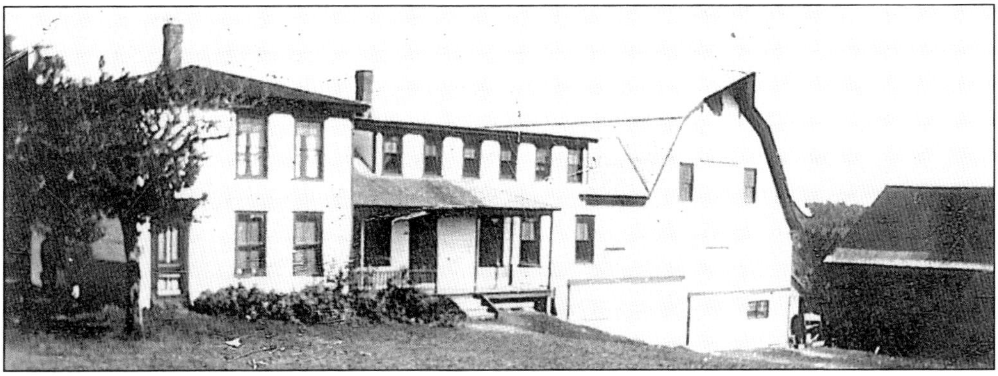

Farrar's Barn, a Hot Spot to Dance. Farrar's Barn was the place to be on Saturday night in Ripley for many years. Built *c.* 1917, it had always been a dance hall. Reginald and Grace Farrar were the owners. Reginald had at one time been superintendent of schools in Ripley, and Grace was a teacher. They moved to Buffalo, New York, in 1924 but came back and ran the dance hall in the summers until it burned in 1950. The barn was a great gathering place; people came from all over. The Annises from Harmony, the Petersons from Hartland, and many other locals gathered there. The Altons, Pages, Richardsons, and Laughtons were known to get into a scuffle now and then. Rumor had it that moonshine was hidden across the road from the dance hall. A woman nicknamed "the Green Hornet" was a regular there for many years.

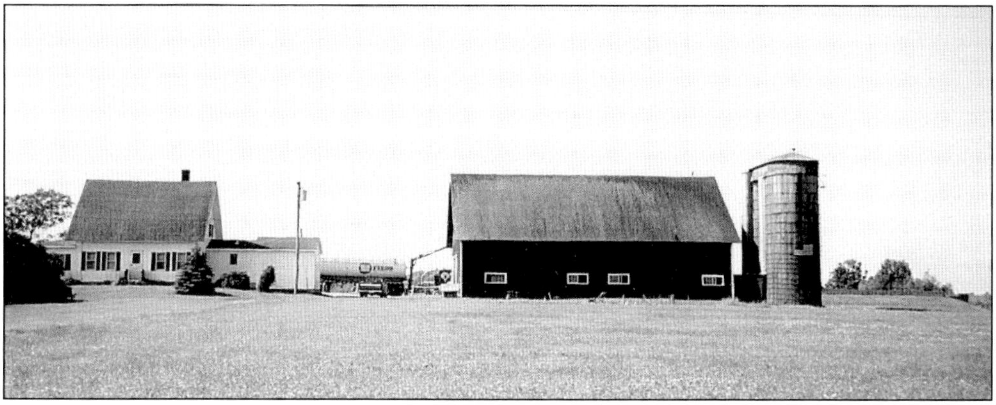

ANDREW SEVEY CARRIES ON A LONG FARMING TRADITION. John Jones first settled here in 1813. Long known as the Jones farm, it was sold in the 1930s to Carlos and Guy Wakefield, who then sold it to Charles Martin. In 1938, John Sevey purchased it. His son LaRoy graduated with a bachelor of science from the University of Maine in 1951. He and his wife, Mary, took control in 1955. His son Andrew also graduated from the University of Maine and went to work on the farm full time in 1982, taking control in 1995. Today, they care for 300 acres of tillable land, own 90 youngstock, milk 80 cows, and ship 500 gallons of milk each day.

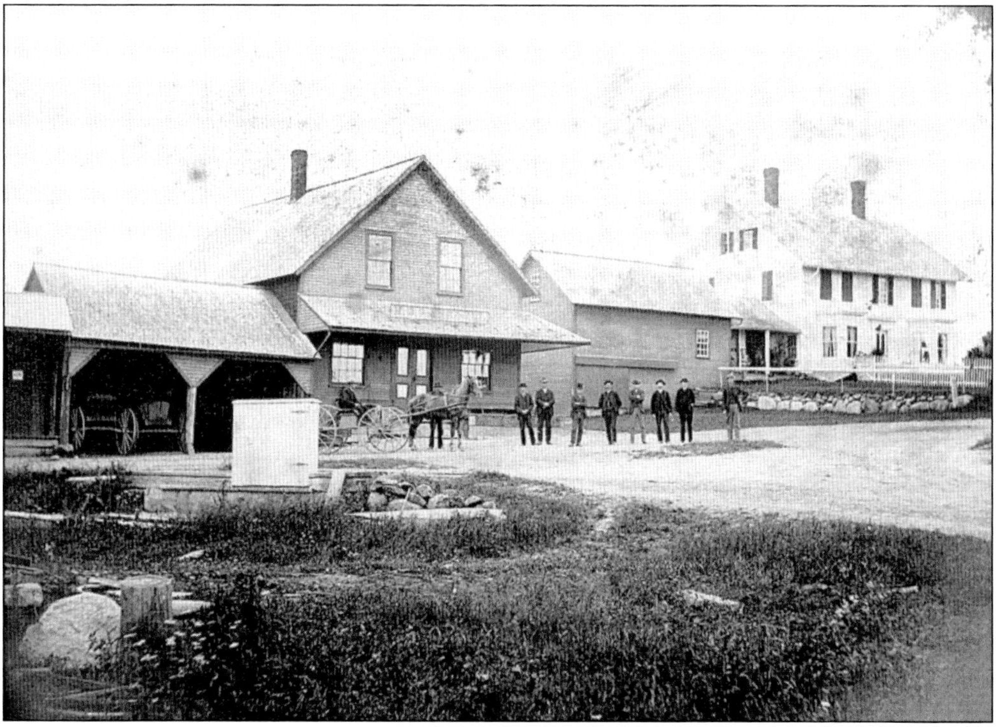

A 1984 FIRE DESTROYS THE FORMER RIPLEY INN. When fire destroyed Jacob Hale's inn (right) on Main Street, the cycle was complete. The inn was built in the early 1800s. In 1829, it was a stagecoach stop with a dance hall and meeting hall. The building was the heart of the town; various businesses sprung up around this central location. There were merchants selling groceries, shoes and boots, dry goods, and meat, along with a library, barbershop, blacksmith shop, cheese factory, and sawmill and gristmill over the stream. Today, there are no longer any buildings on this site where so much happened for so many years.

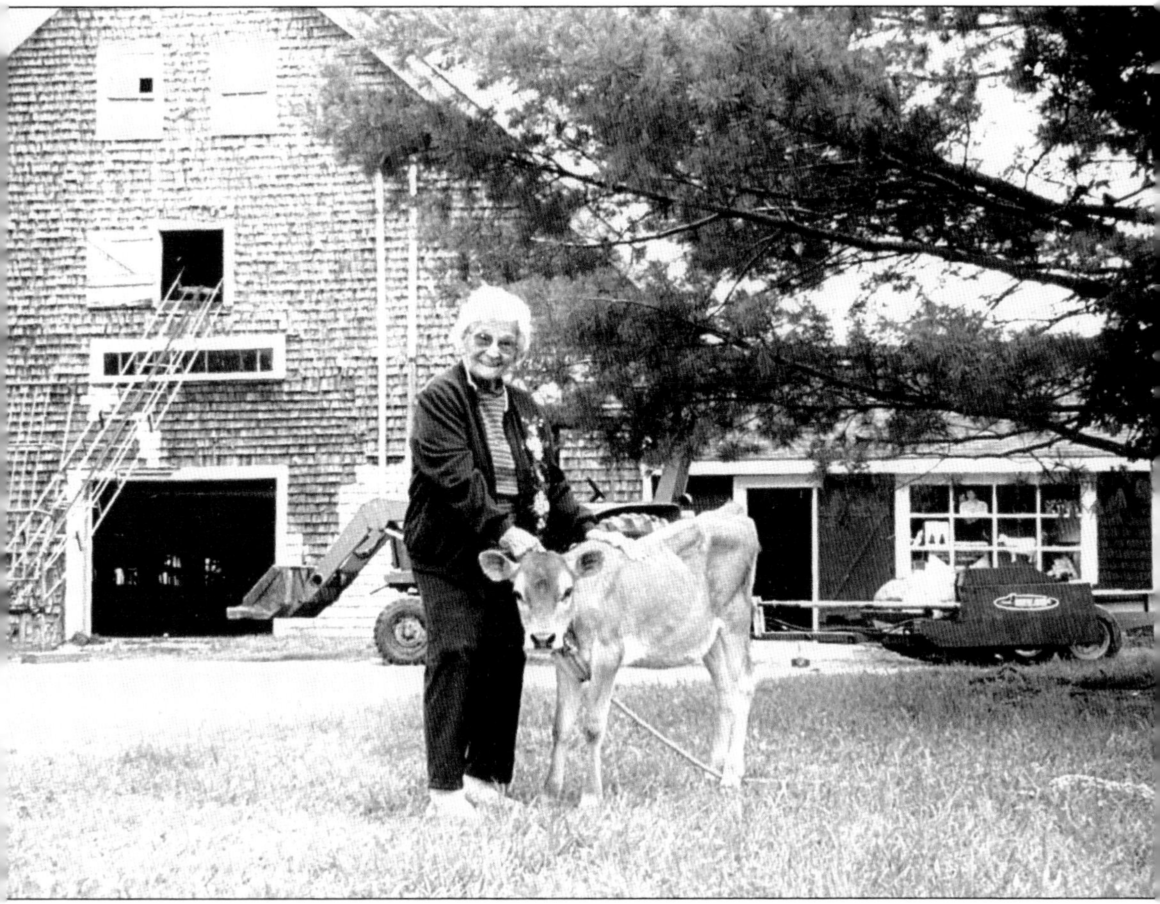

Pauline Folsom Reaches 100 Years Old. Pauline Folsom moved to Ripley in the 1930s and is still there today. Besides raising four children, for a good part of that time, she milked cows on the Chandler Hill Road. Her favorites were the Jersey and Guernsey breeds. She and her daughter milked 15 cows daily on one side of the barn while her husband, Albert, had his 15 Holsteins in a tie-up on the other side of the barn. This 2002 photograph of Pauline with a newborn Jersey calf shows that she has not lost her skill in handling cattle. Pauline turned 100 in 2003. In the background is the barn where she labored so industriously.

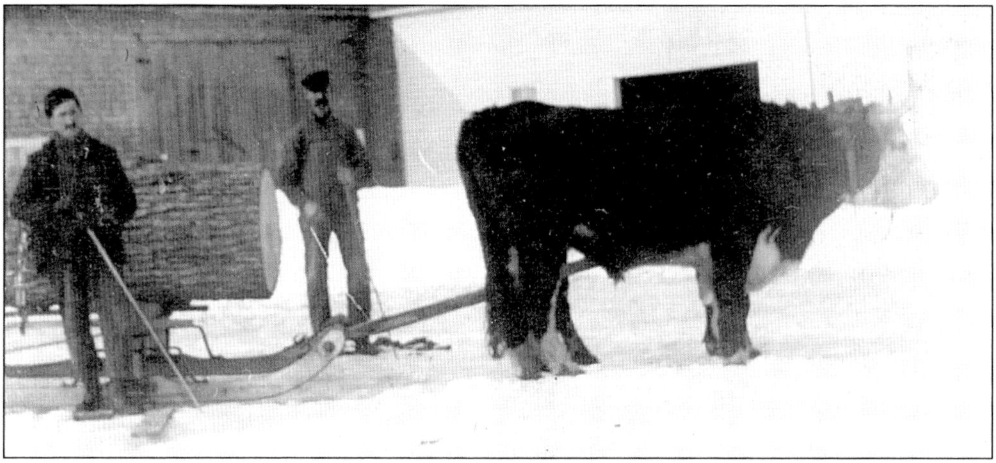

John H. Lane Falls under an Oxen Sled of Logs. John Lane, a 65-year-old farmer on the Chandler Hill Road, was fatally injured on April 12, 1912, while hauling a load of logs to the steam sawmill at the foot of Chandler Hill. The sled struck a stump, throwing him off, and the sled passed over his chest. Lane was one of the best-known farmers in these parts. He was the son of the late Jeremiah Lane and was past master and treasurer of the Dexter Grange. He was also past grand noble of the Plymouth Lodge, International Order of Odd Fellows (IOOF).

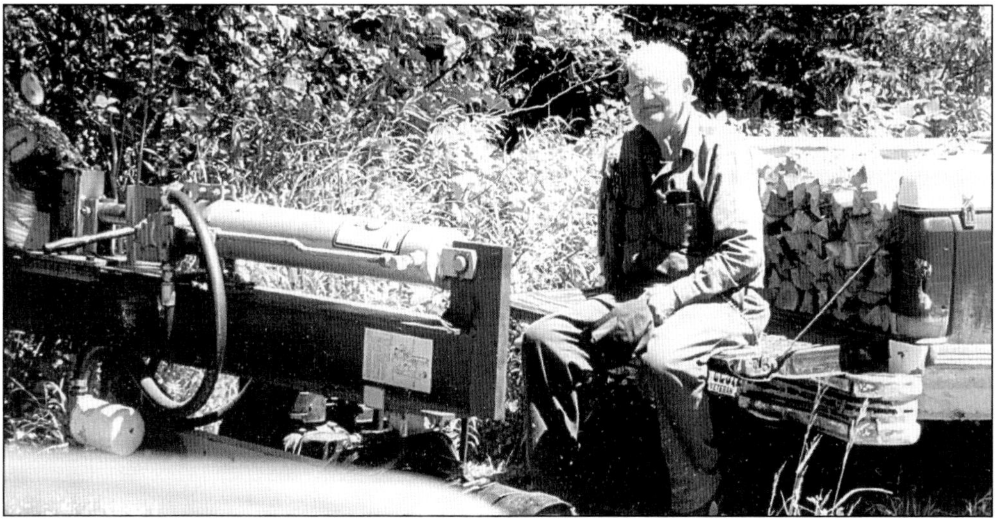

Bob Eaton Putting up His Wood. Bob Eaton is an institution around Ripley. In the woods or in the barn, Bob could be depended on to satisfy. The youngest of six children of Inez and Walter Eaton, he grew up on a beef and dairy farm in Dexter. He remembers "riding on a bull from the railroad station to the Bangor Fair and holding out a tin cup for donations as the entourage made its way through the Bangor streets." He joined the army during World War II and was in China when he got orders to head to Guam and then to Tokyo. He is glad Truman dropped the bomb because he feels he probably would not be here today if he had not. After the war, he was a short-order cook for Bill Nadeau, and then a taxi driver. He raised broilers on the Lane farm and then produced eggs on the Strout farm in Dexter. He drove a cattle truck for the Hanson brothers ("got no money, only an education"), hauling from Canada to Massachusetts. He worked for Rod Hutchins milking and doing field work. Eaton is retired now but recently purchased a 100-acre woodlot, and although over 80 years old, he can be seen regularly on the Lane Road getting out some pulp to sell. He married May Bane of Ripley in 2002.

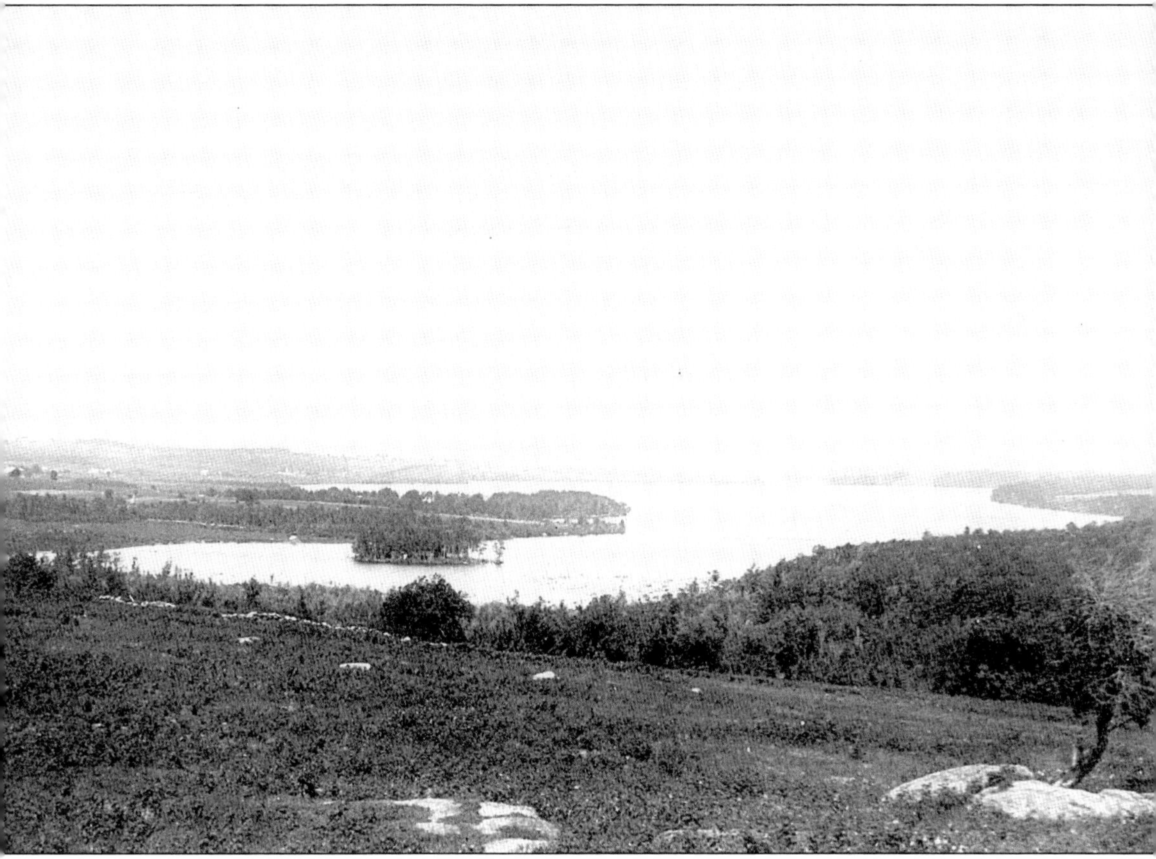

TWO RIPLEY SELECTMAN OUSTED; SEVEN TOWN MEETINGS IN ONE YEAR. This late-19th-century photograph overlooks Ripley's tranquil eastern boundary that goes through Lake Wassookeag by Cook's Island. The Tom Horn farm was on this scenic hill. Thomas Horn was Ripley treasurer in 1817. On February 12, 1821, Horn's wife gave birth to twins, Thomas and Sally. By 1842, the Horn family needed a better road to get from their farm and slaughterhouse to town. At the March 8 meeting, Article 12 to build a road from Chandler Hill to the Dexter town line was bypassed. On March 29, two new selectman were elected; John Hoyt and Joseph Perkins were ousted after only three weeks in office. Three road proposals were put on the warrant at this time. One proposal was to put a road from the Horn farm to the North Road alongside Nutter's property line. The road leading out of the village to St. Albans and from the Lane Road to the Dexter town line was also included in the squabble. At the April 12 meeting, there was a warrant to put a road from Ripley to St. Albans from Main Street. The April 21 meeting had a warrant again to go from the Horn farm along Nutter's line to the North Road. It took meetings in September and October to finally settle the dispute, and a road was voted to be built off Horn Hill to the Lane Road going north to Chandler Hill.

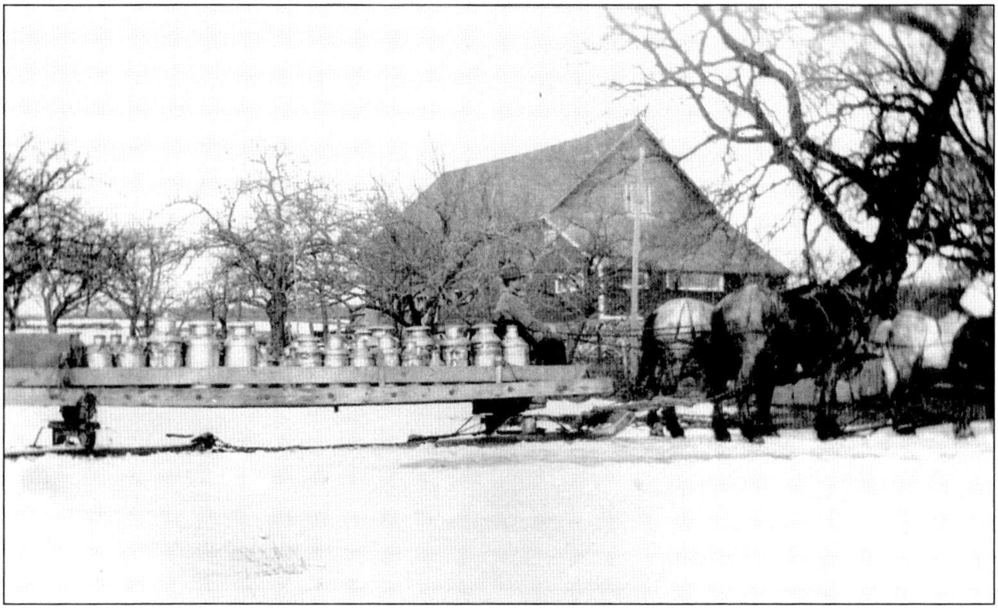

Ripley Roads Easier to Travel on Snow. Ripley has always had a hard time with its roads. At town meeting each year, there are still long heated discussions on how to best maintain and improve the roads. This photograph shows a large sled delivering cans of milk to be processed. Traveling on a snow-covered road made travel much easier—until "mud season" in the spring, when many roads are impassable.

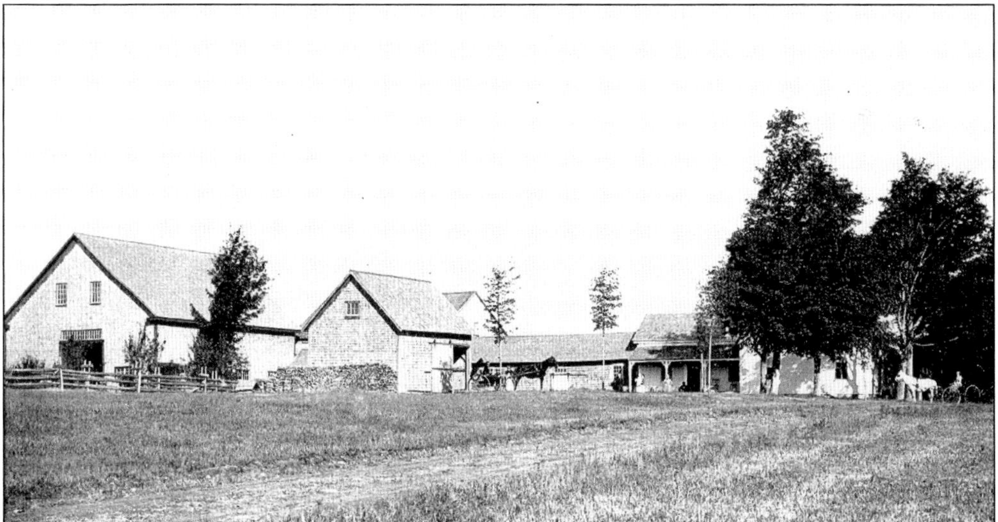

A Tragedy Strikes the Attractive Lane Road Farm. This photograph shows the Lane farm in earlier days. An undated clipping from the *Bangor Daily News* reads, "A May 1965 fire on this farm caused damage destroying 3 barns, 10 heifers, and 50 chickens owned by Rodney Hutchins." Soon after, a "Haying Bee" organized by Dean McKusick brought 50 men and boys to the farm to put up 7,000 bales of hay. Twelve tractors, five balers, and six rakes from 18 local farms could be seen going round and round each field until the hay was hauled in and put in a pile 90 feet by 30 feet and 16 feet high. Roland Kittridge delivered food from his home to the crew, who worked through the night.

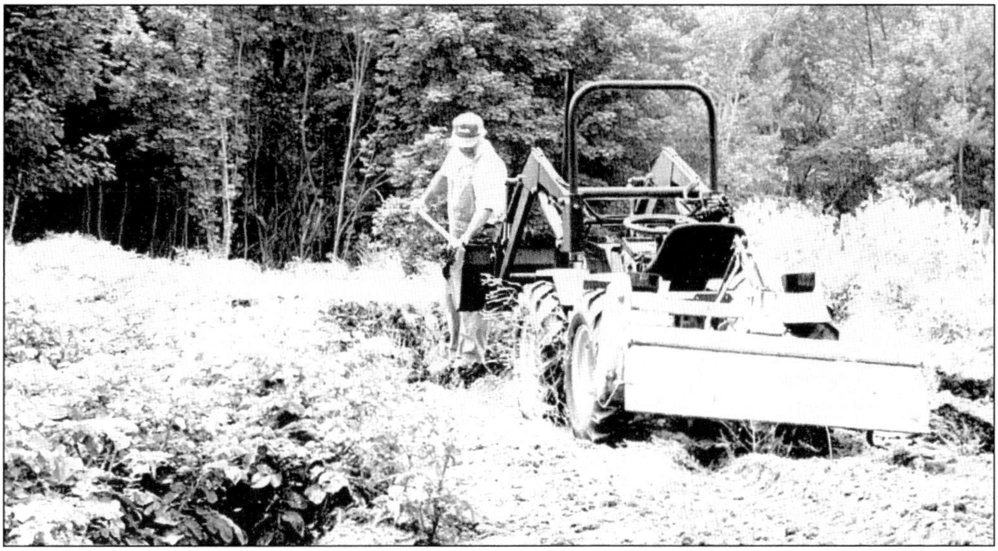

STEVE HOPKINS TENDING ASPARAGUS ON THE OLD JONATHON SEVEY FARM ON THE NORTH ROAD. "Manure is good for asparagus," comments Steve Hopkins as he heaps healthy forks of "dressing" on his well-tended garden. Steve and Sharon built on the Cooley farm some years after it burned. Rumor had it that Cooley had money hidden in various places, and some of the local youth dug around the charred ruins and the foundation for the treasure, but nothing was ever found. Steve's great-uncle Shephard Hopkins at one time was living in Ripley, and Shephard's brother Bradley (Steve's grandfather) thought he would give country living a try and moved in across the road from his brother. After one winter in isolation and mud in the spring, it was too much for his wife to take, and they soon moved back to Dexter.

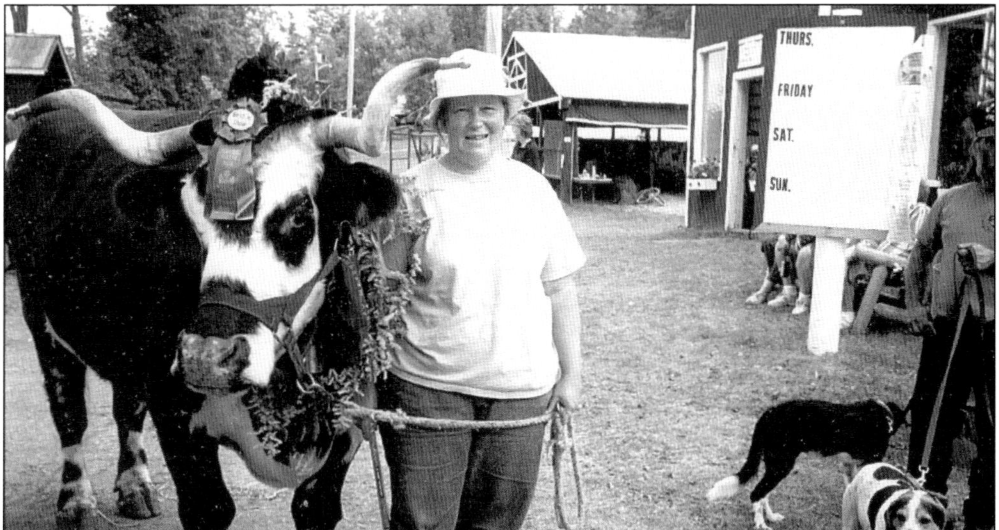

ELLEN KLUCHNIK SHOWS OFF RIBBONS WON BY SPARK. Pictured here is Spark, who is the "nigh" (left) ox of the team. Lion (not pictured) is the "off" ox of this blue ribbon show team. This photograph was taken at Piscataquis Fair in 1995, when the team was 12 years old and weighed 4,600 pounds. The oxen are a Shorthorn-Hereford cross that came from Yarmouth, Nova Scotia. Two dogs, Sammy and Mike, are being held by Harry Roberts to the right.

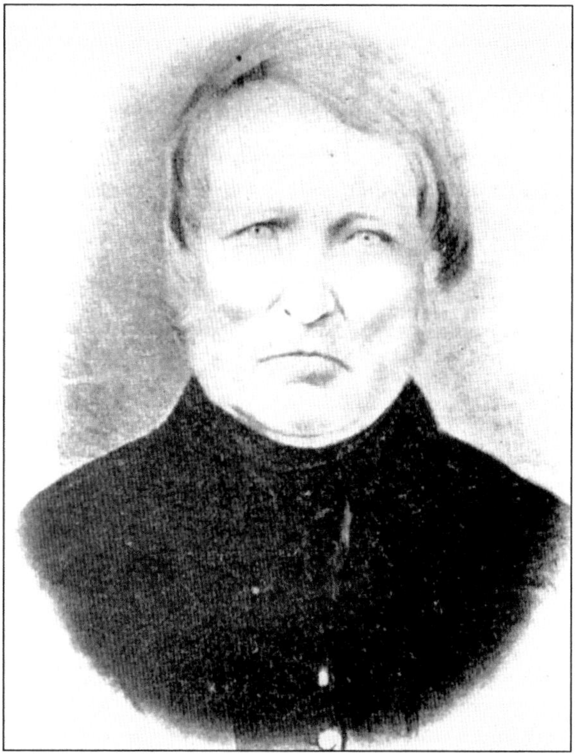

An Early Settler, William Hoyt, Thrown from His Horse. William Hoyt moved to Ripley in 1816 from Bradford, New Hampshire. He first worked at surveying, assisting his brother Stephen in lotting out Ripley and several other towns. He was a mason and was master of the Penobscot Lodge in Dexter in 1822. One evening while riding to attend a meeting in Garland, his horse bolted and threw him off. He continued to the lodge on foot while his horse headed for home. He then walked home after the meeting and stabled his horse before any of the family had wakened and discovered his riderless steed.

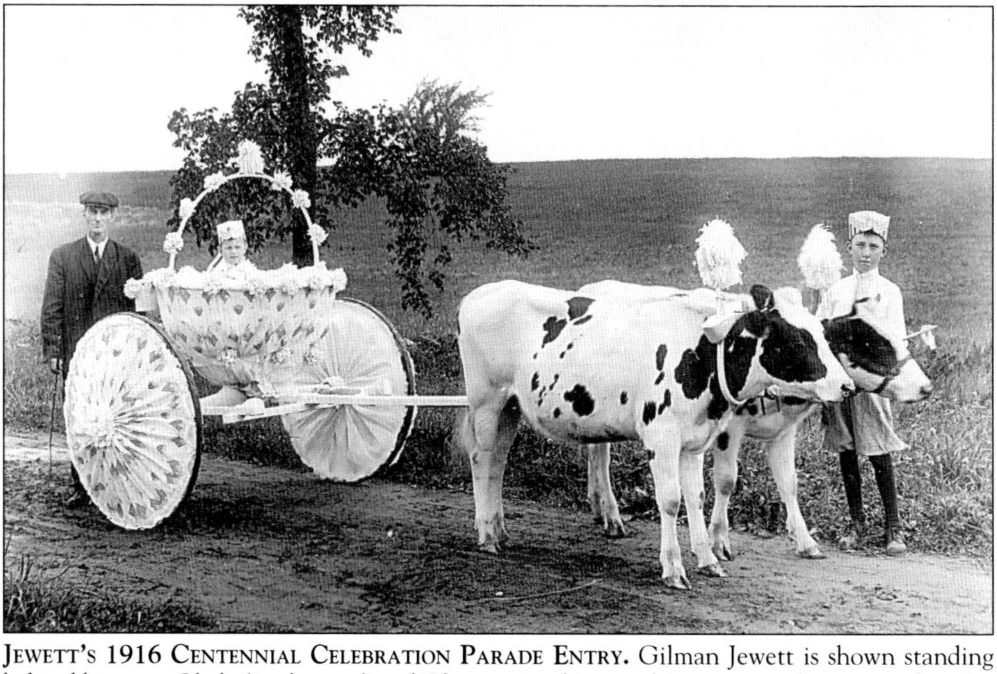

Jewett's 1916 Centennial Celebration Parade Entry. Gilman Jewett is shown standing behind his sons, Clyde (in the cart) and Clayton. Looking at this great parade entry and seeing Clyde's annual entry in Dexter's parades years later, it is apparent Clyde got his creativity from his dad. Clyde and Clayton later owned Eastland Dairies, a modern 32-cow milking operation and a packing plant with a steam boiler to sterilize the utensils.

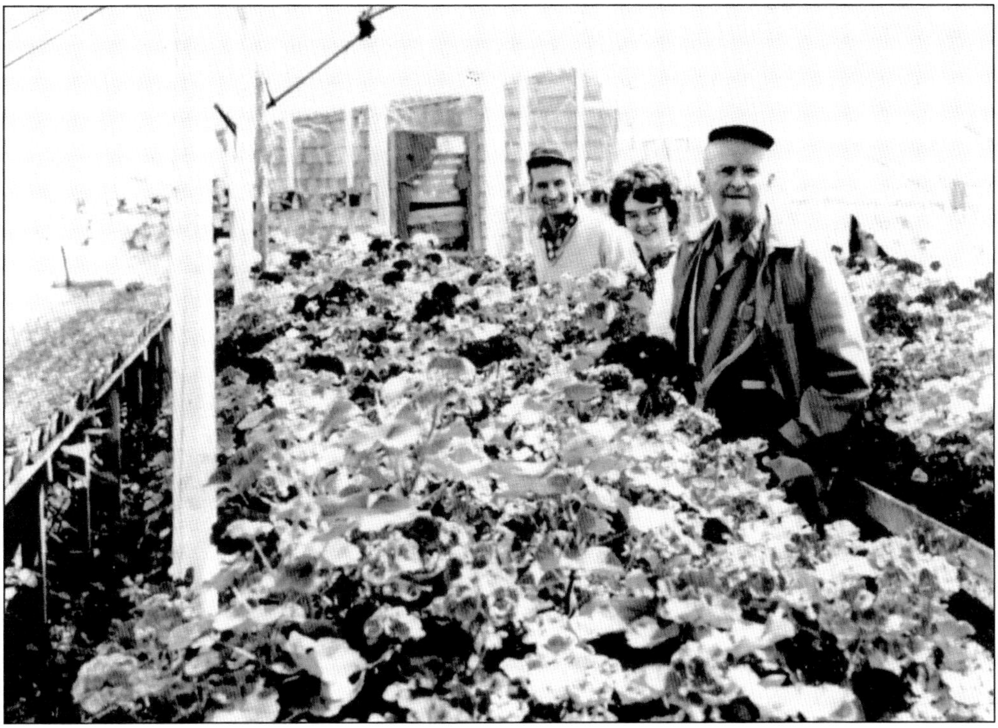

THE GROVE HILL GREENHOUSE, A RIPLEY TRADITION. The Ginseng and Medicinal Plant Gardens, owned by the Hoyts, was the first greenhouse business on the farm and was carried into the 20th century by Fred Haseltine and his family. Pictured, from left to right, are Ken Brasier, Nellie Brasier, and Fred Haseltine. In 1932, the *Eastern Gazette* reported, "F.L. Haseltine's greenhouses are filled to capacity with his plant seedlings, including several thousand tomatoes, celery, and cabbage, also pepper and cauliflower in the vegetable line and many varieties of flowers such as asters, snapdragons, petunias, pansies, carnations, phlox, zinnias, and chrysanthemum."

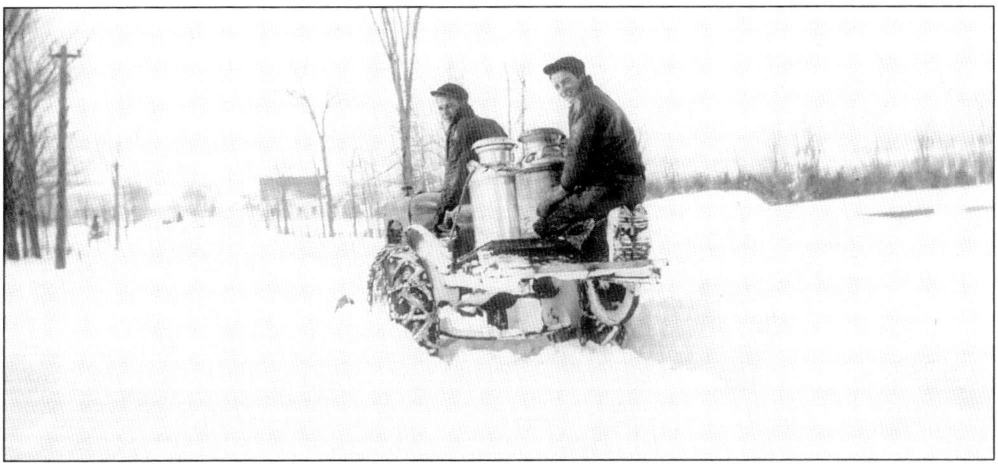

FEBRUARY 23, 1947. On this day, a storm closed the Main Street into Ripley. The only way to get milk to the truck was to deliver it to the Ellms Road, which was plowed. Tim Haseltine (driving) and Ken Brasier deliver cans of fresh milk to the truck at the corner to be hauled to Hood's in Newport for processing.

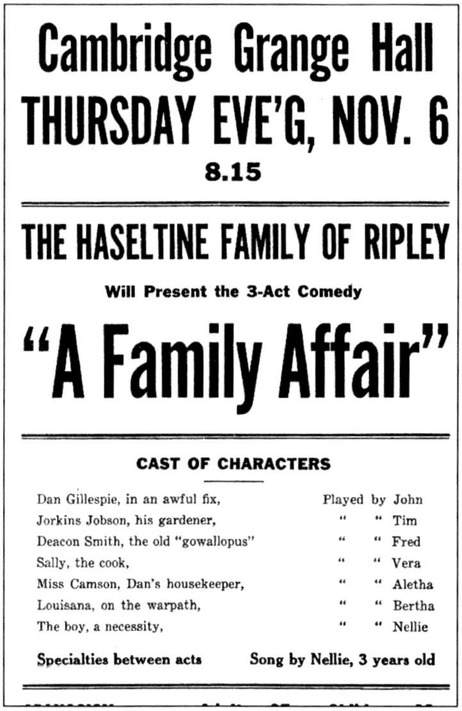
Cambridge Grange Hall

THURSDAY EVE'G, NOV. 6

8.15

THE HASELTINE FAMILY OF RIPLEY

Will Present the 3-Act Comedy

"A Family Affair"

CAST OF CHARACTERS

Dan Gillespie, in an awful fix,	Played by John
Jorkins Jobson, his gardener,	" " Tim
Deacon Smith, the old "gowallopus"	" " Fred
Sally, the cook,	" " Vera
Miss Camson, Dan's housekeeper,	" " Aletha
Louisana, on the warpath,	" " Bertha
The boy, a necessity,	" " Nellie

Specialties between acts   Song by Nellie, 3 years old

A FAMILY AFFAIR: THE HASELTINE FAMILY PUTS ON A PLAY IN CAMBRIDGE. Whether in dramatics or music, the talented Haseltine family is famous in the area. This 1930 playbill lists seven Haseltine family members performing in a play at the Cambridge Grange. Even as late as 1951, they performed benefits for many organizations.

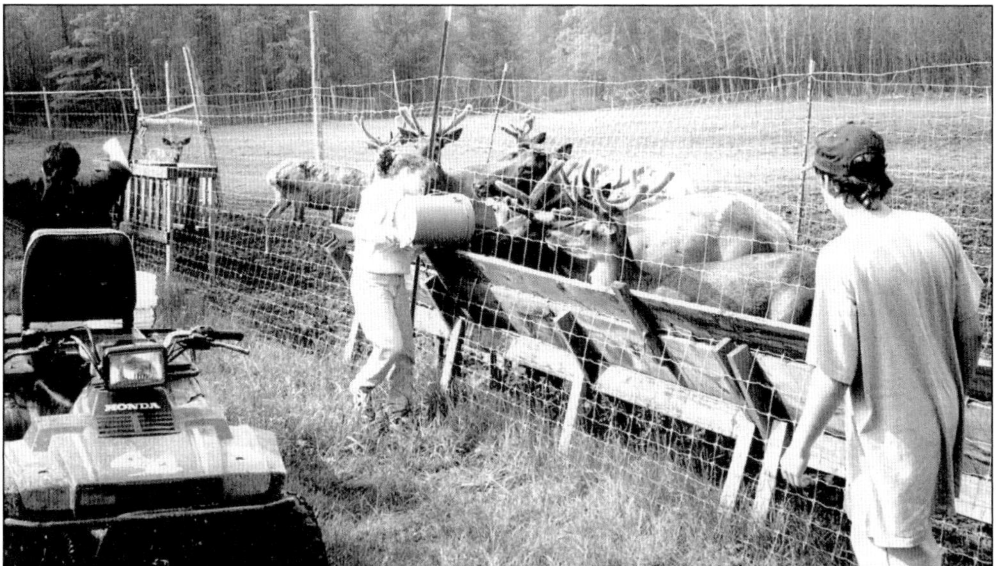

GROVE HILL DEER-RAISING REPLACES GREENHOUSES ON HOYT HILL. One of the earliest farms cleared in Ripley, Grove Hill has been the home of 300 red deer and 100 North American elk for the past 10 years. The owners market this game meat and purchase additional supplies under the Atlantic Game Meats brand. About 150 acres are fenced in. The deer are fed a total mixed ration (TMR) of corn silage, haylage, grain, and dry hay all mixed up and delivered by the Sherburne farm in nearby Dexter. Farm manager Dave Young says, "I can tell when the official breeding season begins. King goes through any fence we put up to get to the females; we can't stop him. And with the unique bugling sound from the elk going on, this place never has a dull moment."

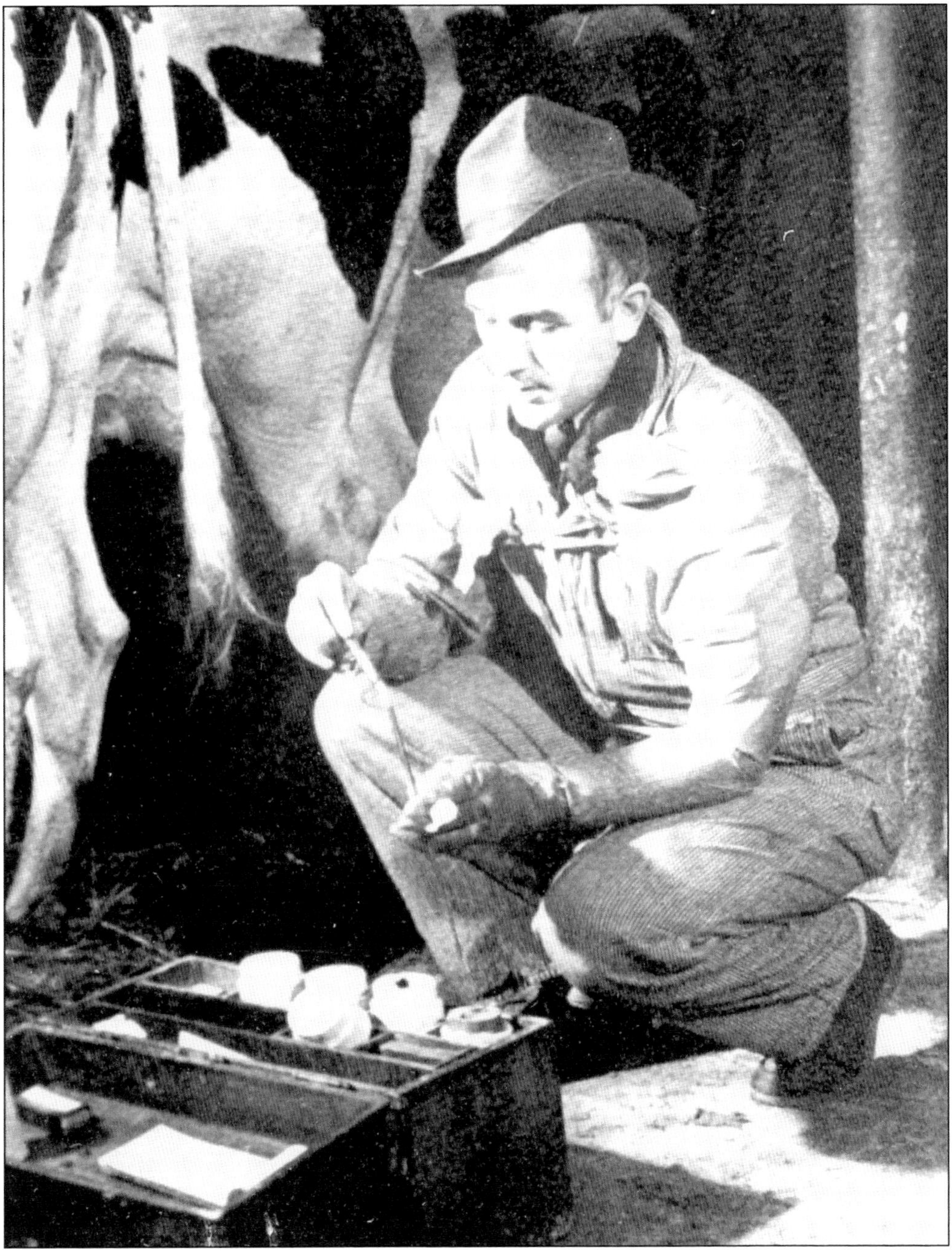

DR. JOHN WOODCOCK, VETERINARIAN. John Milton Woodcock graduated from the University of Massachusetts and Ontario Veterinary College. After graduation, he practiced for a while in New Jersey and then came to Pittsfield, Maine, where he said, "The phone rang off the hook." In 1962, he began work for the State of Maine, becoming the head of the Veterinarian Department, where he remained for 29 years. The Woodcock family was the most ingenious in town, if not the state. Hanging behind the kitchen wood stove was a toilet seat wrapped in cloth. Whenever anyone was going to the "shed," they quietly picked up the warm seat on the way out.

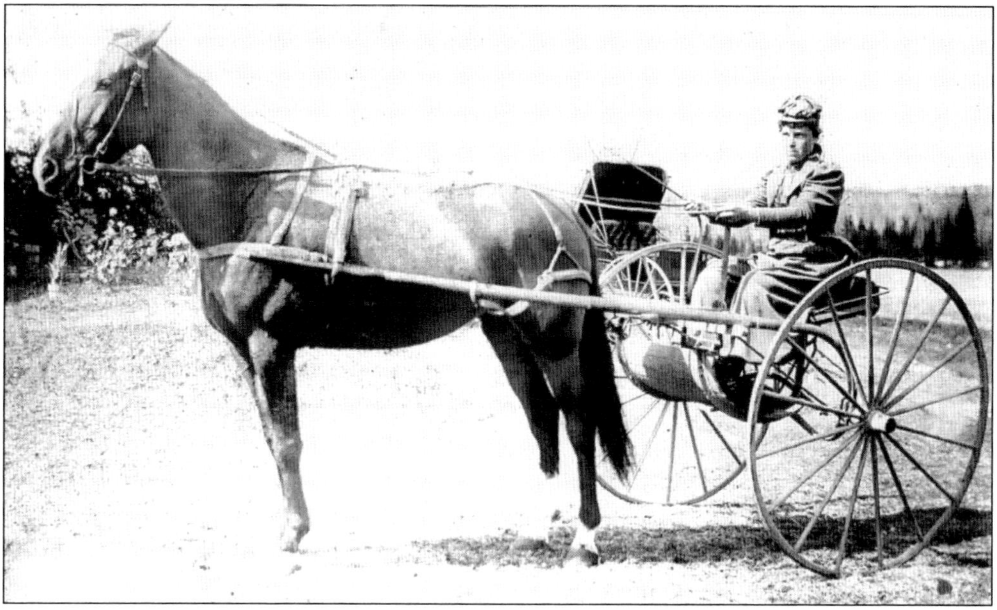

Mae Gould Woodcock Is Ready and Challenges You to a Race. Newland Woodcock's wife is shown driving one of her colts, Nel-Dio-Leo, in 1898 at the home farm. The sire of the colt was Dictator Chief, which had a mark of 2:09. Mae had a reputation as a "finder of lost objects" and was called on often to put her special powers to work.

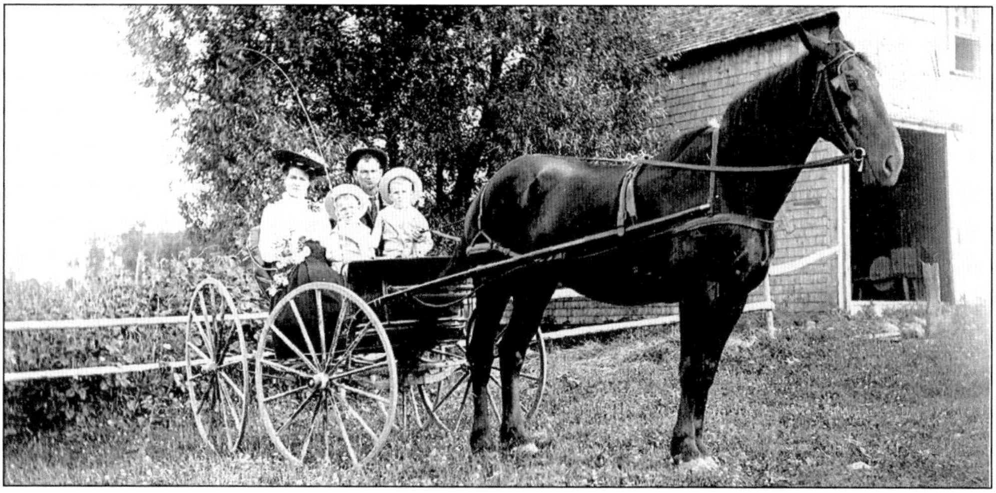

The Nutting Family out for a Sunday Drive. Seen here, from left to right, are the following: (front row) Errol Nutting and Clyde Willard; (back row) Justina Willard Nutting and Mark Nutting. Clyde was a farm boy and remained so. He took over the family farm and milked Jersey cows until old age set in and he retired. Errol did not care for farm animals and developed expert skills in woodworking and metalworking. He worked at the Eldridge Brothers Cabinet Shop and at Fay and Scott to develop his skills. At one time, Errol worked in Chesuncook Village as a builder and improved so that he could make anything. He went to World War I at age 16 and on returning set up shop in Dexter, where he made kick sleds in three sizes. He and his family eventually moved to Dover-Foxcroft, where he owned a sawmill. The interior woodwork in the Governor Brewster house in Dexter attests to his fine workmanship as a finish carpenter and cabinetmaker.

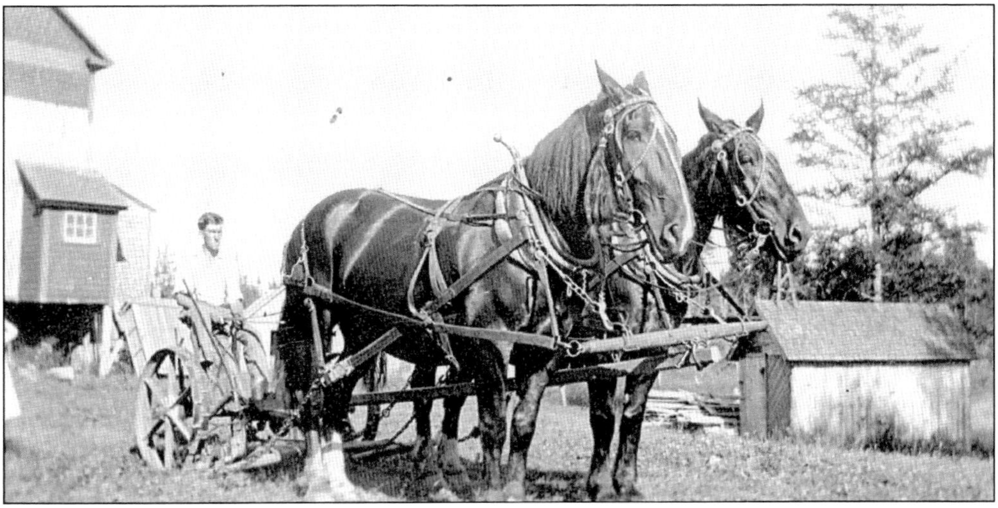

NO TRACTOR FARMING FOR CLYDE WILLARD. Clyde and his nephew Errol were raised like brothers on the Willard farm bordering Main Stream. As teenagers they were hired to stand on the Main Stream Bridge and use pick poles to prevent the logs from jamming up under the bridge. They worked as janitors at the local school and built the fire daily in the winter months. They grew potatoes together and purchased bicycles with the income. They made a bike trip to Bangor once to a relative's house. Clyde also used his money to buy a colt and began his lifelong love of horses. He always used horses, even into the 1960s, when he retired. He never had a tractor. Clyde and his wife, Rose, raised a family of five girls on his milk and wood income and Rose's salary as a nurse at the local hospital.

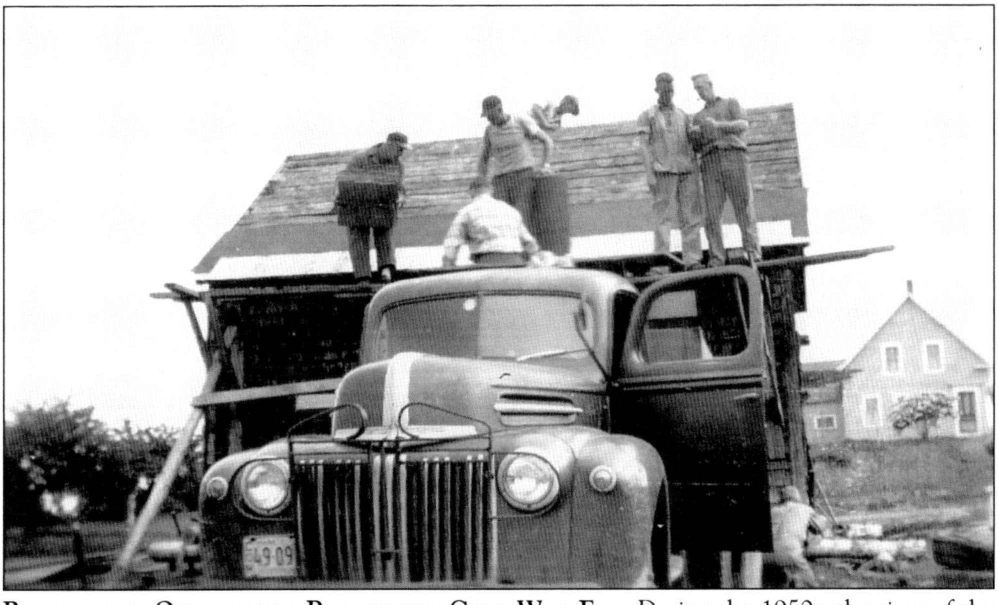

RIPLEY AS AN OBSERVATION POST IN THE COLD WAR ERA. During the 1950s, the time of the Cold War, civil defense was a priority in every community, and Ripley did its part. Fifteen men moved a garage opposite the Mills farm and outfitted it for an observation post complete with telephone and radio. Afterward, the ladies prepared and served a fine baked bean and salad dinner on Linwood Haseltine's lawn. Ken Brasier was director of civil defense. Deputy directors included Bud Ellms, Ernest Sevey, Ethelinda Gordon, and Garnet Bubar.

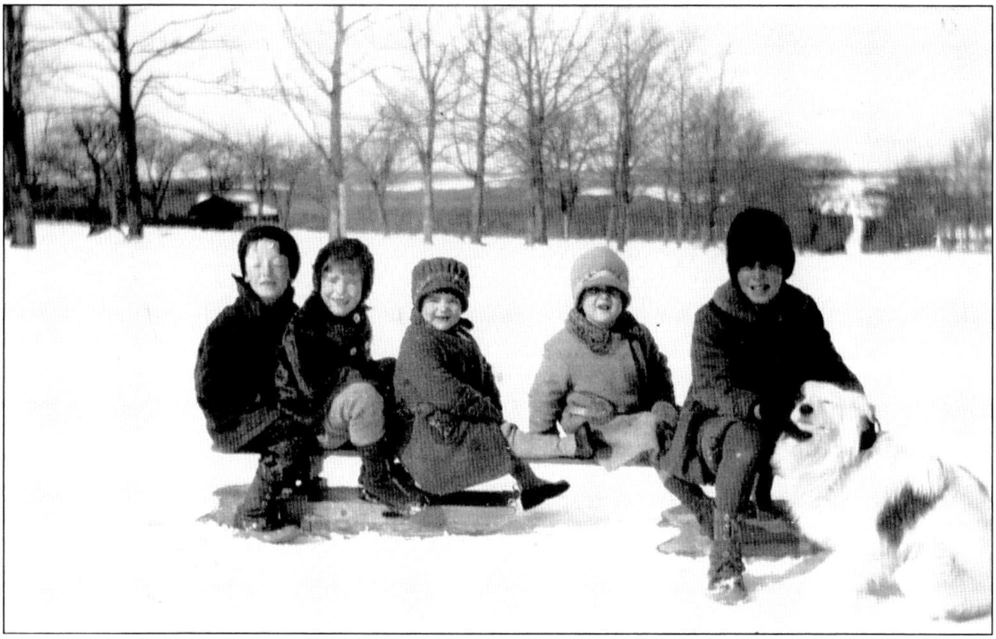

SLIDING IN RIPLEY. In 1929, roads were not plowed, and automobiles did not travel in the winter. The Perkins and Folsom kids knew how to have fun on Chandler Hill. Pictured, from left to right, are Alden Perkins, Barbara Perkins Goulette, Isabel Folsom Ronco, Martha Willard Spaulding, Phillip Perkins, and Peter the dog. This photograph was taken *c.* 1928.

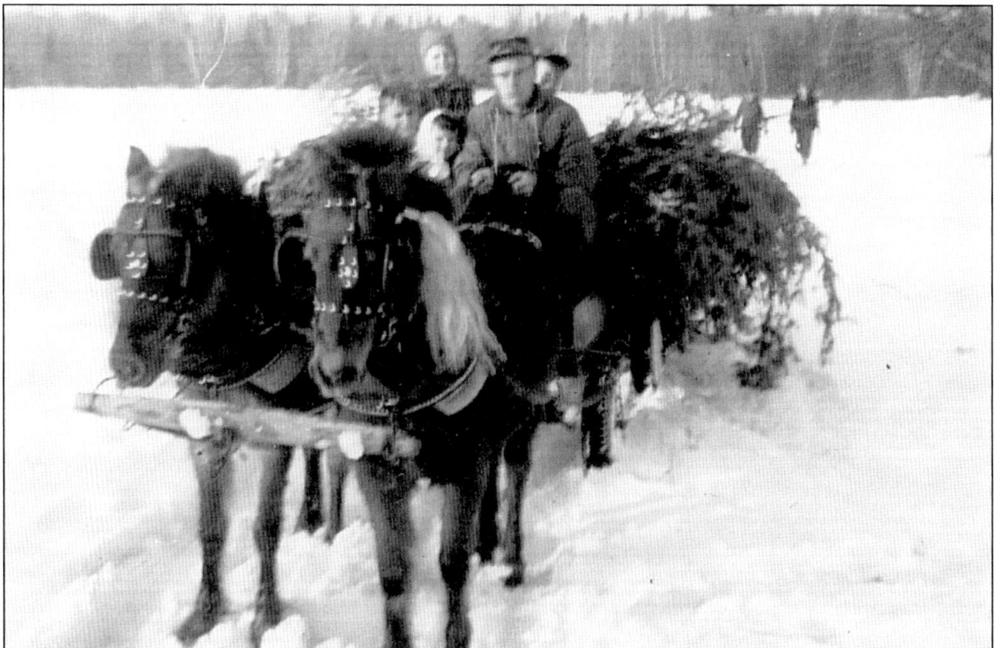

THE DEERING FAMILY GETTING OUT BOUGHS. The Deering family loved to work its ponies, especially when getting boughs to bank the house each winter. Don used Ginger and Cocoa in the woods and at pony-pulling contests. Shown, from left to right, are Jay, Kim, Don, and unidentified. Bringing up the rear are Anita Jewett and Marge Deering.

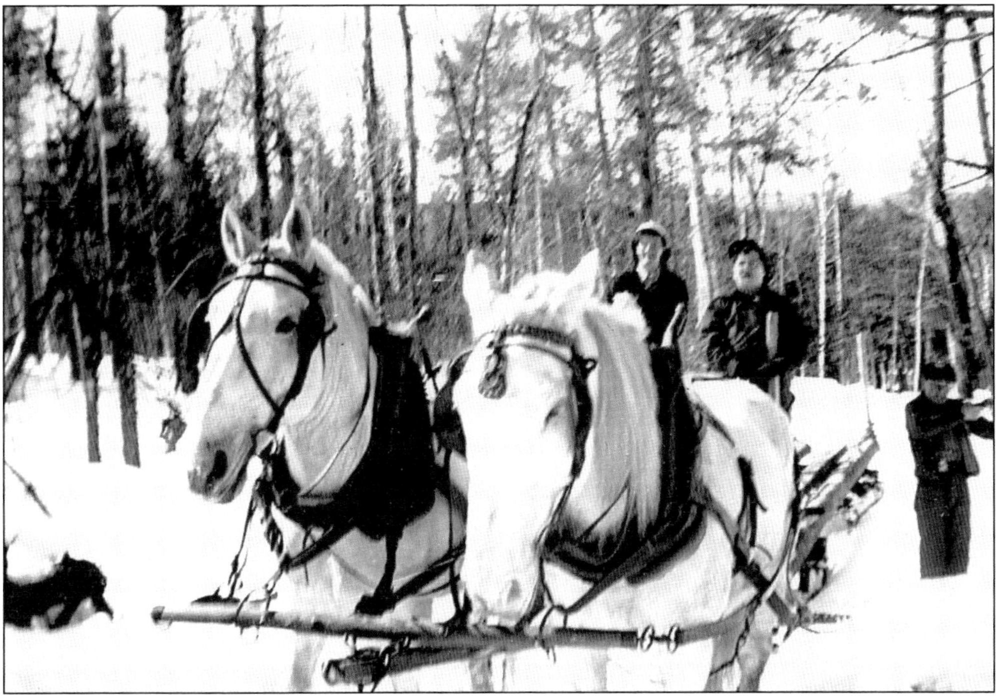

THE GOULD WOMEN KNEW HOW TO HAUL LOGS. Horses Bob and Chub seem eager to get the logs out this fine April 1958 morning on the home woodlot. From left to right are Gertrude Gould and Althea Gould Jewett.

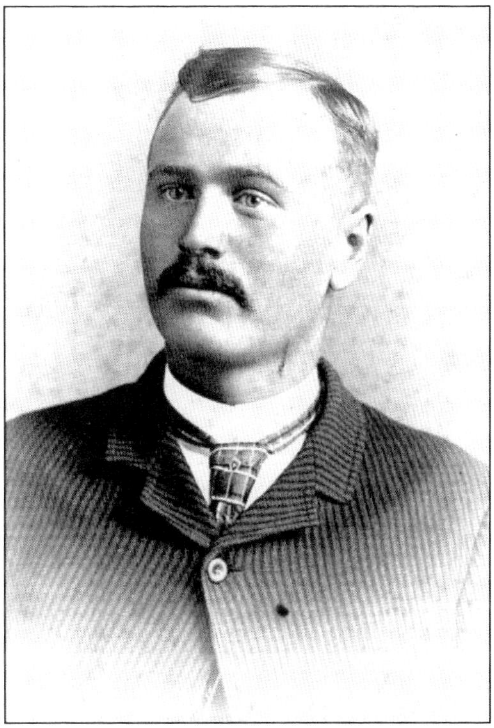

ERNEST L. SEVEY, A MAN OF HIS TIME. Ernest was a lifelong Ripley resident. The son of LaRoy and Annette Jones, he was a farmer and also had an extensive lumber and wood business locally. At one time, he supposedly had eight teams of oxen working in the woods producing logs and pulp. The Seveys farmed at the head of Ripley Pond on the North Road.

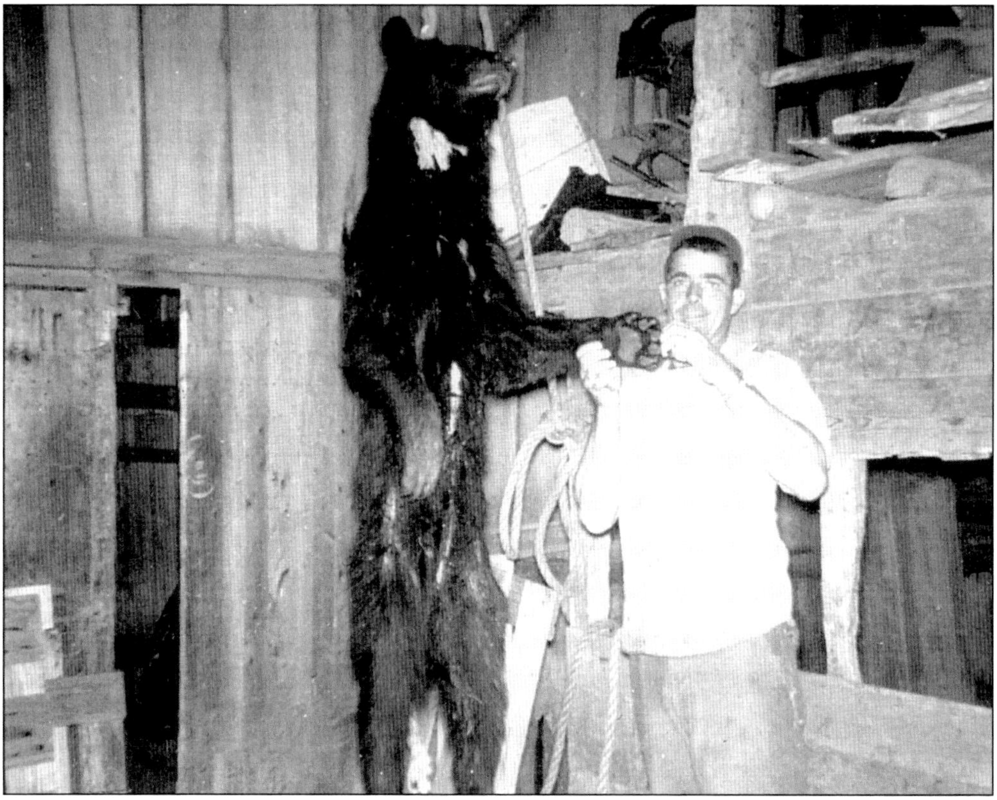

GENE GOULD BAGS A BEAR. "I shot the bear with a 30-30," remembers Gould. "It was out back of my father's place on the Richardson lot. Elmer Sevey had cut the lot and I was cutting in there since I was 14. After I shot the bear it fell onto another one, and that one got up and chased me out of the woods. Wasn't too long after when my dad had sold the farm that it burned down. There were three big dynamite explosions that night it caught fire. Very strange."

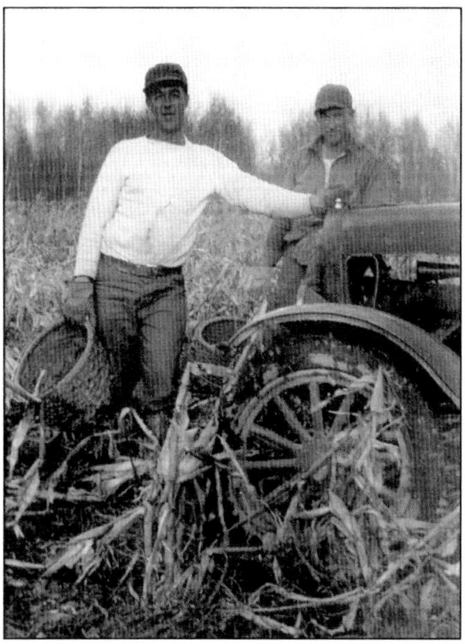

KEN STAFFORD (LEFT) AND AMOS LORD PICKING CORN THE OLD-FASHIONED WAY. Ken worked on different farms in the area. He recently recalled working on the Arthur Buck farm many years ago when Mr. Buck lost his glasses while haying and never found them. The next spring, while Ken was "dunging out," the glasses popped up intact on the manure spreader. They had been lost in the hay, dumped down from the mow, forked in through the swings, into the manger, then into the stall, and shoveled out with the manure and hay during the winter. They never got broken.

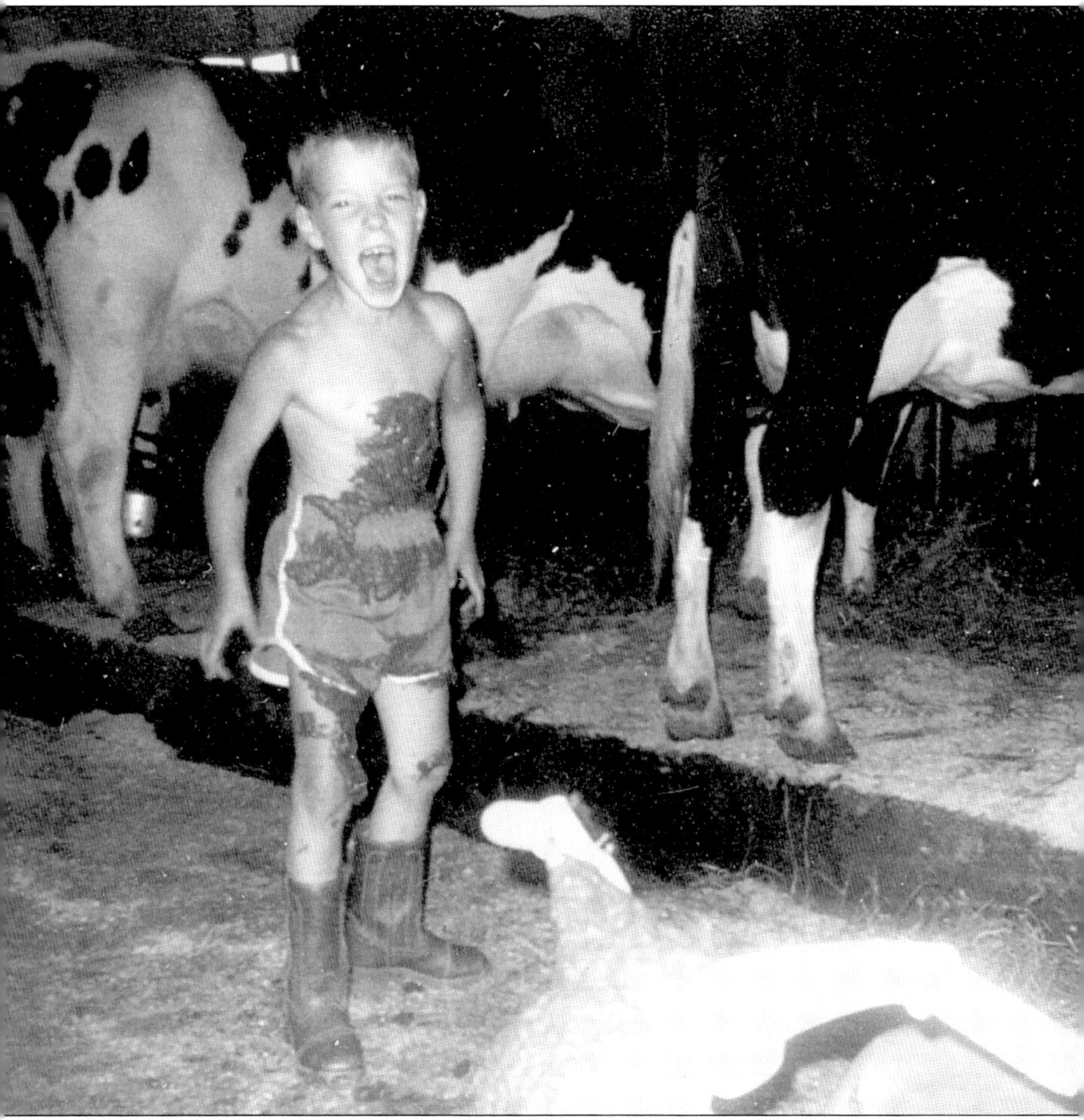

In the Wrong Place at the Wrong Time. Eric Page was five years old. The concrete walk behind the cows was a terrific place to go flying along on his little plastic three-wheeler bike. Joe and Carol Page, his parents, were busy milking. It was early spring. The cows had been out all day on lush, tender, wet pasture. Eric was going too fast, heading into the next barn right into a row of cows. He dragged his feet and stopped barely in time before landing in the gutter. "Momma, it's hot!" Farm people know cows like to cough, and sometimes they do it simultaneously while relieving themselves. Eric was in the wrong place at the wrong time—or do cows carefully take aim and do it on purpose?

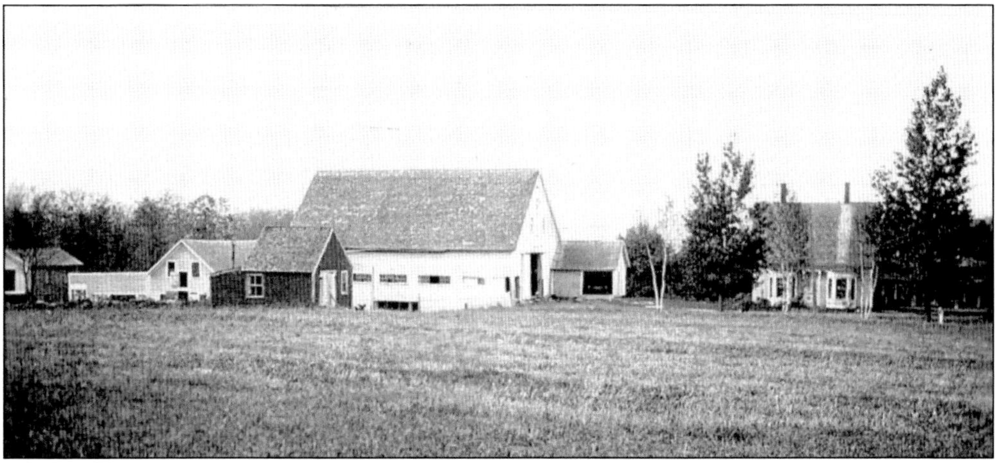

DANIEL RANDALL, A PROMINENT EARLY RIPLEY SETTLER. Daniel walked a spotted trail to lot 22 in 1803. He built a bark cabin, cleared land, and then went back to New Hampshire to marry Abigail Leavitt. Their first child was born in 1804. He was a cooper by trade and was known as a great bear hunter. This photograph shows the Randall farm with the cooper shop, across the road from the barn where the first school in Ripley was held. In 1952, while owned by Harold Dow, the home was destroyed by fire. John, one of the Dow boys, traveled on horseback through five miles of drifting deep snow to notify the Dexter Fire Department.

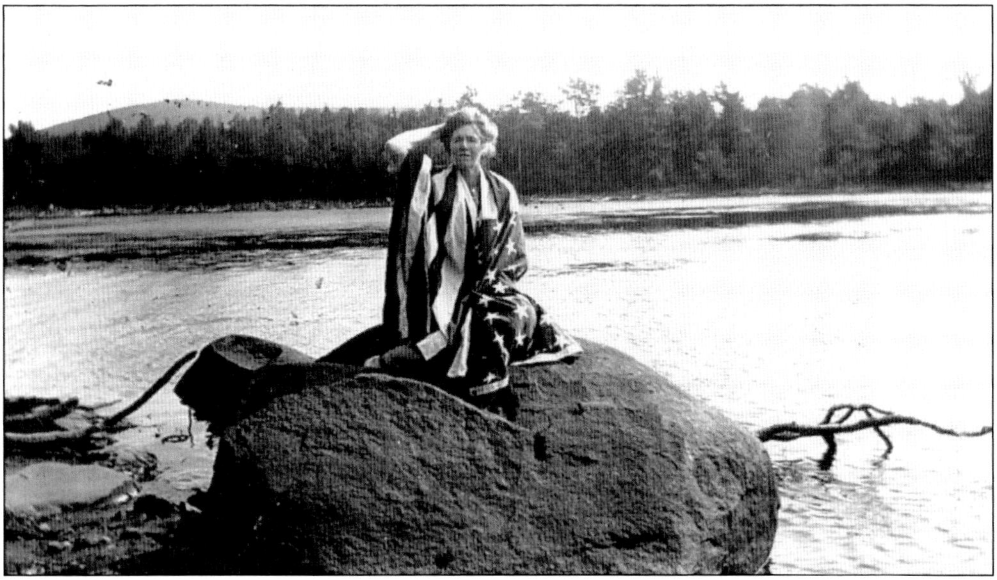

ESTELLE CROCKETT RANDALL WRAPPED IN OLD GLORY AT MAIN STREAM POND. When Estelle married Mellen Randall, she did not realize the lifetime adventure she was getting into. She was the only child of the prominent Crockett family in Dexter and had worked at the *Eastern Gazette* as the local correspondent. At one time, Estelle had a pet monkey named Jocko. Mellen was a cattle dealer and butcher in Ripley, but the couple eventually moved to Bridgewater, where Estelle opened a millinery shop and Mellen became a cattle broker with an office in Boston.

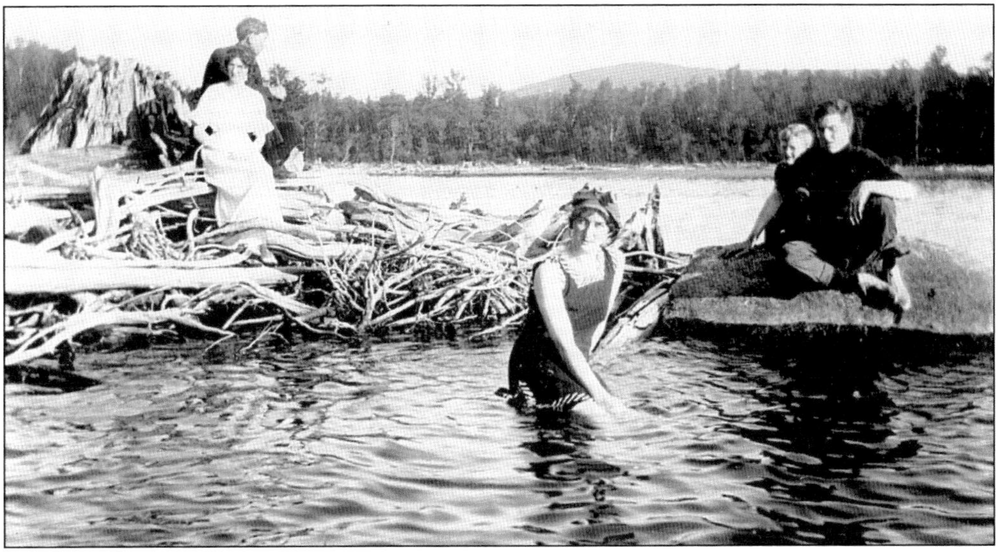

THE INDIAN KNOLL ON MAIN STREAM POND, A FAVORITE SPOT. The Randall family and friends frequently visited their camp on Main Stream. It was on high ground that became an island for a while in early spring. The dam at Main Stream Village held the water back so much that one could row up into Jimmy Brook in the spring. Ernest Blaisdell's camp was near the brook, and one blustery winter day he thought he would drive Mellen Randall's open Model T downstream on the ice to Mel's camp. When they got to the point where Ferguson Stream comes into Main Stream, Alvin Randall and Ed Sawyer got out to check the ice depth with their chisels. "About one inch to two inches of ice," Ed yelled to Ernest. "Oh hell, I can make it OK," Ernest replied. The next thing they knew, Ernest was up to his chin in water, and Mel had bailed out of the automobile wearing his heavy fur coat and almost drowned.

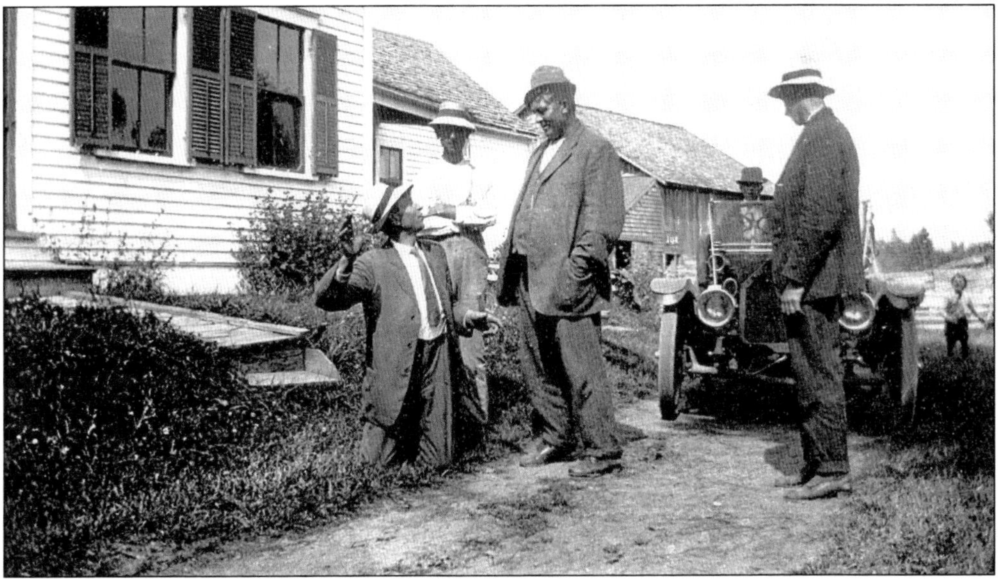

"RETURN OF THE PILGRIMS: MA SAYS THE BOYS WERE OUT ON A TEAR." Mel Randall and the boys liked to have fun. Returning from an outing one day, they put on a show for the family right in the dooryard. Kneeling is Sheldon Huff in front of Mel. The open Model T in the background could be the one that went through the ice on Main Stream.

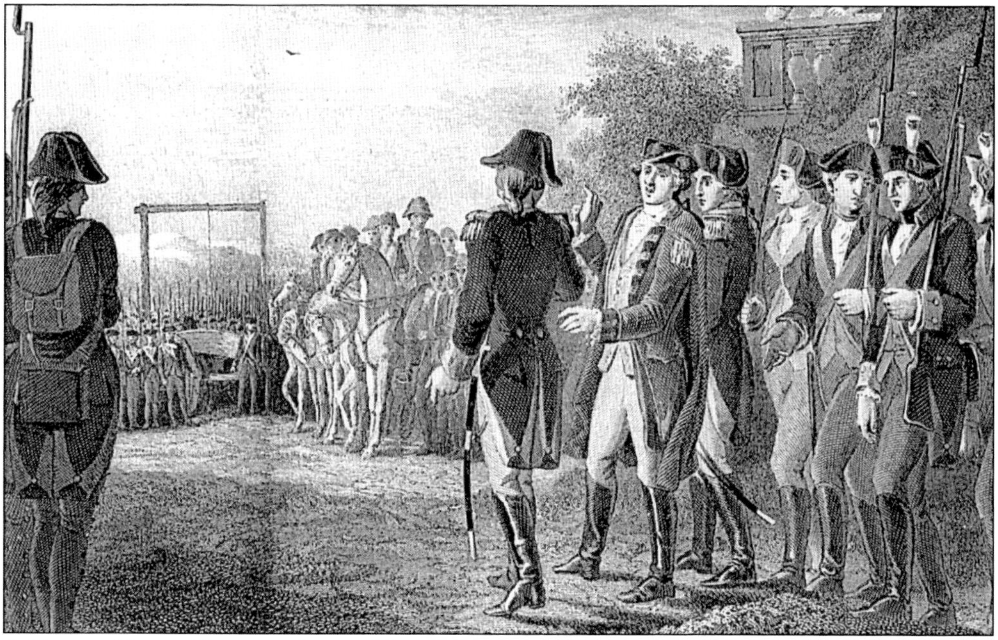

A Future Ripley Resident Leads Major Andre to the Gallows. During the Revolutionary War, Gen. Benedict Arnold gave the plans of West Point to Maj. John Andre along with papers detailing the number of troops and the placement of fortifications. Andre was captured and sentenced to die. John Rogers, sergeant of the guard, was chosen to escort him to the gallows to hang. This surprised Andre, as he thought death was to be in front of a firing squad. John Rogers later became one of the early settlers of Ripley, with many descendants living in the area.

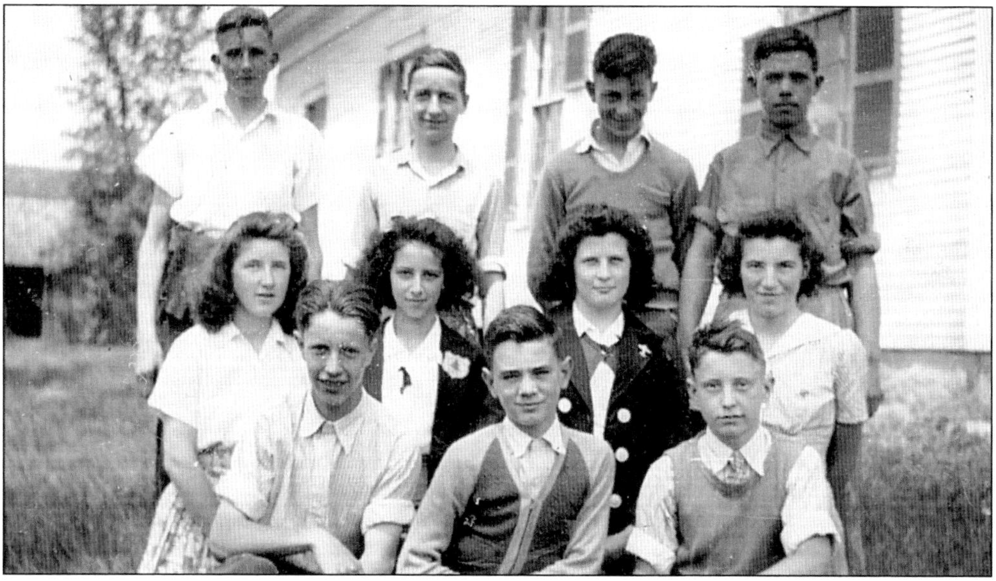

The 1943 Eighth-Grade Graduation Class. Shown here, from left to right, are the following: (front row) Ralph Sawyer, Ernest Sevey, and Harold Sawyer; (middle row) Virginia Farrar Ellms, Dorothy Tewksbury Hutchins, Seretha Sevey, and Kathleen Eaton; (back row) Mel Randall, Ed Farrar, Albert Gould, and Clayton Neal.

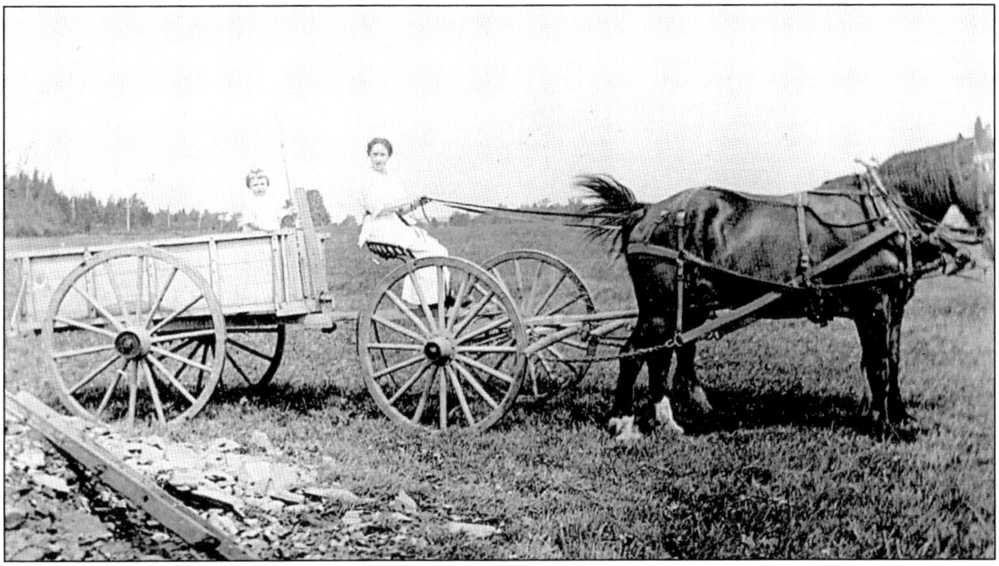

"Ripley Cut off from World by Road and Phone, Asks Aid," *Eastern Gazette*, 1949. The woman and child pictured did not have the problems of future Ripley citizens. They could get through the mud any time with this dump cart. "Fred L. Haseltine told the *Gazette* that Ripley was the only town in the state where a motorist can't get out or in, without getting mired in the mud." In addition, the only phone in Ripley at the time was in a local store and even that was disconnected when the "one-woman switchboard operator decided she didn't want the job anymore." The former Mrs. Winifred Hatch left the job to get married to Charles Johnston. Mrs. Johnston said, "They [the 62 subscribers] were behind on their payments."

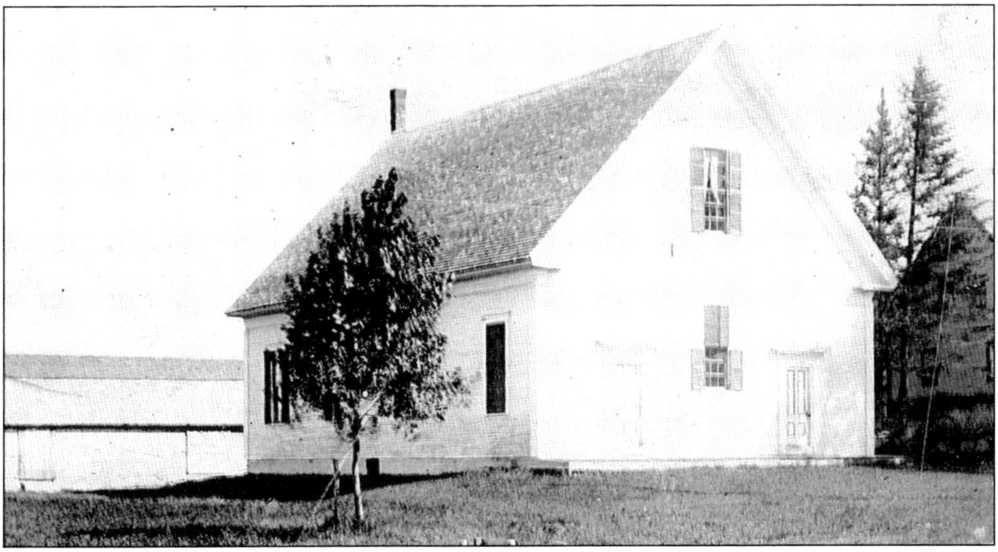

The Ripley Grange Has a Long History. An *Eastern Gazette* article from c. 1930 reads, "The 'Hayseeder's Bawl' put on at the Grange March 25th was a decided success. There were over 100 present, many in odd, freakish and old-fashioned costumes. Mrs. Cora Jewett (in a suit made from feed bags) and Bert Britten (in a much dilapidated dress and hat) were awarded the worst-looking couple. Dancing was the main feature though card playing was a side issue. Refreshments of hot dogs and tonic were on sale."

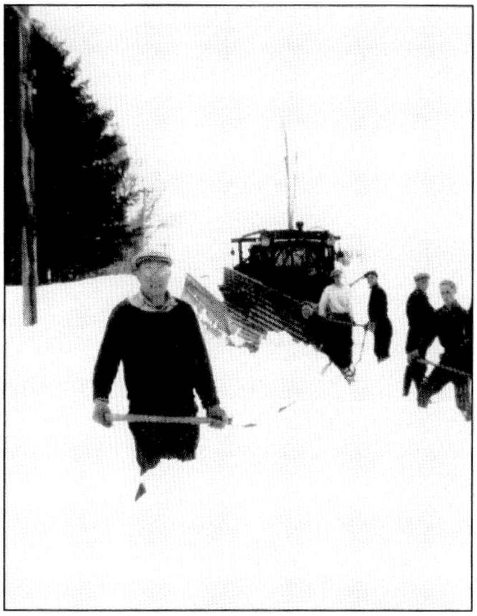

SKIP CLEARING THE WAY FOR THE OLD LINN. Clayton "Skip" Courser did not know the trouble that would be stirred up by his donation of $50,000 in his will to Ripley for the purpose of building a new school. An incredible amount of feuding, rescinded votes, moves, counter-moves, and legal complications delayed the building of the school.

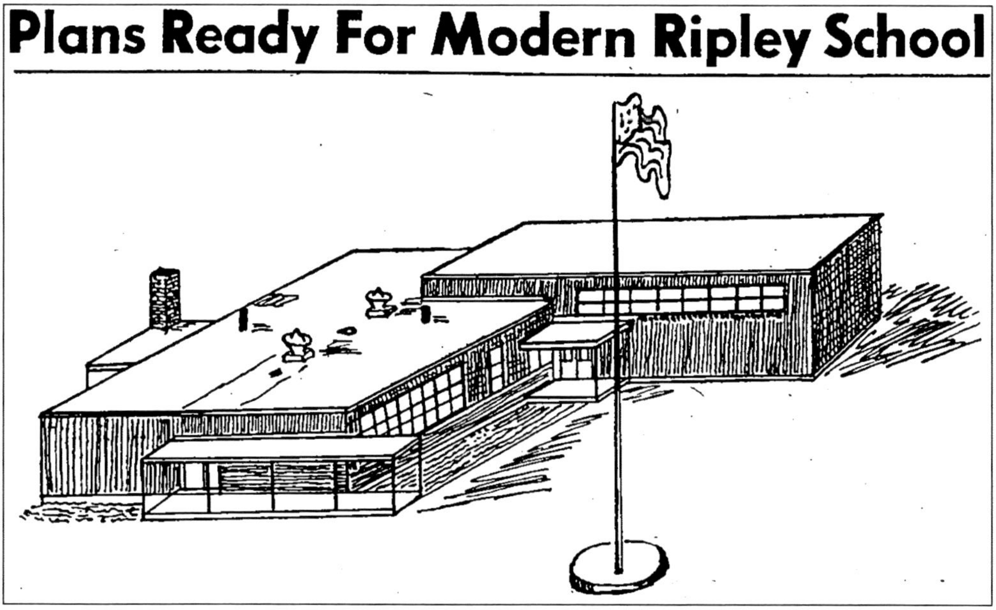

THE NEW SCHOOL FEUD GOES ON MORE THAN TWO YEARS. Pictured here is Ripley's new school—or is it? This original flat-roofed design with cafeteria and gym at a cost of $47,000 was debated at a town meeting, but at a special meeting by a vote of 64-41, the design was changed to "a 4 room, two pitched roof smaller building of 'sturdier build.' " Three members of the building committee resigned, and a new nine-man committee was formed. Two out-of-town lawyers were present at this special meeting and helped only to complicate matters more. The following week, charges were aired that the selectman were "not properly elected," which resulted in one Ripley resident refusing the selectman on his property to assess his home. Later on, when a structure with brick facing was proposed, protesting committee members threatened to bring a court injunction against awarding a contract on present bids. Finally, at another special town meeting, a brick building it is by an 88-31 vote! Clyde P. Jewett had the lowest bid and got the job. More than 200 people filled the hall, and many harsh words and pointed questions enlivened the evening meeting. The meeting was kept well in order by moderator Tim Haseltine.

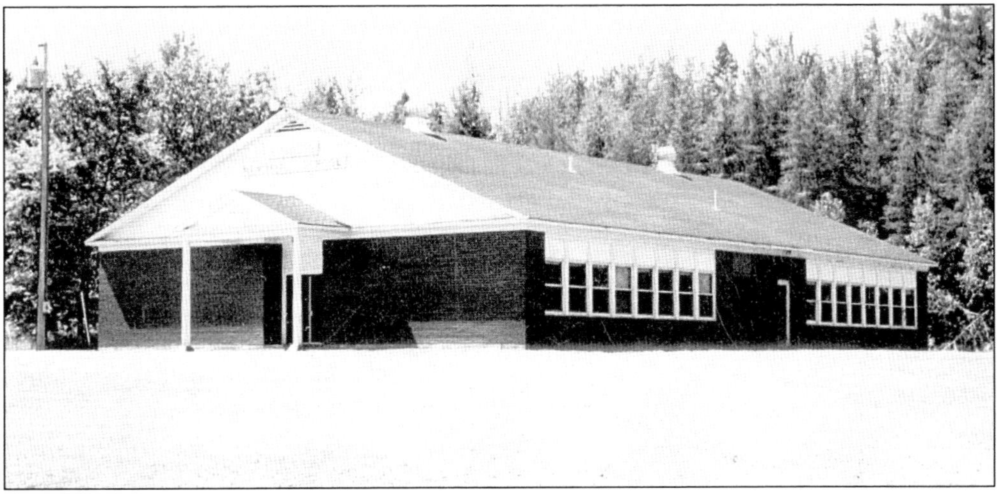

Ripley Votes for a New Brick School. The *Eastern Gazette* reported on August 16, 1956, "Shortly after the meeting, the selectmen signed a $49,592 contract with Clyde P. Jewett of Dexter, head of the Jewett Construction Co., which had submitted the low bid on this type of structure. The opponents of the present plan still insisted that the type playroom provided would not be adequate and that the brick veneer was an unnecessary expense."

Moses Rises from the Dead. "In the 1850s when in Rio de Janeiro he was stricken with yellow fever and after a brief illness was taken from the hospital to the 'dead house' where he awaited burial. There he laid for 2 days." (From a clipping in the Ellie Hurd scrapbook, at the Dexter Historical Society.) When officials were bringing more dead bodies in, they saw Moses sitting up! He was taken back to the hospital and recovered. After 14 years following the sea, Moses L. Arno returned to Maine and purchased a farm on Chandler Hill. Moses is pictured in front. Behind him are Ruth Hill (with the baby) and Ellie Hurd, Moses's grandniece and niece.

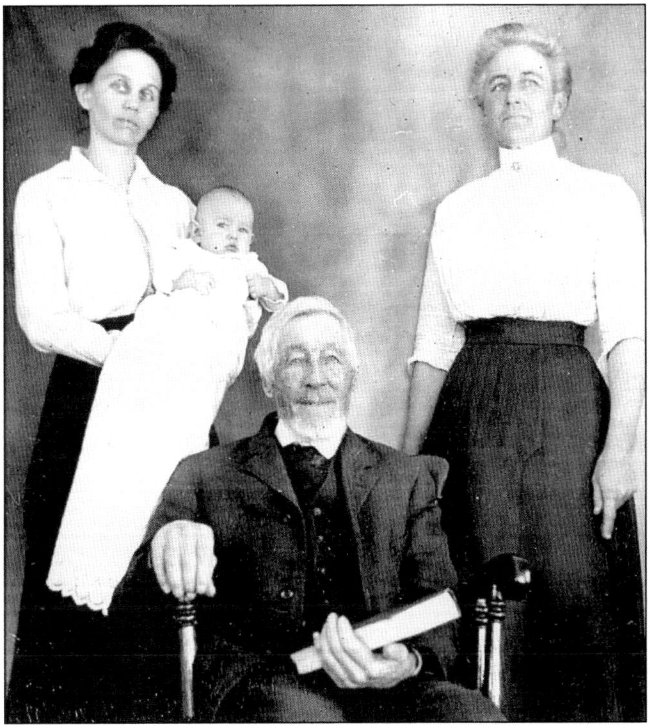

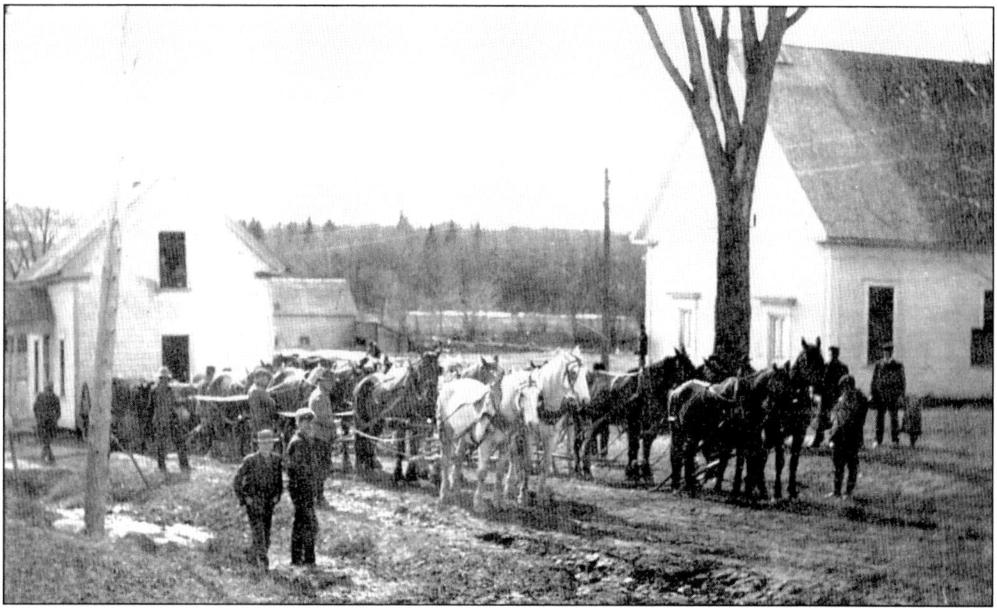

Moving the Felker House in Ripley Village, c. 1897. William Felker moved a building from Main Stream Village with eight teams of horses. This photograph shows it passing by the Grange hall on the way to the Fush Hill area of town. But it got stuck in the mud in the middle of the road just above the Grange hall. A lot was quickly purchased to provide space for the house. At one time, the building was the local telephone office and Hatch's Auto Garage and Gas Station. Today, it is a private residence.

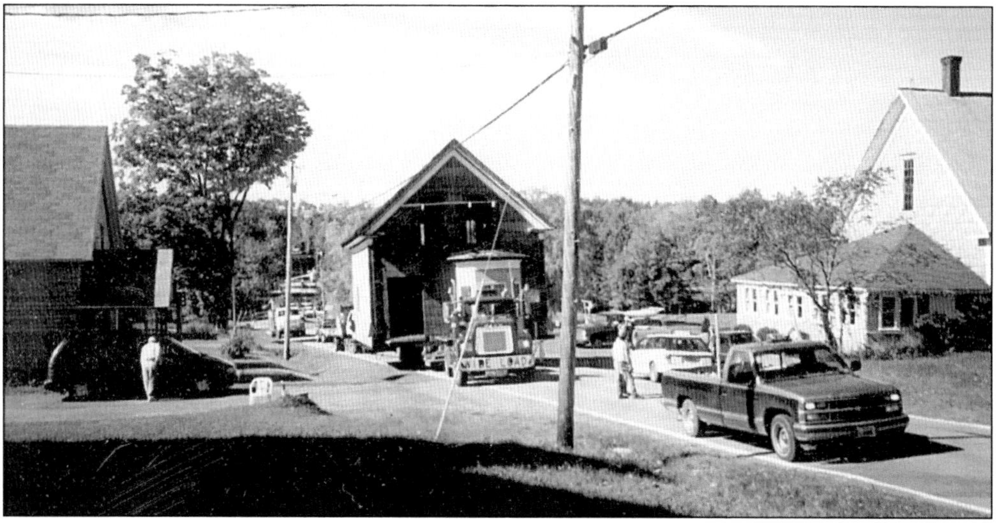

Moving the Bane House in Ripley Village, c. 1997. Ernest Sevey offered this house to David St. Germain if he would move it to another location. St. Germain thought it over and decided to take on the job. It was exactly 2,000 feet to Gary Hanson's field, and a house mover from Skowhegan could be hired to do the job. The move went off without a hitch until just above the Grange hall the truck's steering box broke and the house blocked the road, tying up traffic for part of a day. The post-and-beam construction of wooden pegs kept the house tight and straight on the trip up the road. This photograph shows the house being moved just as it is passing the Grange hall.

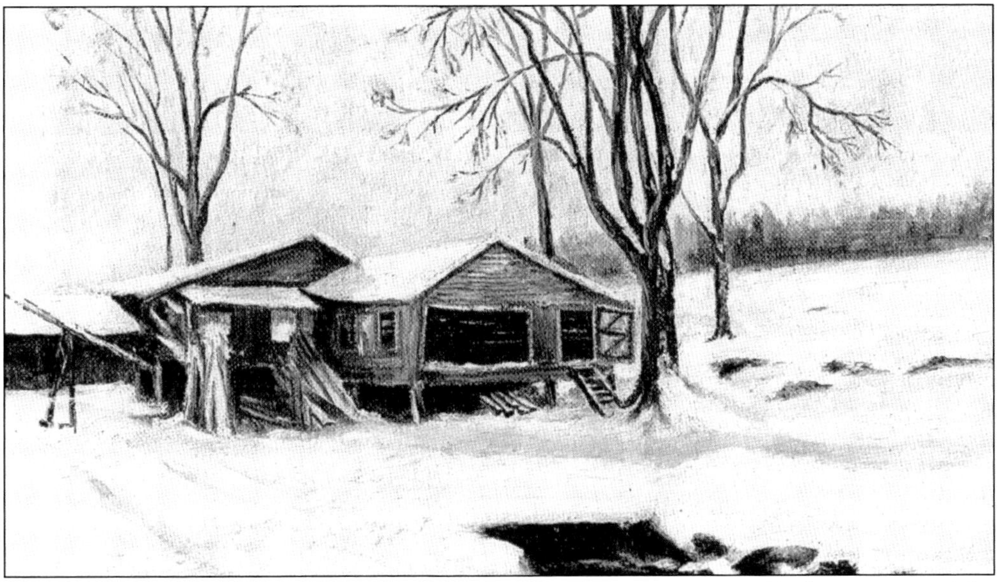

The Long Sawmill History Ends in a Feud. The waterpower site in Ripley was one of the earliest places to be developed in the new settlement. A sawmill and gristmill were top priorities in any community. The gristmill had ceased to exist by 1920. The sawmill ended in 1969, when Galen Goulette sold it to Ernest Sevey "on the very day Astronaut N. Armstrong landed on the moon." Then there was a feud about the water rights for a while. Today, Sevey has a hydropower unit on the original sawmill site. It is a five-kilowatt unit that supplies power to his home nine months each year and, at times when there is a surplus, to Central Maine Power. This is the smallest independent hydro producer in Maine.

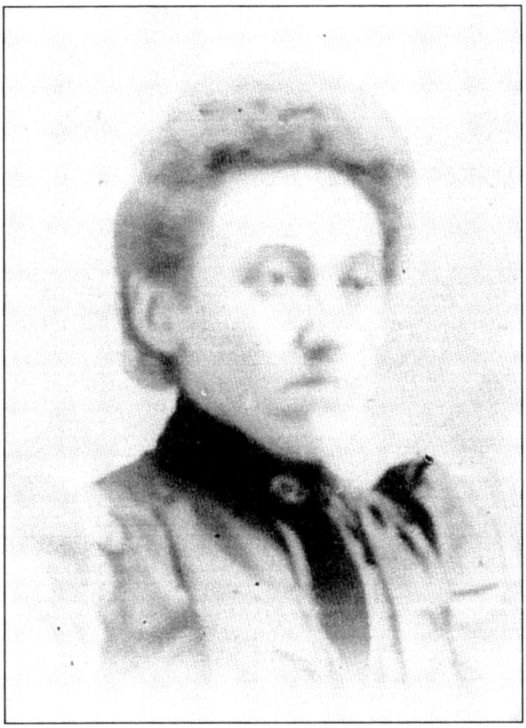

"Affrays and Disturbances" Common on Fush Hill. In the 1870s and 1880s, Turner H. Lord's name frequently came up whenever there was trouble. At one time, Lord was accused of tying up and whipping his stepson, Charles L. Davis, then a mere child. The Wednesday after "the great storm" was a "cider induced affray." When the fight was over, Turner Lord had a broken nose, John Bowdoin had a black eye, and Frank Lord was scratched and battered. Charles Thurston apparently came out of it unscathed. The image shows Effie May Lord Cooley, Frank Lord's daughter, who totally disapproved of her father and uncle abusing cider. Rufus Cooley is Effie's great-grandson. Rufus and Janice Cooley have a large dairy herd and farm on the Frank Lord property. And there is no feuding on Fush Hill today.

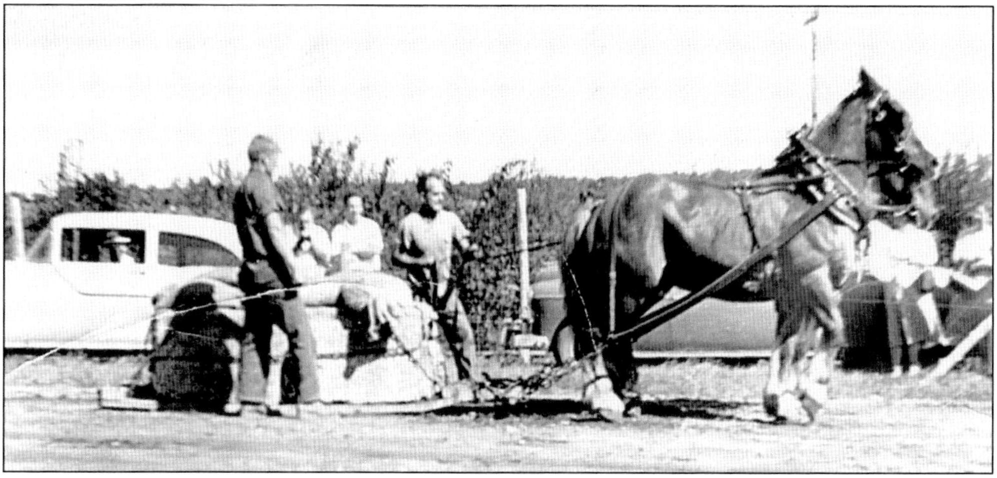

VERNAL M. SINCLAIR WINS ANOTHER HORSE-PULLING CONTEST. Joe and Ginger always pulled well for Vernal. In this photograph, Vernal gets ready to start, with Carl Davis beside the sled. Vernal milked cows and plowed snow in the winter but always had horses. His mother, Violet, always had horses and ponies to feed, even into her old age. Despite his love of horses, Vernal bought a brand-new truck in the 1940s, and one stormy winter day, he hooked onto the Linn tractor to help the boys out, but his new truck got stove up. He could not forget that for a while.

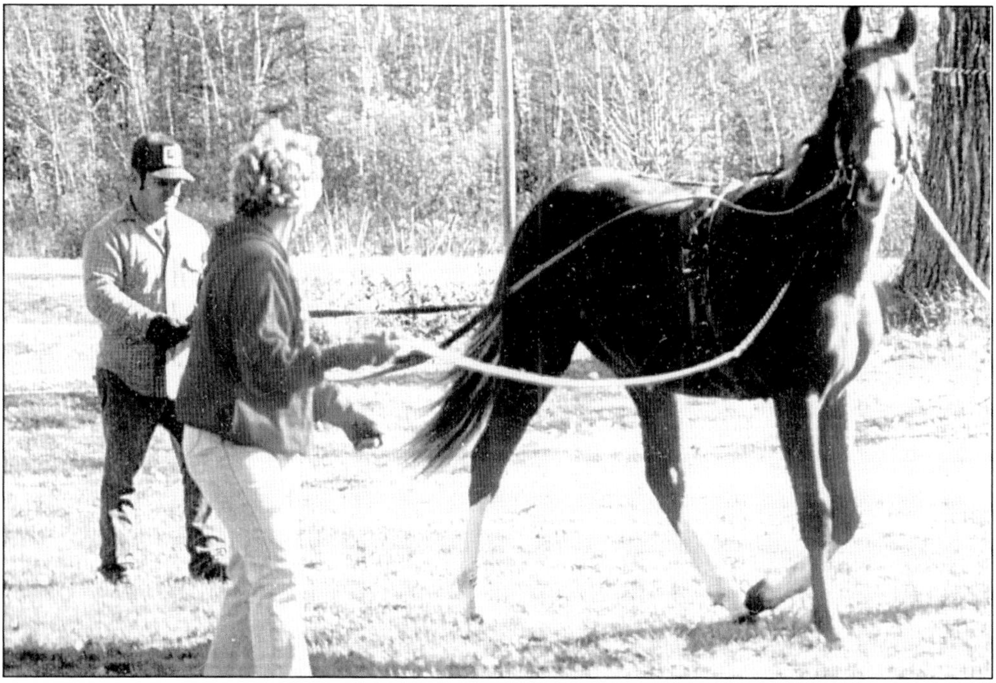

VERNAL AND JERICE CARRY ON THE SINCLAIR TRADITION WITH HORSES. Vernal has raised and raced horses ever since he can remember. He started working with his father as a teenager, "right out of high school." Around that time, his father switched from pulling draft horses to harness horses. Young Vernal also got involved and has had horses for 40 years now. Vernal and Jerice are shown "line-driving" a two-year-old Standardbred named Rita. That is how they break a young colt to pull a sulky.

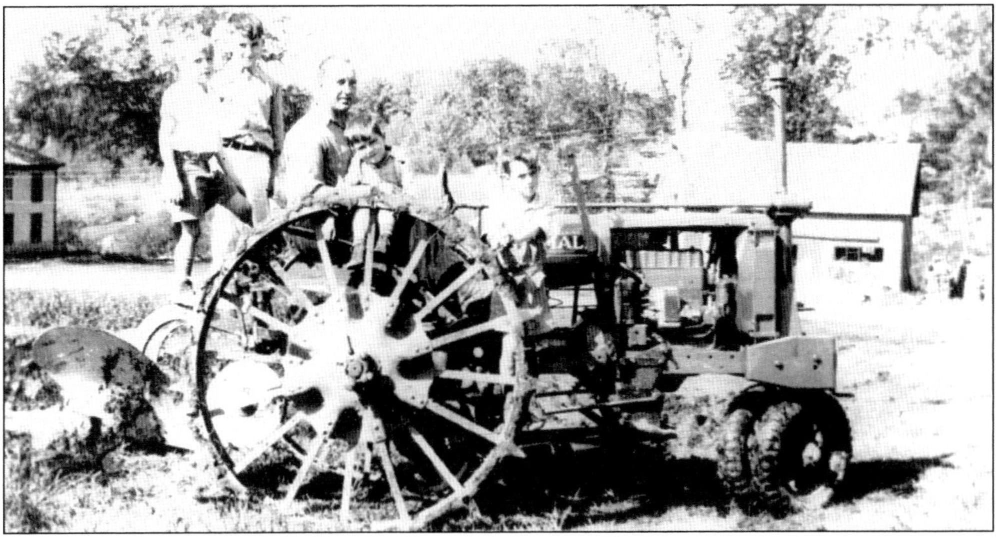

The Sevey Family Poses on an Early Farmall Tractor. Bert Sevey takes some time off from plowing a garden to pose his and Del's children on his Farmall tractor c. 1935. Pictured, from left to right, are Richard Sevey, Almond Brann, Albert Sevey, Howard Sevey, and Ernest Sevey. Bert and Del bought the Arthur Buck farm, and the Sevey family moved into it on June 1, 1940. They milked a few cows and had a variety of crops and animals. Del later taught school when the boys got older.

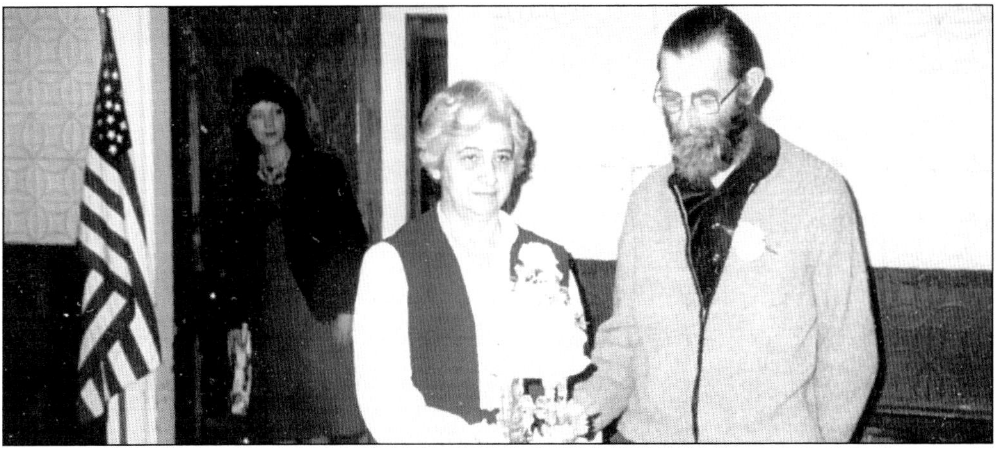

Rodney and Dot Hutchins Celebrate 25 Years of Marriage at a Surprise Party. Their daughter invited them out to dinner, and on the way they passed the Ripley Grange, the parking lot filled with cars. Dot said, "I wonder what's going on at the Grange? I don't know of anything supposed to be there today." Her daughter Charlotte suggested they go in and see what was going on, and that is how they walked in on their own surprise celebration. Rodney and Dot were presented a boutonniere and corsage. Henry Nutter made the cake, and Tim Haseltine played the organ. Rod was a farmer and a woodsman all his life. His father, Hugh, and his ancestors Harry and Ben all farmed on the Shore Road in Dexter. Rod came to Ripley c. 1947 and bought the Amos Lord place on the Lane Road. He loved his draft horses and always had a pair on the farm. Dot is a lifelong Ripley resident and was raised on the typical self-sufficient small farm of its day. She has been the town treasurer for 25 years, Grange master, deputy of the Pomona Grange, Ladies Aid chairman, County Extension chairman, and local church secretary.

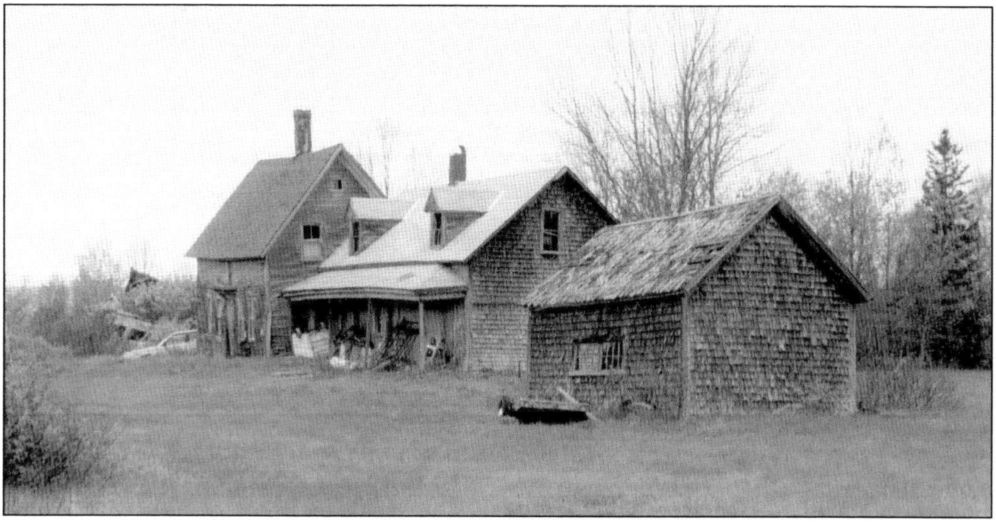

Maine's Oldest Cow Receives Congratulations from Borden's Elsie. The *Eastern Gazette* of May 27, 1948, reported, "Lila Vittam's 28-year-old cow recently calved for the 26th time having a bull calf. Her milk output at this advanced age is over 10 quarts per day. Last summer the dean of Maine herds had her production up to 18 quarts per day. Elsie, the Borden cow, sent a telegram of congratulations to, 'Mother's cow,' the name she received from Lila's mother, Mrs. Mel Thurston who considered her a pet. The farm has 7 cows, 3 calves, 2 pigs, and some sheep and lambs," similar to many small subsistence farms in Maine in 1948. The barn had fallen down by the time this 2001 photograph was taken.

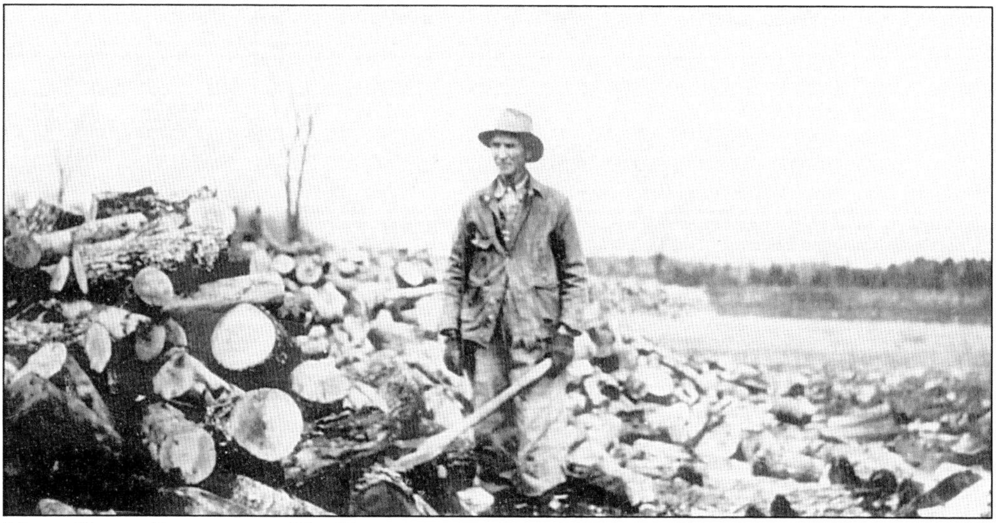

Mont Ellms Putting up His Firewood for the Winter. Alonzo Lemont Ellms came to Ripley to farm in 1902. He was a mild-mannered, kind person of few words. He and his wife, Eva, raised two boys, Edward Horace and Charles. Charles stayed around locally. His many interests included raising turkey, working as a mechanic, working at Fay and Scott, for Checkerboard Feed, and for his son Bud in the construction business. He was a daredevil as a child, and rumor has it at age two he was found on the peak of the new barn the family was constructing. Ed graduated from Bowdoin College and Massachusetts Institute of Technology. He became a chemical engineer and architect and spent his life in New York working for Allied Chemical, only returning to the home farm when he retired.

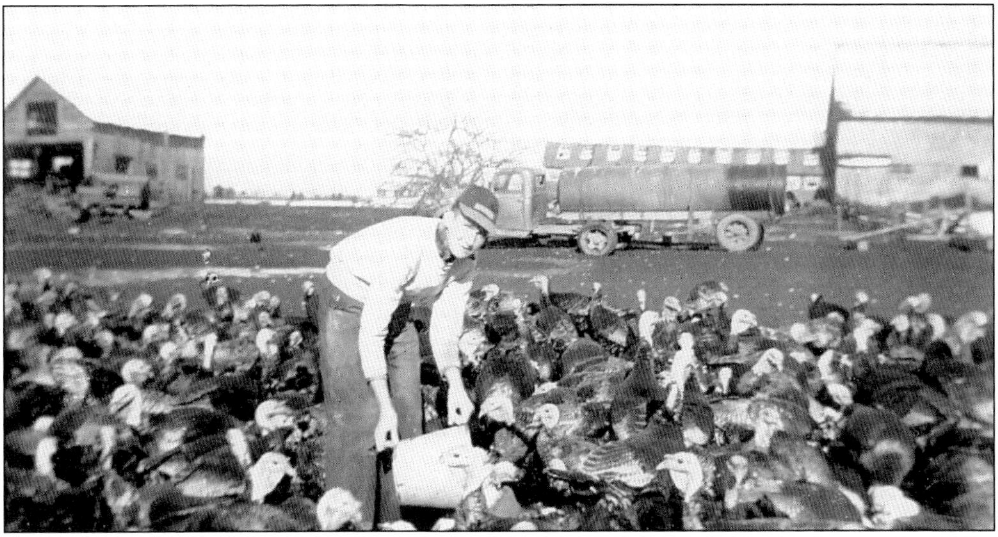

TURKEY RAISING ON THE ELLMS ROAD. Charles Ellms Sr. had a large flock of turkeys in the 1940s. It was mostly a family affair on the property where Ginny Ellms lives today. She remembers picking the feathers off the birds to get them ready for the market. Turkeys were sold as far away as Greenville for Thanksgiving season. Mel Randall is shown feeding the flock. The building behind the truck is the former horse stable that was moved from the Grange hall.

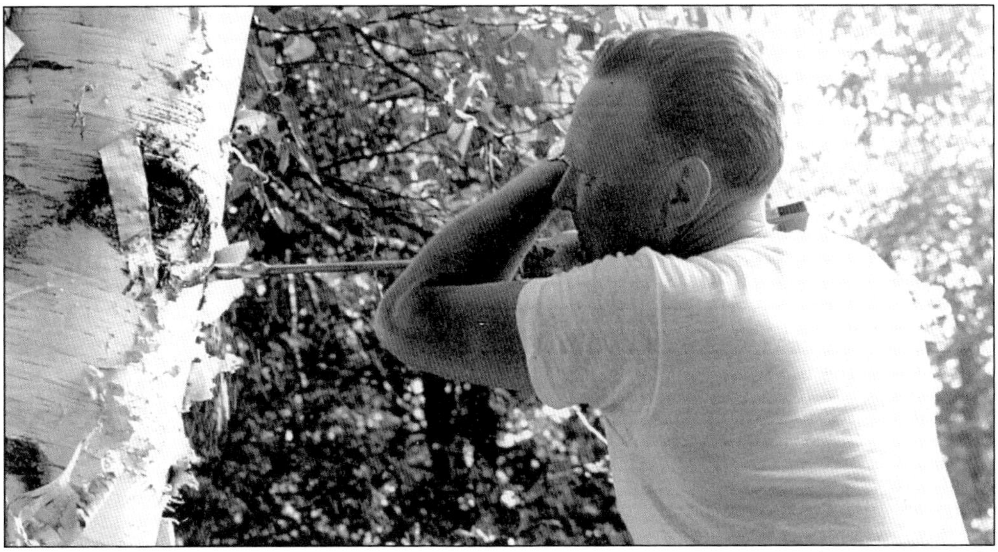

BUD ELLMS DELIVERS A TRUCKLOAD OF SNOW FOR MAY 1. It all started down at the soda fountain at Joe Bush's Dexter Rexall Drug Store. Over a cup of coffee and during a February blizzard, Joe remarked that he would like some more snow. Bud said he had a lot of orders ahead. "But you'll get delivery. When do you want it?" Joe, always the wisecracker, said, "I'll take two loads for delivery on April 30 at 50 cents a load." So on April 30, two dump truck loads of snow were delivered to Joe Bush's home by police escort. Bud was always full of fun. He was a Ripley Church board member, a Dexter Kiwanis member, a Dexter Fish and Game member, and a Ripley selectman for 14 years. He was always there to help his fellow man, always with a smile and a laugh. His wife, Ginny, drove the school bus and worked for School District 46 for 27 years.

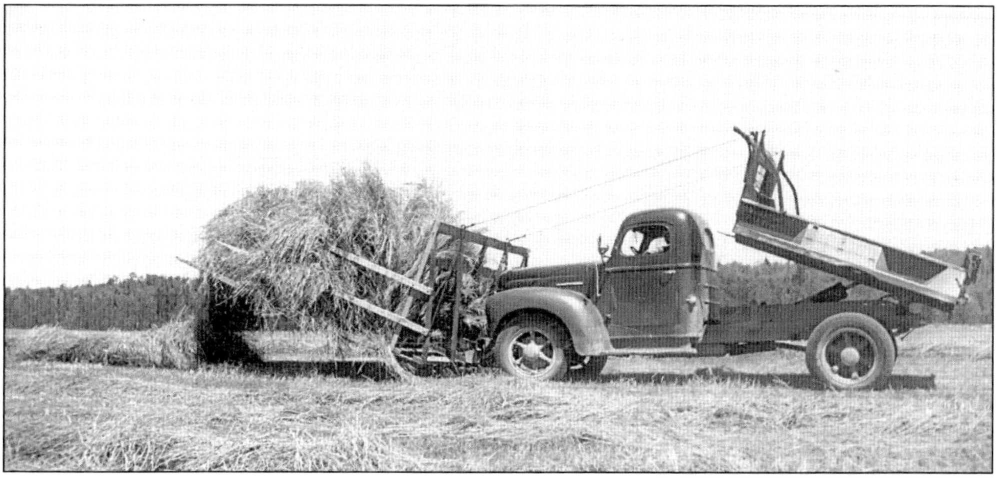

Farrar's "Buck Rake" Spears an Automobile. Ed Farrar and his dad, Raymond, were proud of their new rig used to haul hay to the barn. It could get hay in so much faster. There were 10-foot tines on the loader to hold a vast amount of hay. Ed was pulling out of a field with the rake loaded. He stopped and looked both ways at Todd's Corner. A car went by and Ed slowly pulled out behind it. Then it happened. The car had missed the St. Albans Road turn and was backing up. The car backed right into Ed and his load of hay. Ed had speared the rear end—putting a tine through the trunk and up into the roof. The driver and his friend had just been over to Glen Ring's getting some potatoes and did not seem too indignant about the accident at the time. They just wanted to be on their way. But it was not too long before an officer from Pittsfield showed up in the Farrar's dooryard demanding $75 for the damage to the hot-shot lawyer's car.

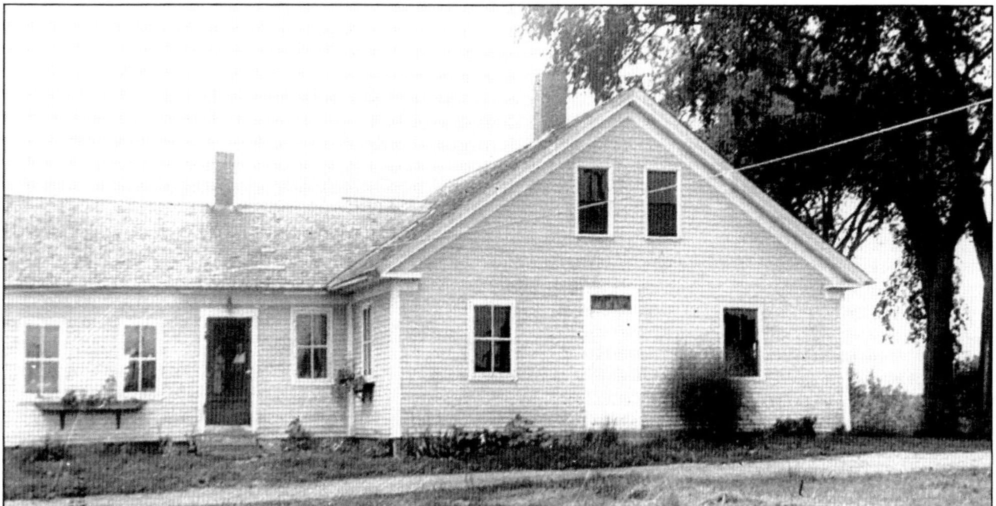

Dr. Todd of West Ripley Requests a Bill Payment. "Dr. Todd, Sir; My brother told me that you was here yesterday, to see me about that money I was owing you and have not the means to pay it untill I sell my farm. I have bargined [*sic*] it away and expect to do the writings in a few days. I expected to nex Saturday but I saw the man that is to have it today he says he shall not be able to do them under about ten days then you shall have your money. Yours in haste, George R. Watson, Cambridge, Maine. August 6, 1858." Shown in the photograph is the Dr. Todd farm, at Todd's Corner.

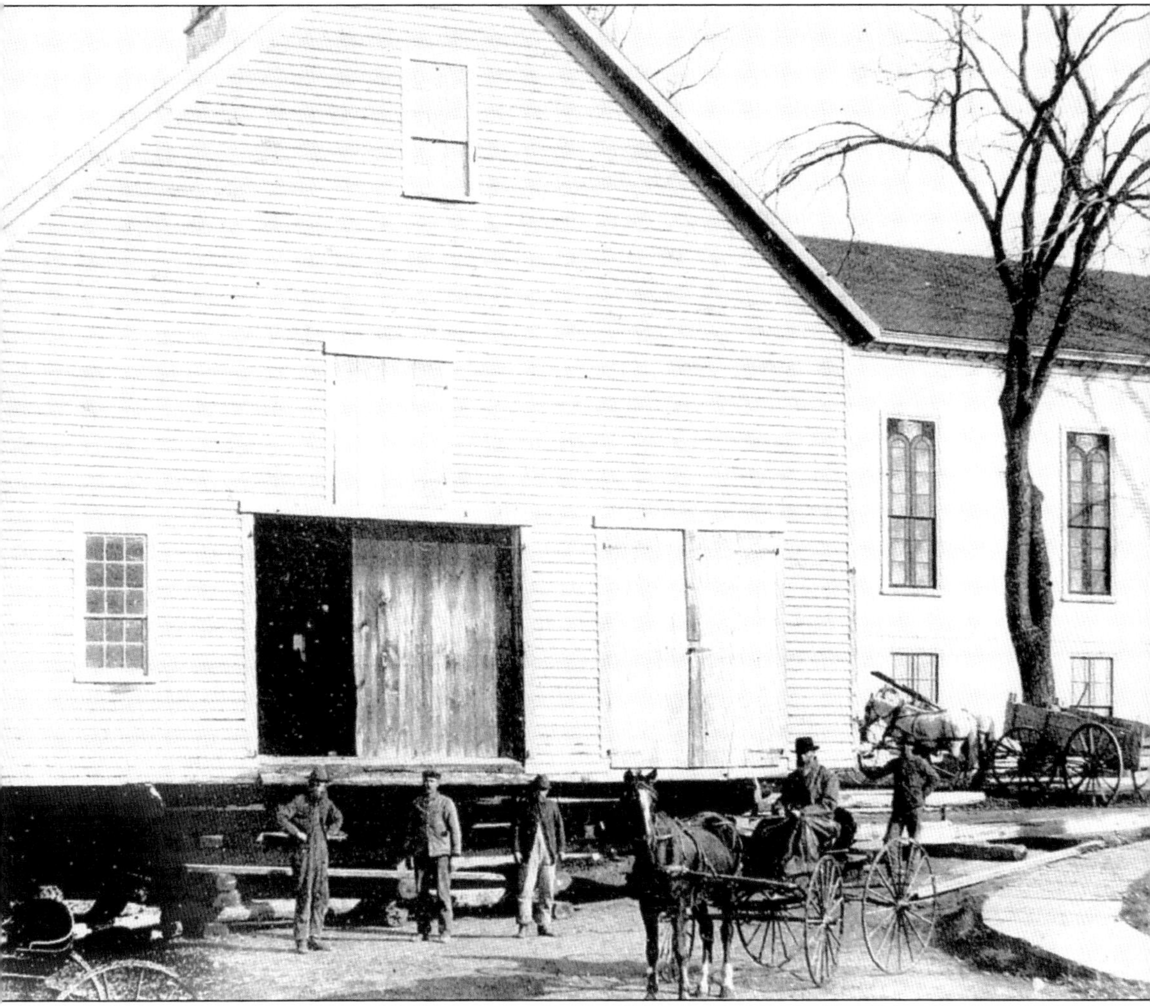

THE SEVEY FAMILY, BARNMOVERS EXTRAORDINAIRE. Making room for the Abbott Memorial Library to be built on the Dr. Burleigh home site are, from left to right, LaRoy S., Ernest L., and Albert L. Sevey. George Abbott, who donated the library to the Town of Dexter in 1895, is possibly sitting in the carriage. In the photograph, the barn is in the middle of Church Street, just below the Universalist church and not far from the present traffic light. Tragedy struck the Sevey family in 1908. LaRoy died of pneumonia on April 12 at age 69, his son Albert died of pneumonia on April 14 at age 31, and Uncle Moses Sevey died on May 30 at age 76.

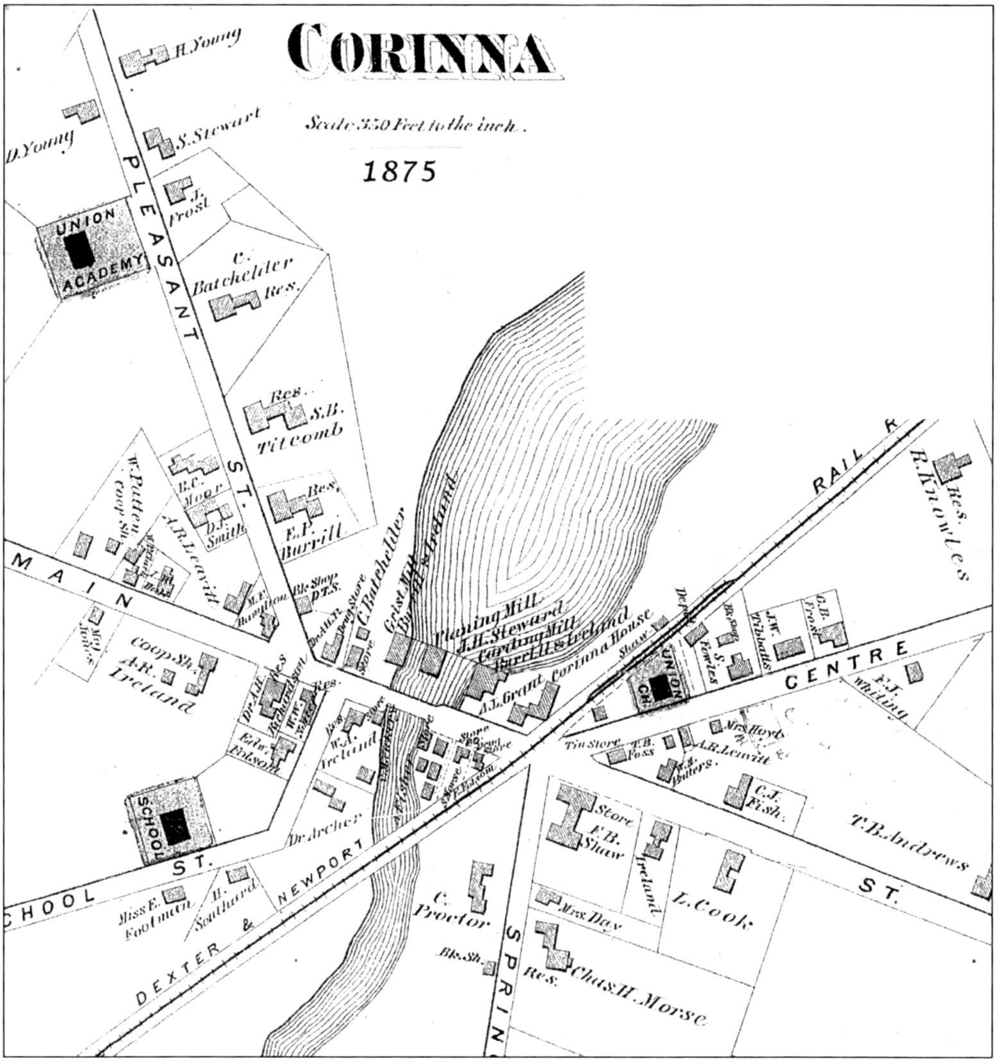

A Map of Intown Corinna, 1875. Corinna at this time had 32 merchants and 35 manufacturers. The town also had two physicians, three lawyers, six justices, one constable, one printer, one silver-mining company, one hotel, and one newspaper (the *Corinna Herald*).

Two

CORINNA

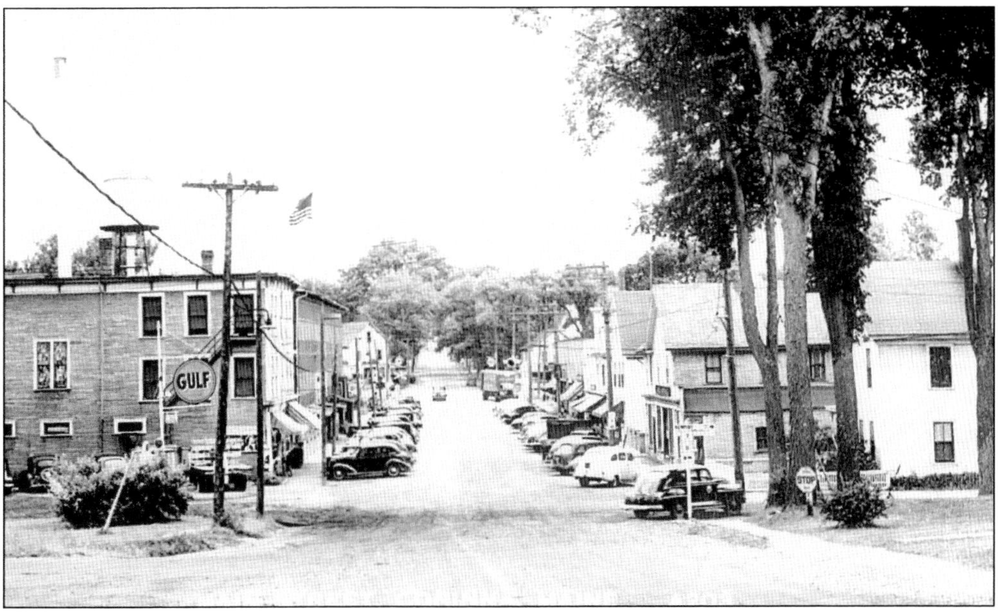

MAIN STREET, CORINNA, MAINE. Corinna was purchased from the Commonwealth of Massachusetts in 1804. A Mr. Chase was one of the first settlers, but he soon left, deserting his family here. The first permanent settler was William Southworth (Southard). The town, first known as Moor's Mills, was incorporated in 1816 and was named Corinna *c.* 1818. Its population in 1900 was 1,170. By 1990, that number had risen to 2,196. In 2000, Corinna's population was 2,145.

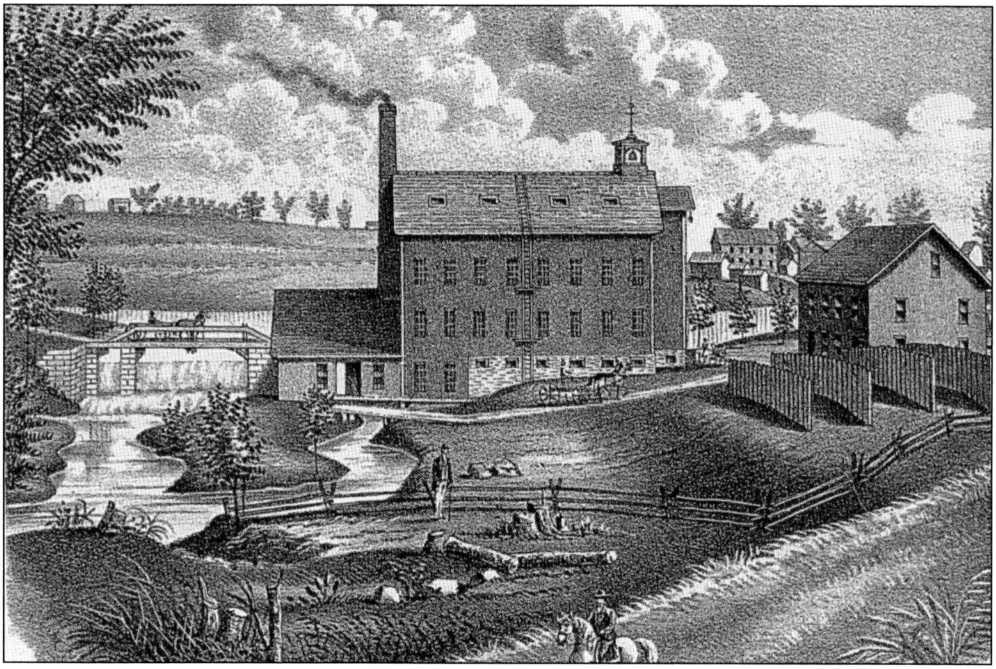

GREENWOOD LANDS IN THE UNITED STATES WITHOUT MONEY OR FRIENDS, 1850. It is a long way from emigrating from England to establishing a successful woolen factory in Corinna, Maine. But that is what Charles H. Greenwood did. After 15 years working in woolen mills in various parts of America, he settled in the town as proprietor of the Corinna Woolen Mill. His large family of 11 children worked in the mill alongside him. In the Depression era, the name was changed to the Moosehead Woolen Mills. In 1942, an entirely new mill was built near the old one. In March 1950, the mill complex burned completely and was never rebuilt.

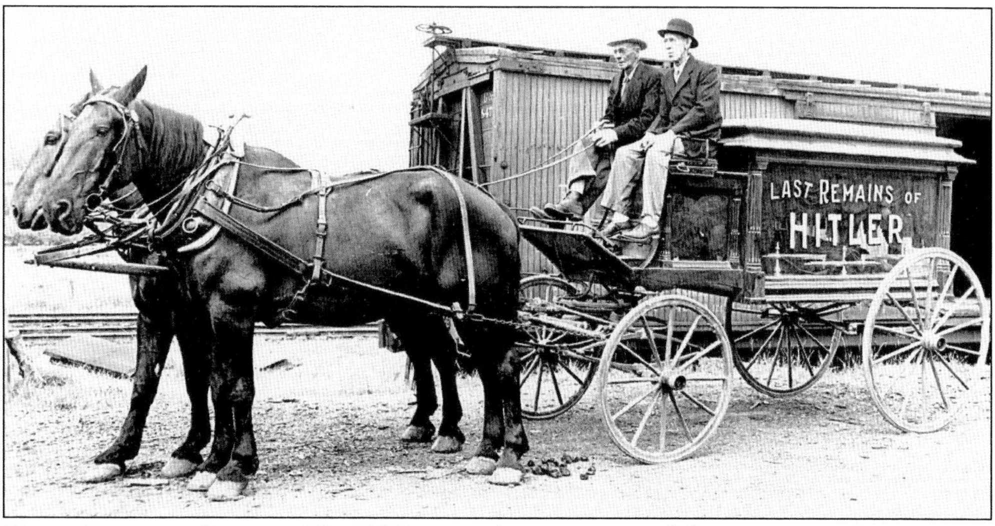

HITLER BURIED IN CORINNA. The V-J Day parade in 1946 was jubilant. Leon Dearborn (driving the hearse pictured) was the local "Express Man." He delivered coal to town residents in canvas bags. Ed Brann (beside Dearborn) always hung around with Dearborn and worked in the local mills. We do not know how the town got Hilter's remains, but they were paraded through Corinna in the hearse for this parade that celebrated a special day in American history.

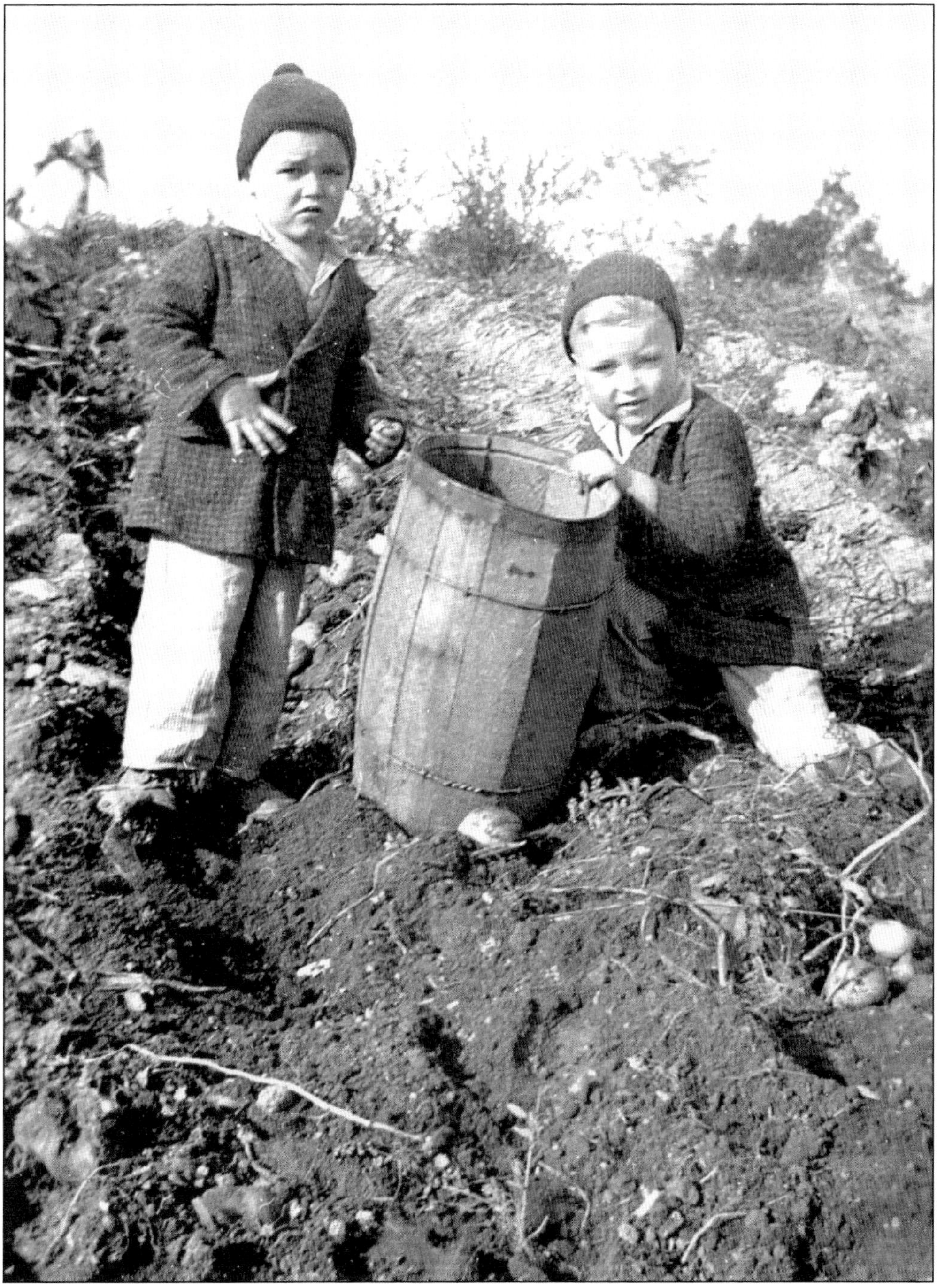

"Dad, We Got This Row Picked. Where Do We Go Next?" Keith Smith's boys learned early about potatoes, including the hard part, harvesting. From left to right are Stewart and Carl Smith. Beginning in North Newport, the Smith potato business moved to Corinna, where Hillacre Farms became a prosperous potato and corn rotation enterprise. Carl and Stewart were involved in starting the Sebasticook Valley Potato Warehouse. The object was to supply the potato chip market and have a large supply of potatoes under one roof.

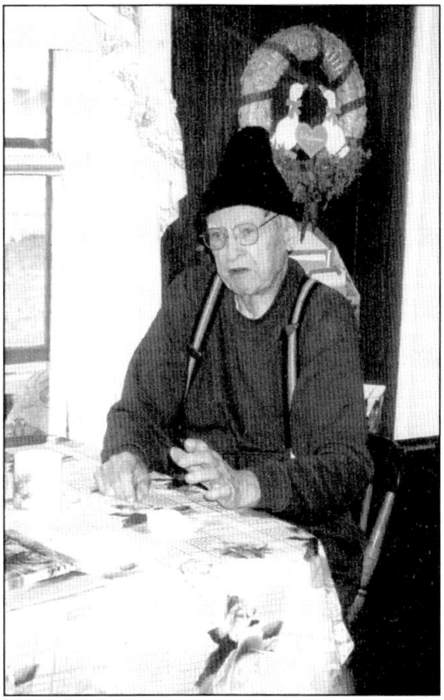

Well-Liked Stan Leavitt Receives the Gold Cane. Stan Leavitt just turned 98 years old. Whenever anyone wants to know about the last 100 years in Corinna, they ask him. He spent his life working in the local mills, and at one time, his wife, Grace, sold doughnuts to local homes. Leavitt is a dedicated Odd Fellow, likes to recite poetry, plays the spoons and hand saw, and loves the "fake" wrestling shows held in Bangor.

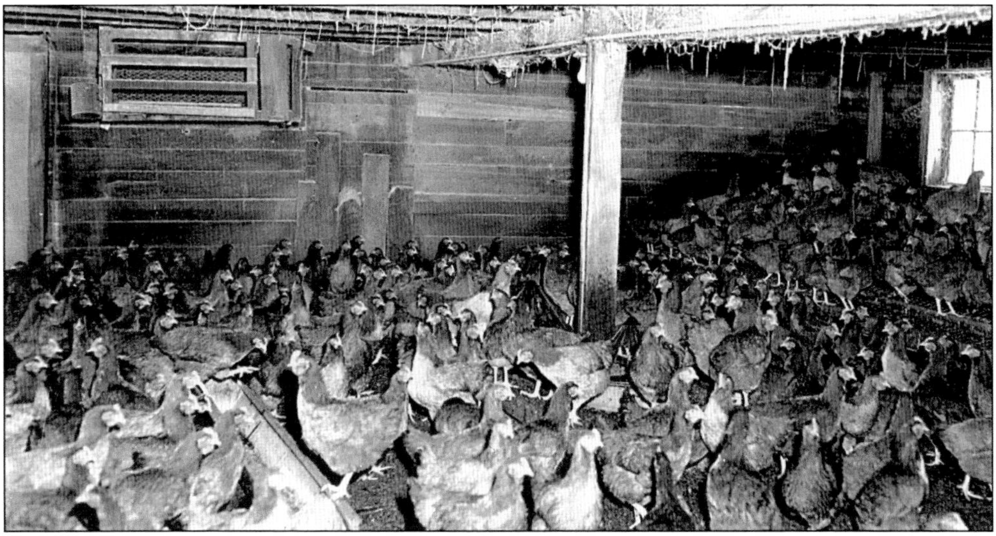

Sen. Jerome Emerson Revolutionizes the Poultry Business in Central Maine. The first poultry Jerome Emerson had were Rhode Island Reds and market eggs were sold. In 1938, he began producing 30 dozen hatching eggs daily from mating New Hampshire Reds with the Barred Rock cockerels he raised. The eggs were shipped to Venezuela, and each individual egg had to be stamped. The business eventually grew into a table-egg-processing plant on his farm that included cold storage. He went from 25,000 to 100,000 laying birds put out on contract to many farms in the area They were a sex-link cross of Rhode Island Red and Barred Rocks. The business prospered until 1974, when transportation and grain costs killed the egg and hen business in Maine. When Emerson's father became ill, he was elected in his father's place to the state legislature. In 1978, he ably represented his district in Augusta as a senator and a member of the transportation committee.

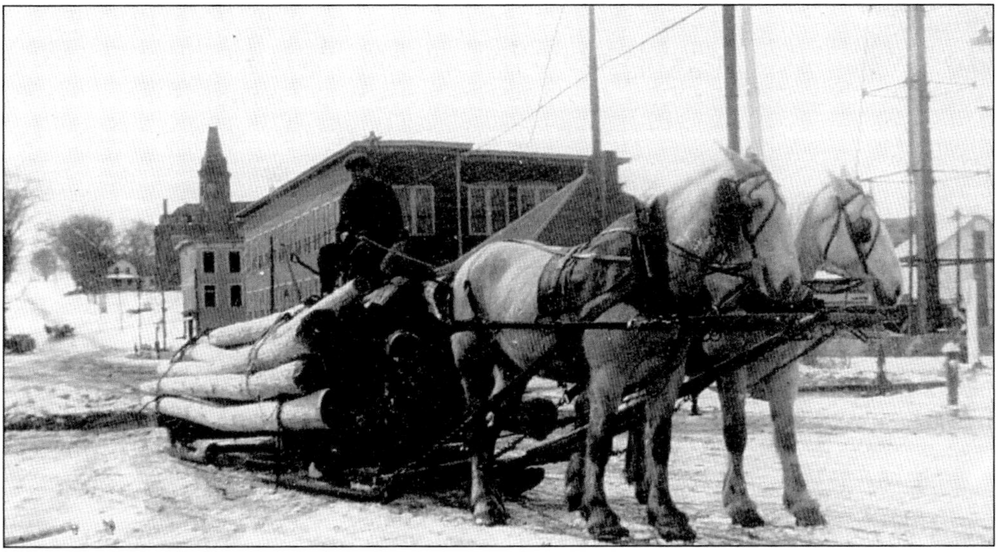

Jim Emerson Delivering Telephone Poles to Be Shipped by Rail. Jim always had a woods operation going in addition to his 40 milking cows. At one time, he operated a saw and finishing mill in Newport near the armory and American Legion hall. The cedar poles pictured came off his woodlot and are being hauled to the rail line in Corinna Village for delivery all over Maine. Emerson's wife, Zelda, was a teacher for many years.

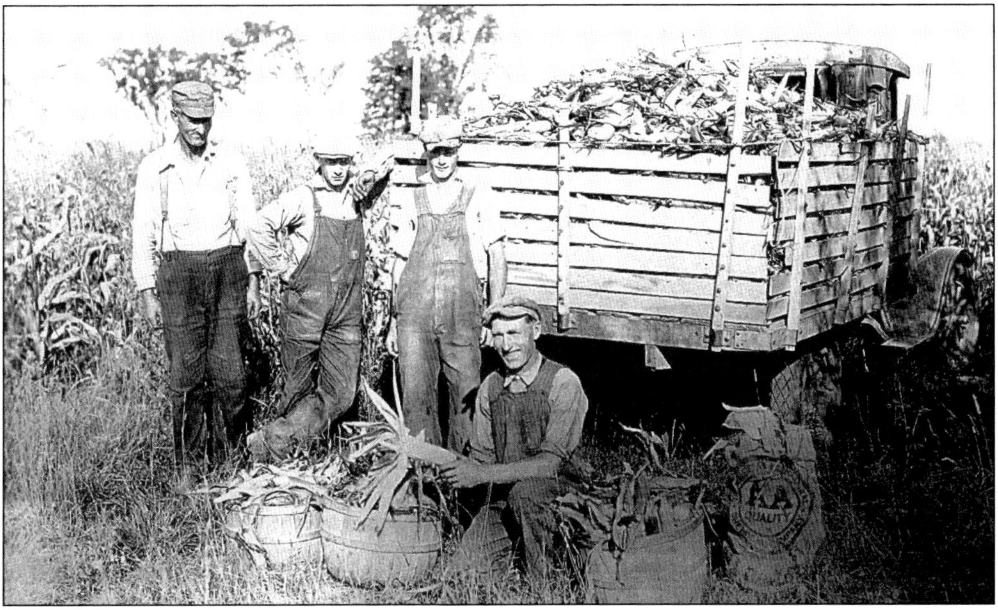

Picking Sweet Corn to Sell. Pleasant Vail Dairy was started by Jim Emerson in 1931. A milk-processing plant was built in a section of a former poultry building. His son Jerome learned how to operate the steam boiler, cream separator, pasteurizer, and bottling equipment. The milk was delivered locally. In this photograph, Jim and his crew pick sweet corn and throw it into the truck, one ear at a time. Someone got smart and made a "corn boat" of two poles and a frame to hold a barrel. The horse pulled it through the rows, and then the barrel was dumped into the truck at the end of the row. Standing, from left to right, are unidentified, Erwin Jones, and Don Knowles. Jim Emerson is kneeling.

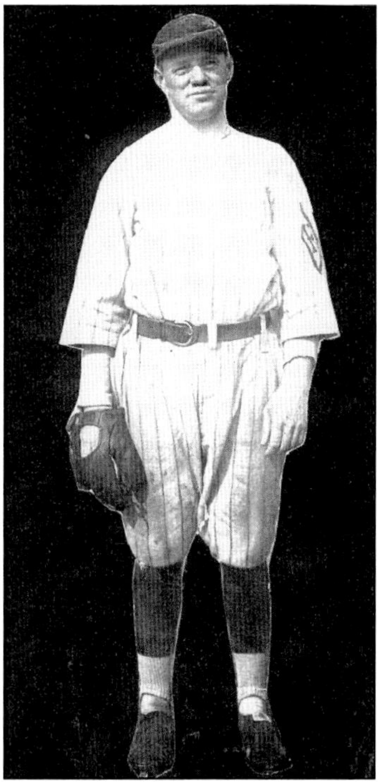

A Major League Baseball Prospect in Maine's Hall of Fame. "The late William S. (Sheriff) Buckland of Corinna is said to have pitched more baseballs, won more games and pitched more no-hitters than any other Maine star in his long career. Chalking up more than 500 wins in 750 games makes him an easy choice for the Maine Baseball Hall of Fame." (From the *Maine Sunday Telegram*, November 6, 1977.) He began at Maine Central Institute in Pittsfield and, after graduation, pitched for Winthrop, Skowhegan, Rockland, Corinna, Dexter, Portland, Guilford, Greenville, Millinocket, Old Town, and Milo. He went out of state to Maryland twice and pitched for Sherbrooke in Canada. "He possessed a great fork ball but was known as a smart slow ball moundsman. He pitched at least 17 no-hitters and averaged nearly 14 strikeouts per game. He pitched his last game at age 56."

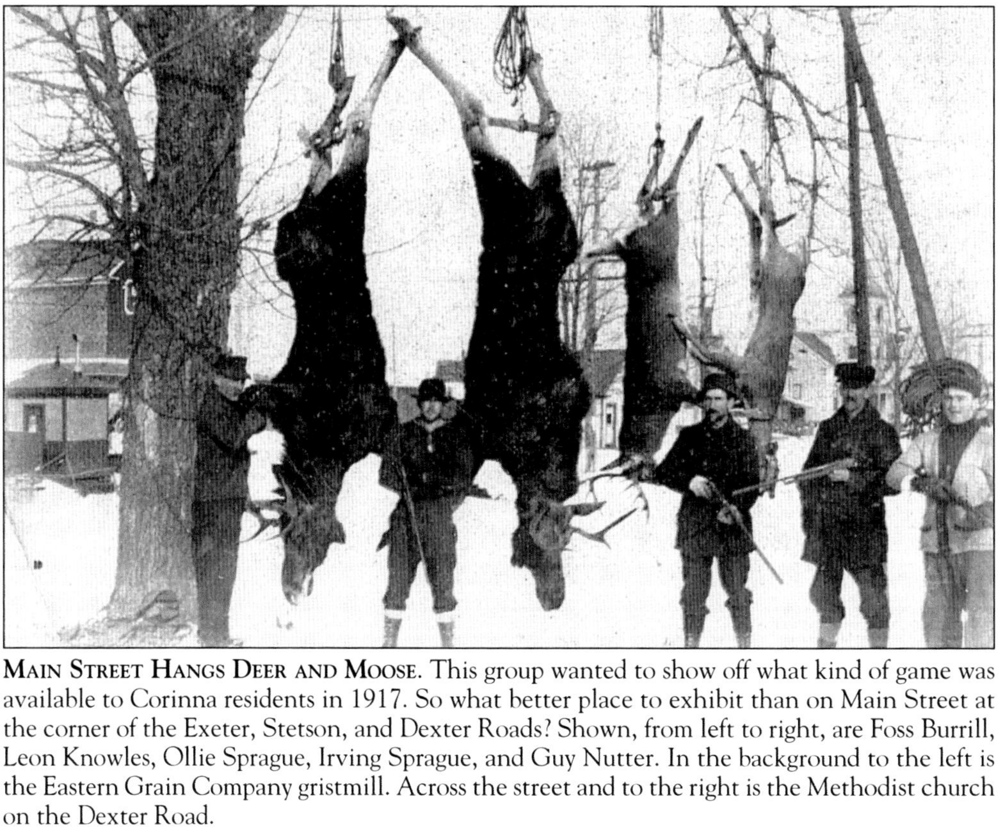

Main Street Hangs Deer and Moose. This group wanted to show off what kind of game was available to Corinna residents in 1917. So what better place to exhibit than on Main Street at the corner of the Exeter, Stetson, and Dexter Roads? Shown, from left to right, are Foss Burrill, Leon Knowles, Ollie Sprague, Irving Sprague, and Guy Nutter. In the background to the left is the Eastern Grain Company gristmill. Across the street and to the right is the Methodist church on the Dexter Road.

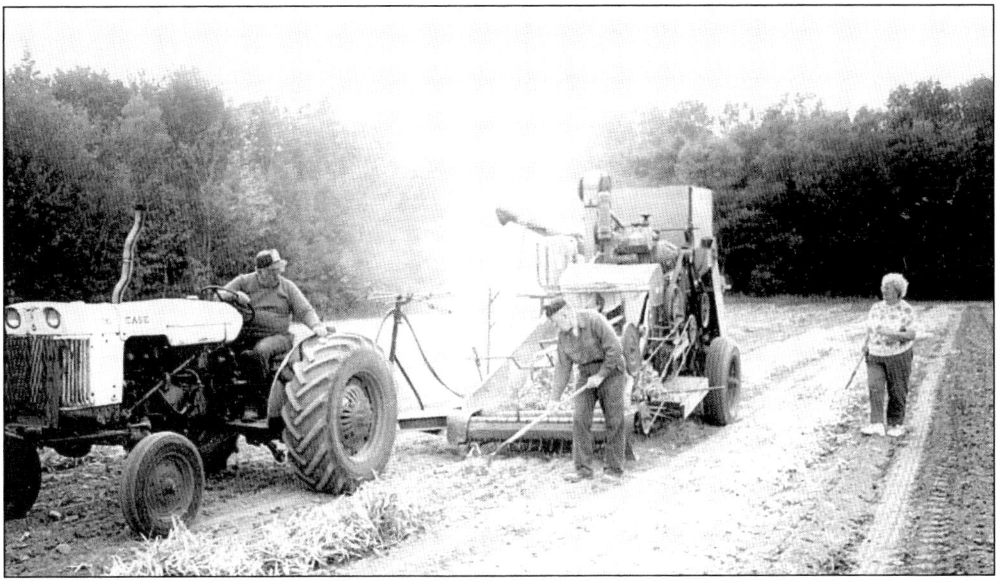

THE BOLSTRIDGE BEAN CREW HARVESTING BEANS. Notice who is riding and who is walking. Lloyd Bolstridge is driving the Bidwell combine. His brother Leslie is keeping the windrow in order. Audrey Bolstridge is busy pulling back the beans at the end of the rows so the machine can make the turn. After pulling and rowing the beans, the combine thrashes, fans, and deposits the beans in a holding tank. A truck then takes them to the beanery warehouse, where they are cleaned, inspected, and dried to 18 percent moisture.

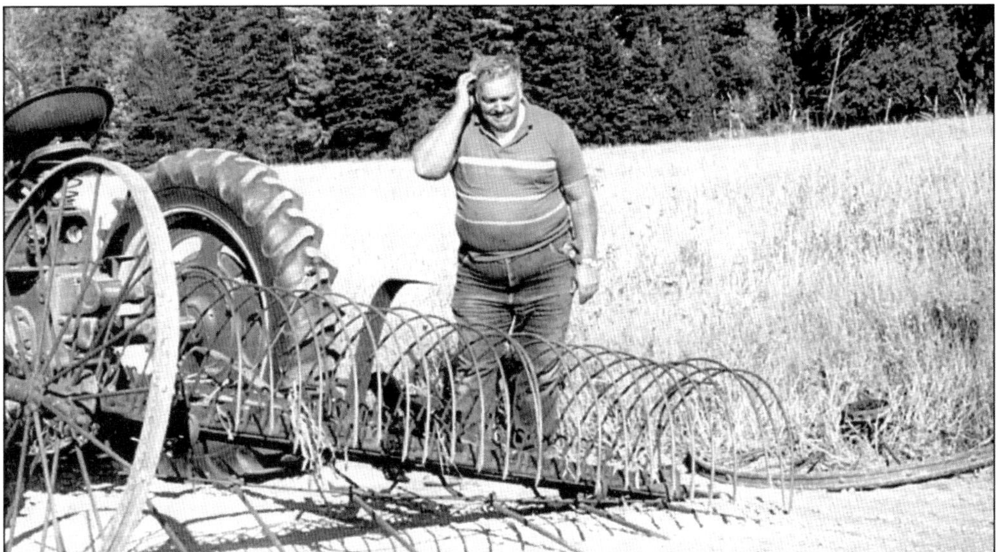

HORSE-DRAWN RAKES ARE NOT MADE FOR MODERN-DAY FARMING. Dump rakes were made to be pulled slowly by horses. Lloyd Bolstridge found that out the hard way. He and his wife, Audrey, have been farming for many years. At one time they were producing 18,000 eggs per day from 20,500 hens. They won the world's largest egg contest at Pittsfield on three different occasions. Soil cultivation includes the organic methods of rotating dry beans and corn. Cover crops have been seeded into the corn by helicopter in August to prevent soil erosion over the winter. Some beans are sold to Johnny's Selected Seeds and Fedco.

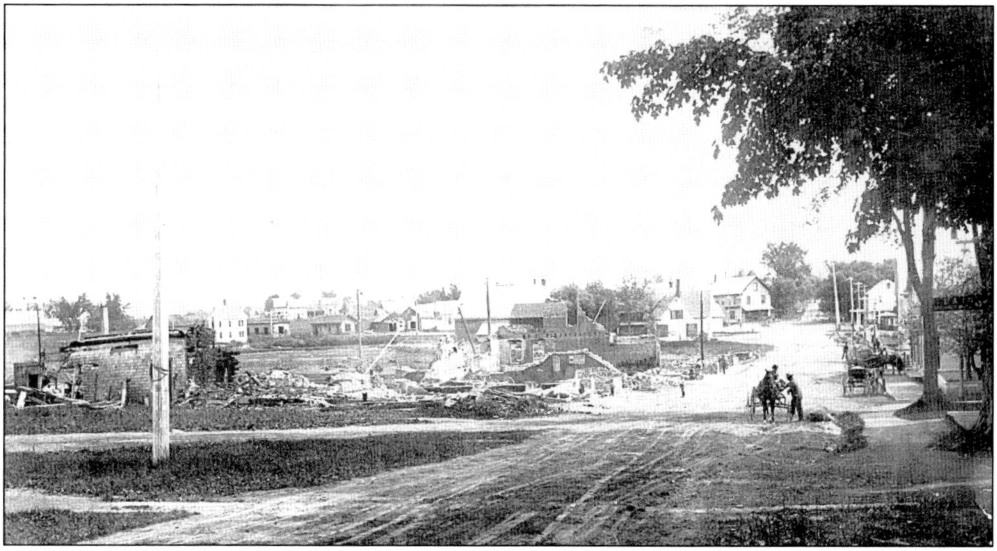

A 1904 Fire Ravages Main Street. In the 1870s, a stone dam and a brick gristmill were built. In 1877, the Eagle block was added, which contained stores, lodge rooms, and offices beside the grain elevator in the rear. On July 4, 1904, a fire destroyed it all on that side of Main Street. A new elevator was built by Leslie F. Ireland in 1912 where Corinna Manufacturing later stood. In the 1890s, Ireland installed an electric light plant in his mill, and it ran daily until 11:30 p.m. Ireland drowned in the millpond while removing splashboards at the upper dam. Another fire on September 11, 1911, burned the gristmill, two other business blocks, and two dwellings. It was rebuilt and became the Eastern Grain Company.

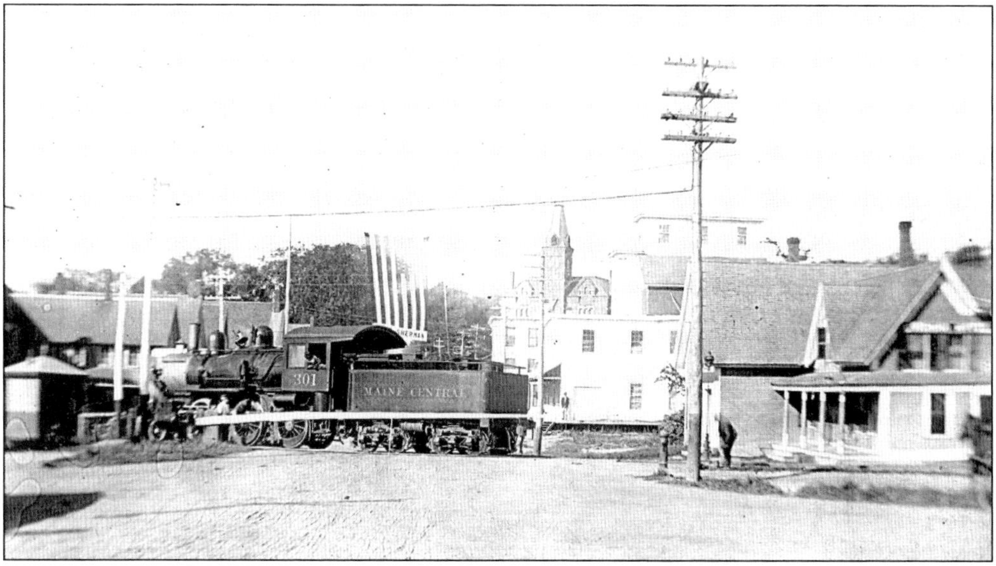

Corinna Lends $50,000 to Build a Railroad. The Dexter and Newport Railroad opened up the area. Becoming a boomtown, Corinna had two trains daily pass through and connect to Newport for travel to the rest of Maine. A Western Union telegraph office was soon opened. Principal products shipped on the railroad were hay, potatoes, grains, eggs, apples, and wheat. Several cattle buyers shipped meat to the Brighton and Boston markets. Ship timber was also loaded on the railroad from the surrounding towns, to be sent to Belfast and neighboring ports.

ELDER LEVI M. STEWART (1823–1910). In *The Life of Levi Merrick Stewart* (1932), Maynard W. Quimby writes, "A poor woman who lived in one of the many houses which the 'Elder' owned and rented had been ill for a long time. The collecting agent had told her that unless she paid her rent immediately she would have to move. The next day the woman came to Mr. Stewart and told him what the agent had said. He told her to come back to his office on the following day. When she did this Mr. Stewart handed her the deed to the house in which she was living."

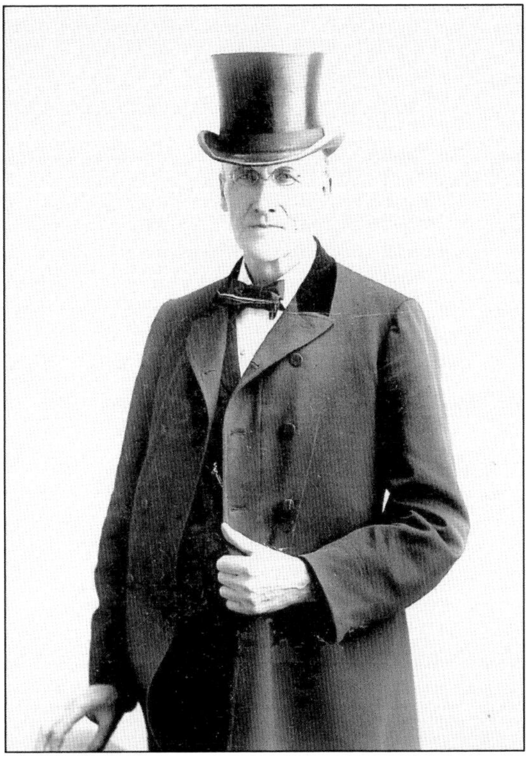

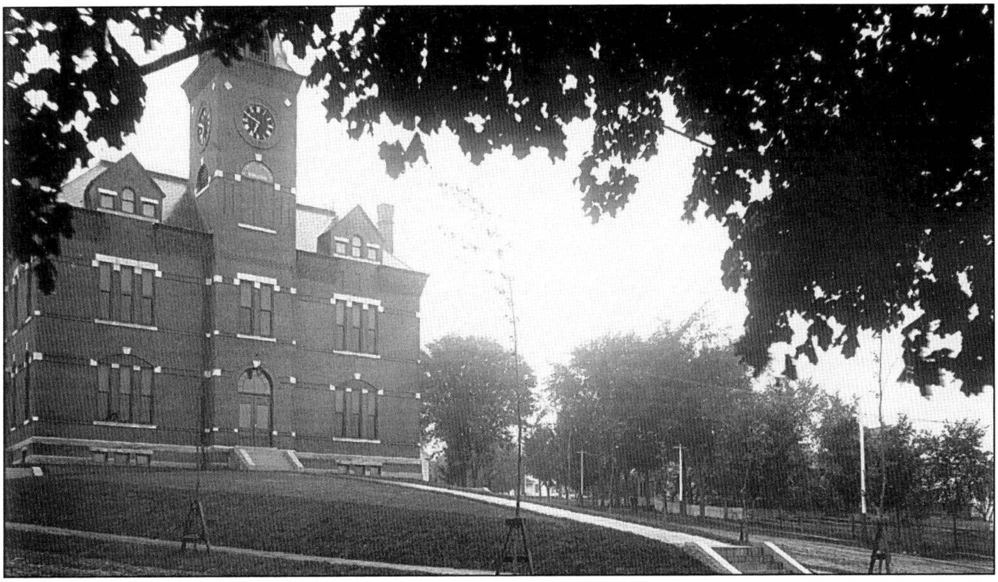

THE LEVI M. STEWART LIBRARY. Quimby continues, "Elder Stewart was very fond of fine books there can be no doubt. His own library consisted of more than 6,000 volumes of which over 2,000 are law books. His Civil War collection alone numbered 400 volumes. In the Napoleon collection there were 250 separate books. He also had in his library a collection of 75 volumes concerning Abraham Lincoln." Levi's will stated, "Sixth I give and bequeath unto the Stewart Free Library of Corinna Maine all of my books, and also the sum of $50,000 to help maintain the same in a state of excellence."

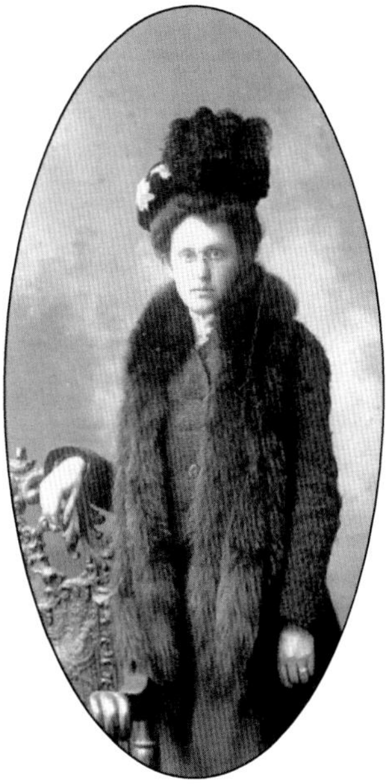

EDNA EMERY HUTCHINS WAS RIGHT; THE TOWN DID NOT LISTEN. The town fathers should have heeded Edna's advice. "Don't trust Striar's; make them pay their taxes like everyone else," she admonished years ago. When Eastland Mill recently declared bankruptcy and left town leaving a big tax bill unpaid, Edna was vindicated. She was a milliner by occupation, but her real value to Corinna was her civic activities. She was a longtime school board member, local PTA member, librarian, and a member of the Order of the Eastern Star, the Garden Club, and Morse's Corner Baptist Church. Her caring interest in her community touched many Corinna residents. She organized the school's hot lunch program, as well as the church community workers of the Methodist church. She was active in the Republican Party and served on the town committee. As a school board member, it usually took a giant snowstorm for her to ever call off school.

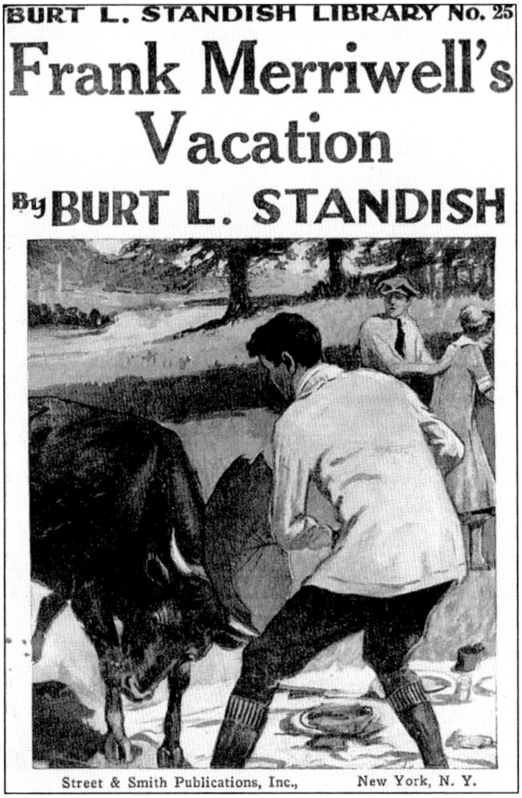

A CORINNA NATIVE AUTHORS 600 BOOKS; 200,000 SOLD WEEKLY IN THE UNITED STATES. He was known to the literary world as Burt L. Standish, one of many pen names, but was actually William George Patten. Born in Corinna in 1866, he founded the *Corinna Owl*, a weekly newspaper, just after graduating from high school. "Patten was probably the most prolific writer who ever lived. He turned out more than 20 million words about the Merriwell brothers, Frank and Dick, between 1896 and 1916. Without a doubt, Frank Merriwell was the most popular fictional character in American literature." (From *Frank Merriwell's Father*.) Leslie Bolstridge collected 200 volumes of Frank Merriwell books and donated them to the library.

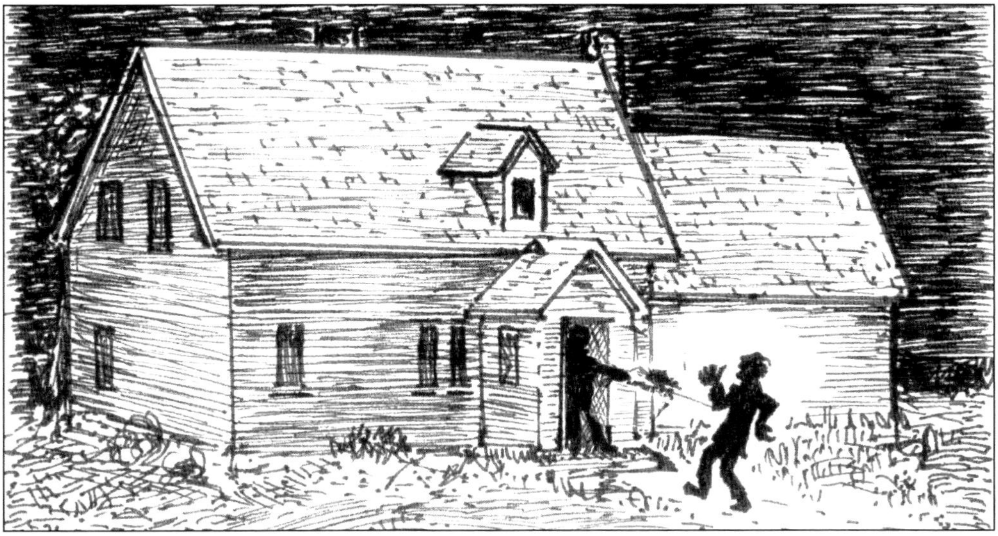

A Corinna Murder Case Baffling Officials, August 12, 1913. "Deputies Welch and Levenseller stated that there were no statements to be made public as yet. Wayland Philbrick when shot was thought standing on the board about 6 feet from his doorway where his assailant was standing. The report that Wayland told his mother and a friend the name of his murderer are denied. As he left for the hospital he remarked to a neighbor, 'I'm not afraid to die. The only thing I regret is that I can't leave my mother better provided for.' Everywhere there is a prevailing feeling of insecurity, and doors and windows are carefully locked at night and people hesitate to leave their homes after nightfall." (From a clipping in the Ellie Hurd scrapbook.) This sketch was done by Dave Pearson.

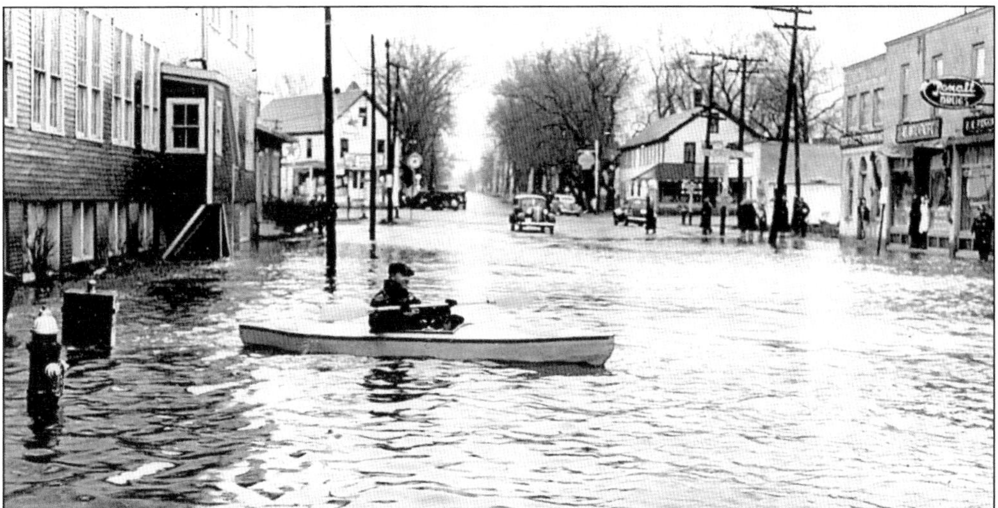

Pearl Shepherd Tries Fishing in Main Street after the 1936 Flood. The floodwaters on Main Street looked calm enough to fish in, but behind the woolen mill to the left was a torrent of ice chunks and rushing water. Henry King had fallen off the Upper Dam and looked like a goner. As he fought to stay afloat among the ice heading down stream, he came upon the Main Street Bridge. At the last moment, he dove down as deep as he could to avoid the bridge and miraculously surfaced on the other side. He was fished out of the turbulent waters downstream and survived.

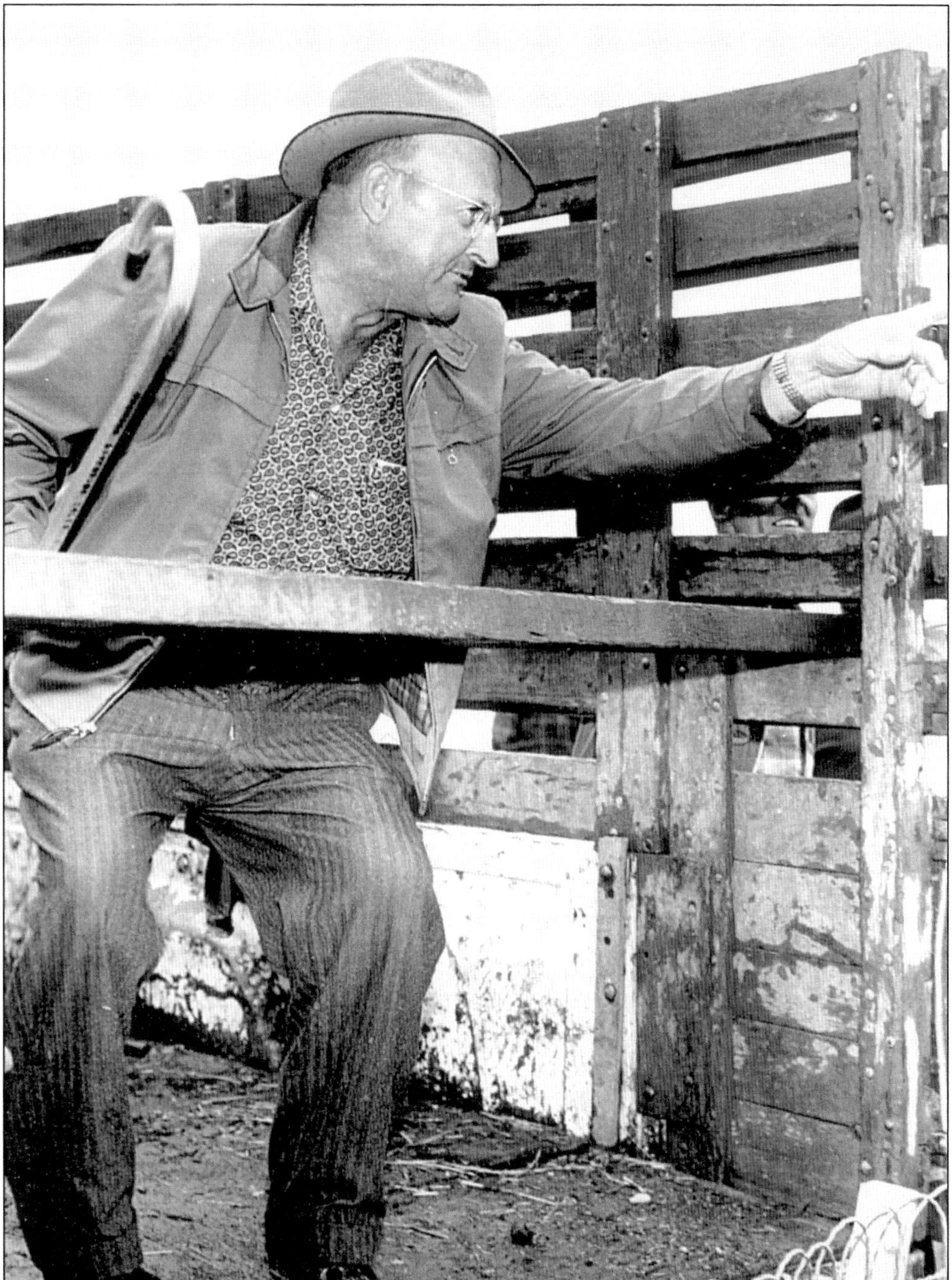

Razor Getting Another High Bid. Oh how he could work a crowd! One time, at Hammond's barn at Exeter Corner, a "poor" draft horse was brought in. When Razor started the auction off at $100, the crowd howled with laughter. So he dropped the starting bid to $60 and began his stories and chatter to warm up and distract the crowd. Gradually the bids started flying. When the old horse got up to $160 he shouted in wild glee, "Ha, I knew what the old S.O.B was worth!"

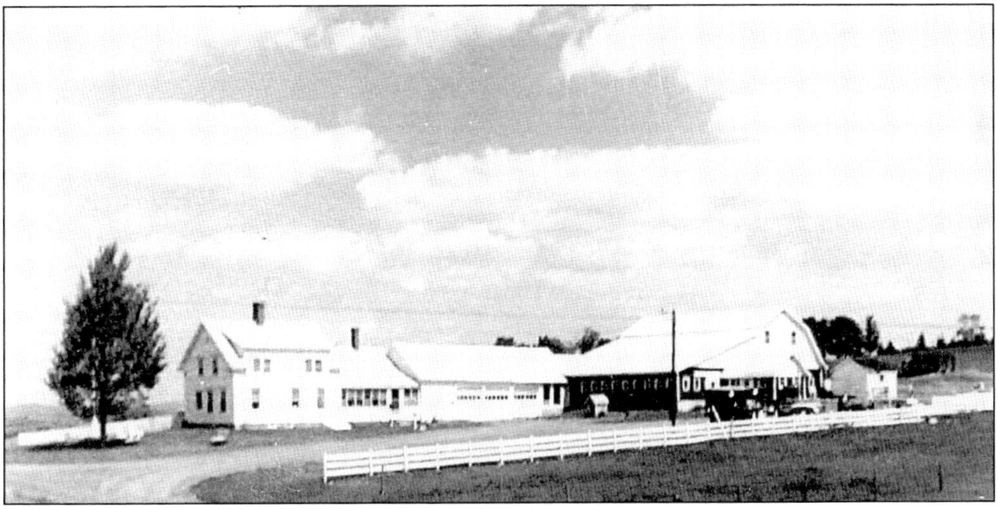

The Auctions at Corundel View Farm. At one time, Razor had 100 purebred Guernseys at Corundel View Farm, and he continued auctions there with his wife, "Mike," for many years. People would come from all over every Thursday to Corinna. Razor was county commissioner, Grange master, president of the Eastern Maine Development District, and very active in 4-H Club auctions and oxen pulling.

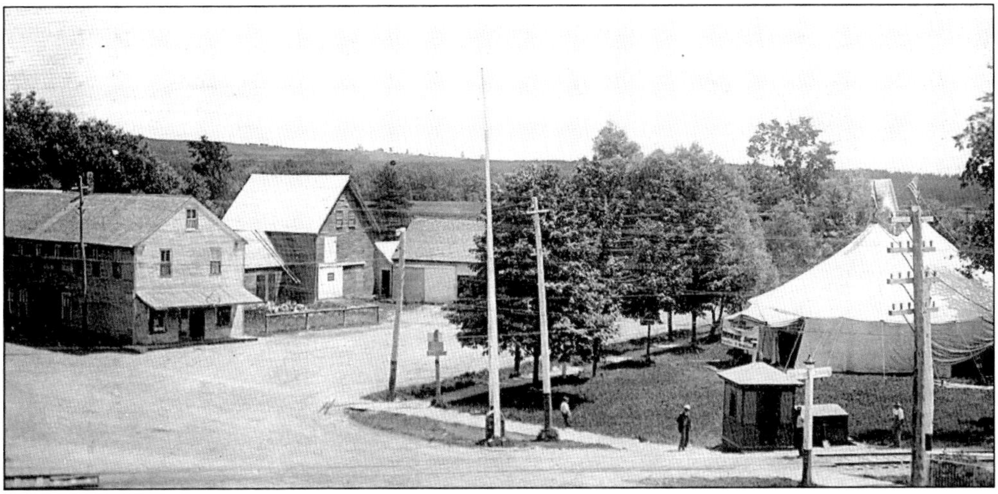

The Religious Revival Circuit in Corinna to Save Souls. Camp Meeting Day arrived sunny and bright. With a large tent set up on Main Street at the Stetson Road corner, everyone expected a good crowd. "The big wind blew into Corinna. It came in the form of an Adventist preacher, John Nickerson. He claimed to have figured out the exact date when the world would come to an end. He stood the town on end and shook it. He packed the old Union church to overflowing. All Corinna seemed tense as the day of the great event drew near. The day wore on. Nothing happened. Morning came again. It was another day and the Prophet John was discredited. He left town and settled in Dexter where he became a boot and shoe cobbler. There was a report that he had turned atheistic." "I'm through trying to be a benefactor to humanity," he said. "Hereafter I'm going to look out for myself and let humanity go to hell." (From *Frank Merriwell's Father*.)

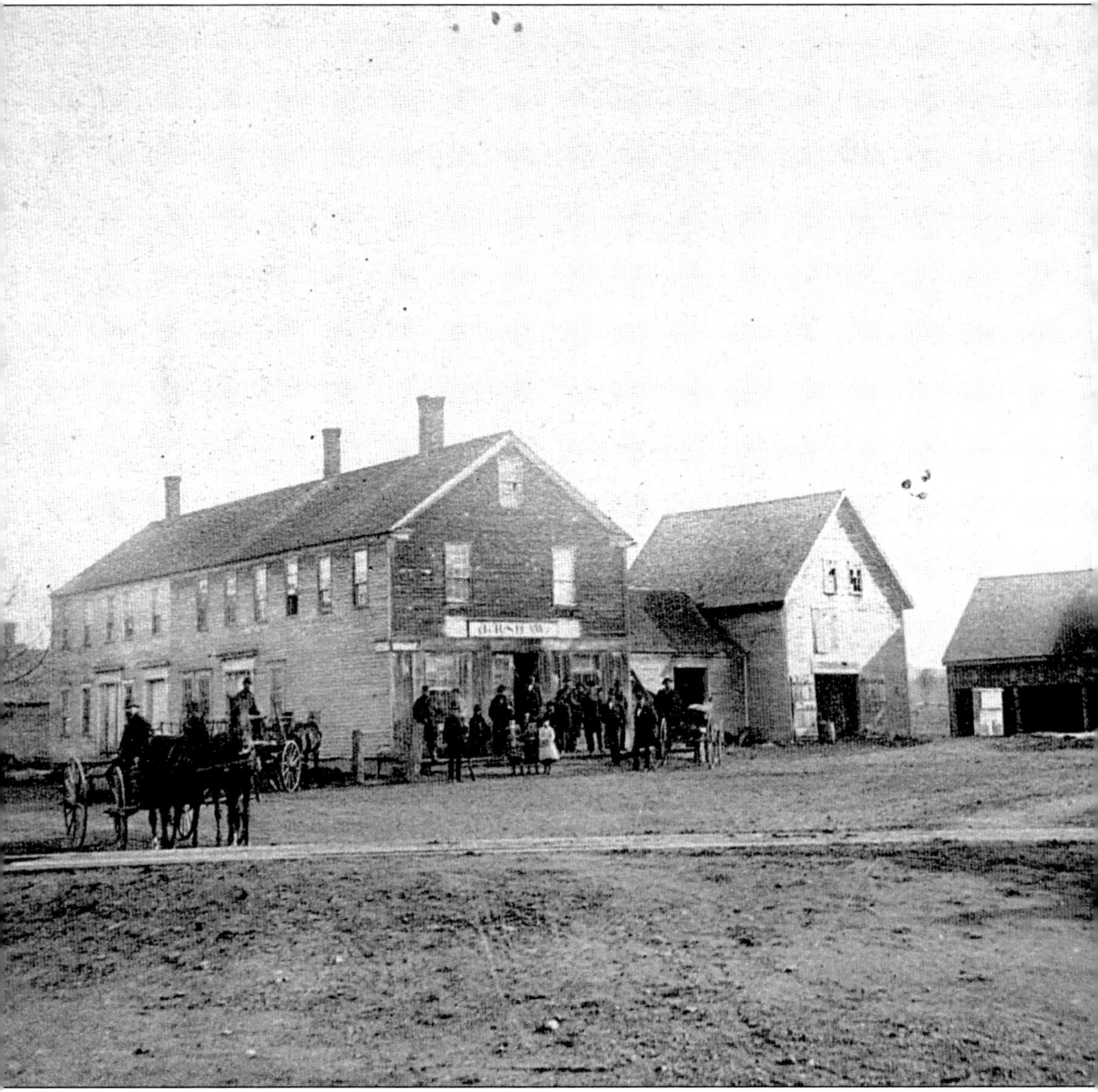

THE MYSTERIOUS DISAPPEARANCE OF CORINNA'S 1881 TAX REVENUE. Indignant Corinna taxpayers are seen gathering in front of Flavel Shaw's store at the corner of the Dexter, Exeter, and Stetson Roads discussing Corinna's enormous town debt of $4,315.58. Part of this debt was a mysterious disappearance of $1,522.34 revenue from tax collecting. Town records reported the following: "Amount of receipts found for which no credit was given on the books, $169.51. Amount sworn to have been paid and no credit given on the books, $438.79." The total tax bill to be collected was $1,825.72, but treasurer Samuel Copp received only $303.38 cash. What become of the missing $1,522.34? Anyone who can shed light on this 1881 mystery, please call the town office.

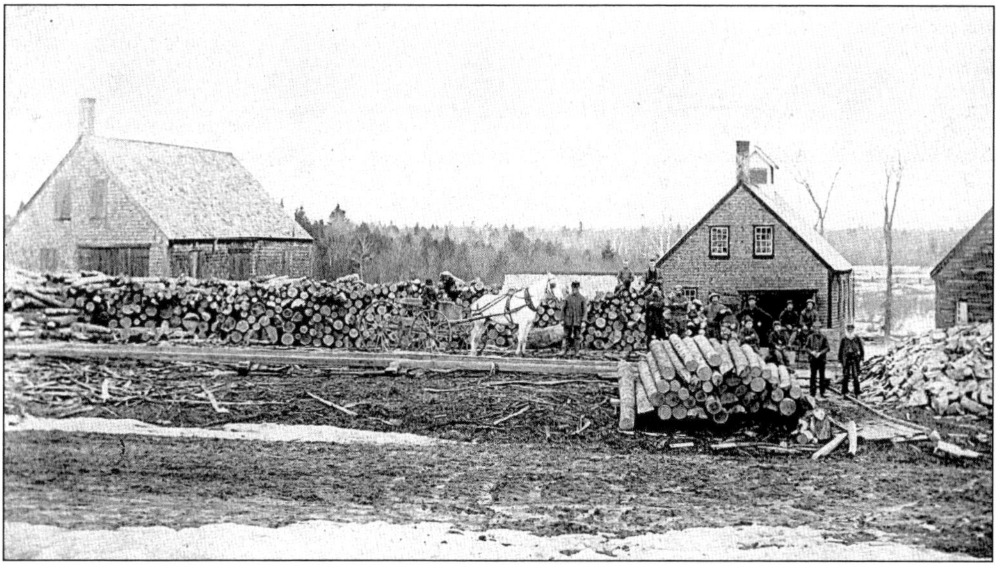

THE WATER-POWER OF MAINE (1869), BY WALTER WELLS, SPT. HYDROGRAPHIC SURVEY OF MAINE. "First, on the Dexter stream, Moody's Mills [photograph shown above] 8' head, various saws. Second and third, below, unoccupied; 10' head each. Fourth, Lincoln's Mill, 10' head, 2 shingle mills, privilege capable of doing much larger business. Fifth, Village Mills, 12' head, grist, shingle, cloth-dressing, and carding mills. Sixth, unoccupied, about 8' head. Seventh, on Alder Stream, Shepherd Mill, saw and shingle machine; now unoccupied. Eighth, Welch Mill, below, 9' head, saw mill. Ninth, Burrill Mill, 7' head, shingle machine. Tenth, in south-west corner of town, Nickerson Mill, shingle mill. Eleventh, in the east part of town, a saw mill."

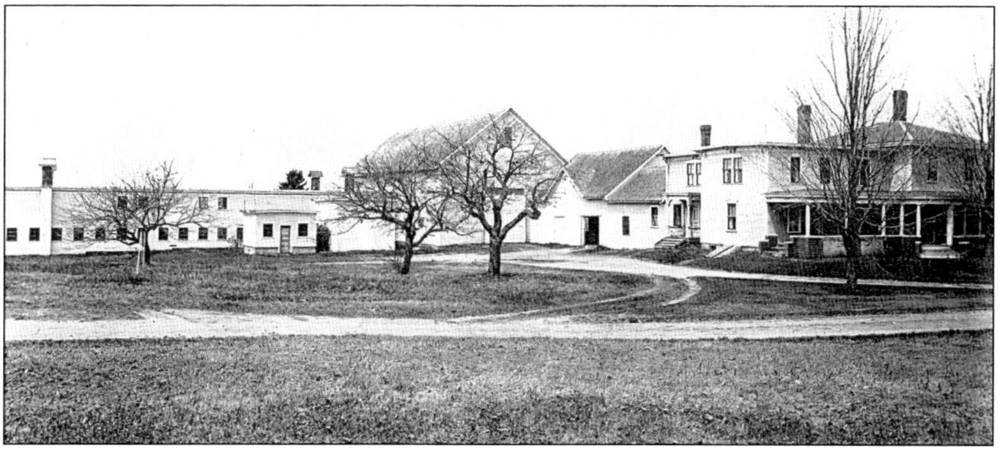

MORSE'S CORNER TRICKEY FARM, 1917. The Carrol J. Trickey farm was completely modernized, with a new stanchion-style tie-up for 55 milking cows and a cheese factory on the property. In the early 1930s, a fire started and it was determined that the only way to save all the buildings was to dynamite the shed to stop the fire from spreading. Ted Peavey set a charge on the shed floor. What Ted did not know was that there was also a large cache of dynamite stored upstairs in the shed. When it all went off it blew out windows across the street at the church plus the Holt house. Fireman Herb Dow Sr. was at the well getting some water, and when the explosion happened it almost blew him into the well. But the fire was stopped and the barn saved.

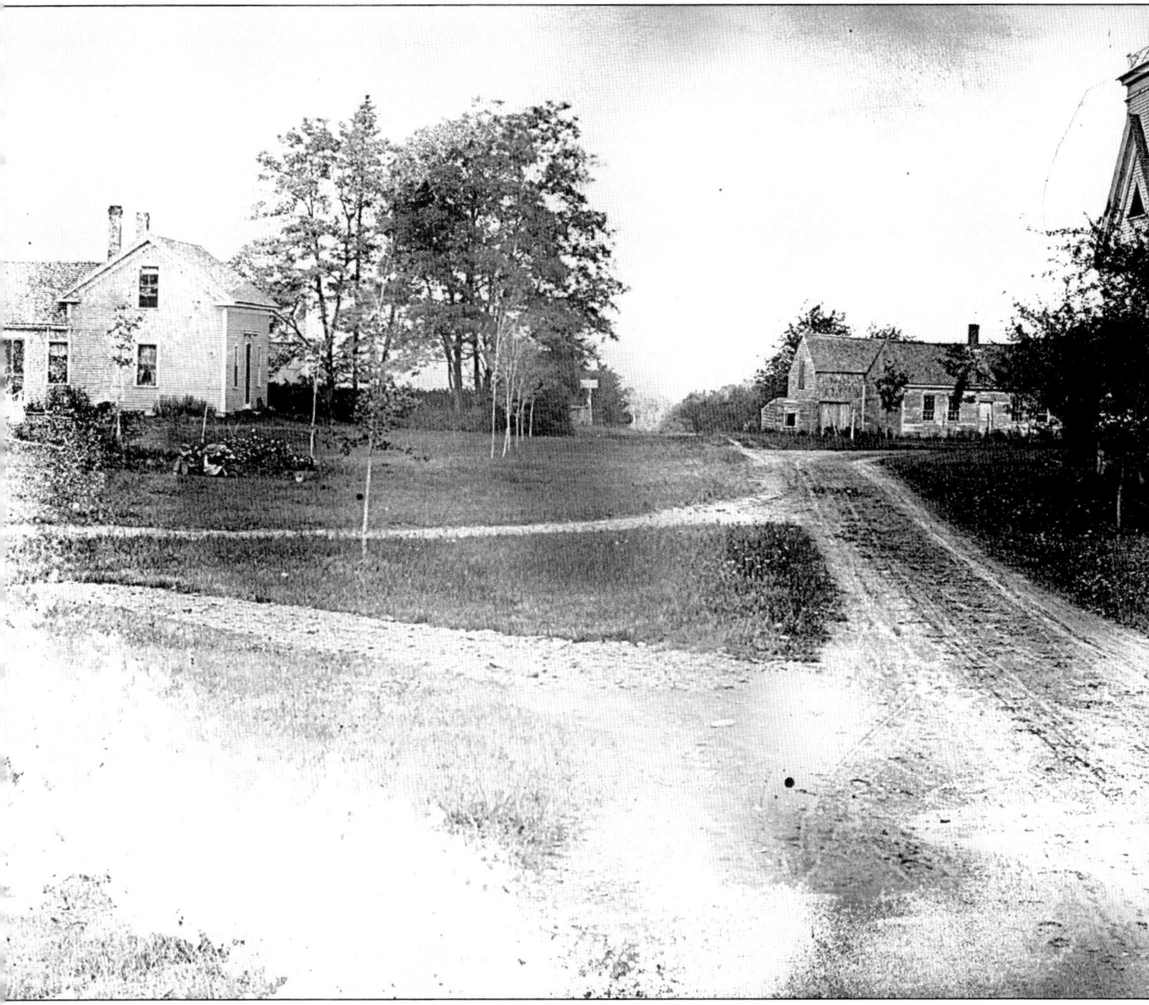

William "Tame" Hole Puts Rocks to the Town Farm Windows. Nobody knew where he came from. It was rumored he was a stowaway in the hold of a ship from eastern Europe. William Hole was dark and foreign in complexion and appearances, and his nationality and origin were unknown. His name, "Hole," developed from his manner of coming to America—in the hold of a ship. He was a blacksmith at Morse's Corner who liked his rum. He would go to Bangor, returning with a keg of rum strapped to two poles from the saddle. He was a signer of the Incorporation of Corinna in 1816 and had five children born between 1809 and 1821. In 1839, at the town meeting, Hole wanted to divide up the surplus funds from the Jackson administration among the townspeople, but it was voted instead to buy a farm for the poor of the town. In a state of intoxication, he went to the town farm and shattered every pane of glass. It was ironic that his son Walter and his wife, Lefa, became town charges and lived there years later. Tame lived to be 100 years old. This view, looking north, shows Morse's Corner. Hole's blacksmith shop would be just to the right of the photograph.

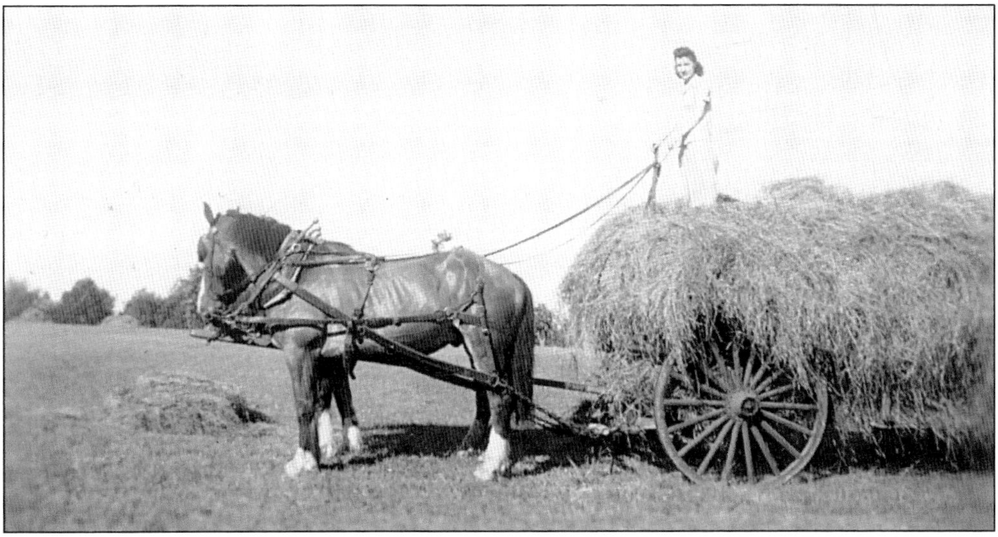

Haying at Morse's Corner. "I was the outside crew," Doris White McKenney said recently. "I never worked in the barn or fed up, but Grampa Pratt showed me how to drive the horses to get in the hay, and I did it. Never got in any trouble either. I loved horses, even though I never had one of my own." Doris hayed at Morse's Corner c. 1942 while her husband, Richard, was stationed in the army down south. The barn is still standing.

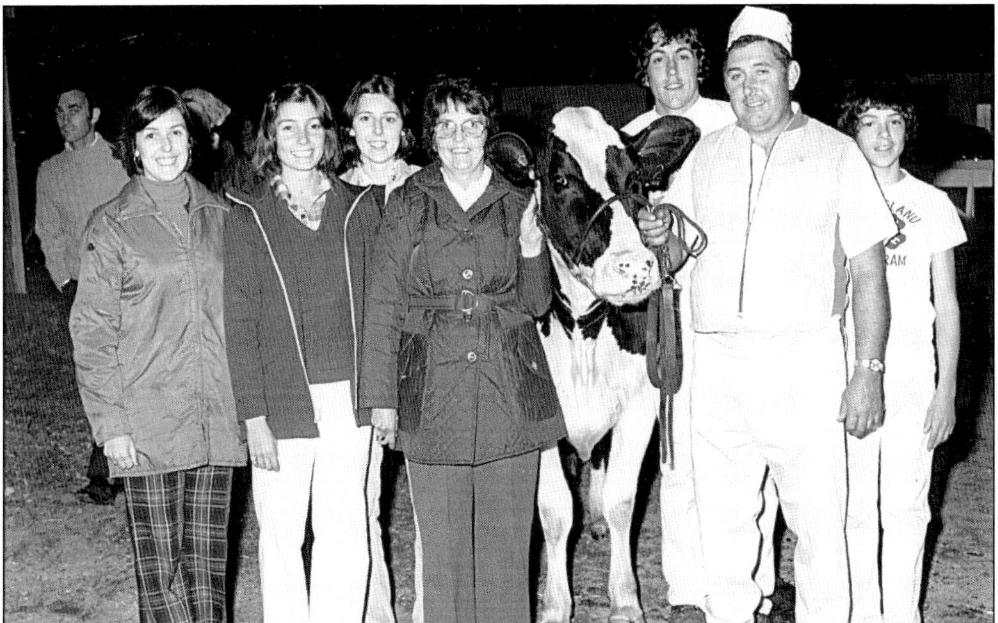

Ken Veazie's Veazland Farm Started with 11 Cows in 1951. It took 32 years of hard work, but by 1983, the Veazie family was voted Dairyman of the Year. By then, the farm had grown to 800 acres and 240 cows and heifers. Four generations of Veazies have farmed where Ken got his start. Ulysses G. Veazie started farming *c.* 1900. Today, Ken's two sons, Richard and Robert, run the operation. Shown here are, from left to right, Patti, Kathy, Sharon, Virginia, Richard, Kenneth, and Robert Veazie.

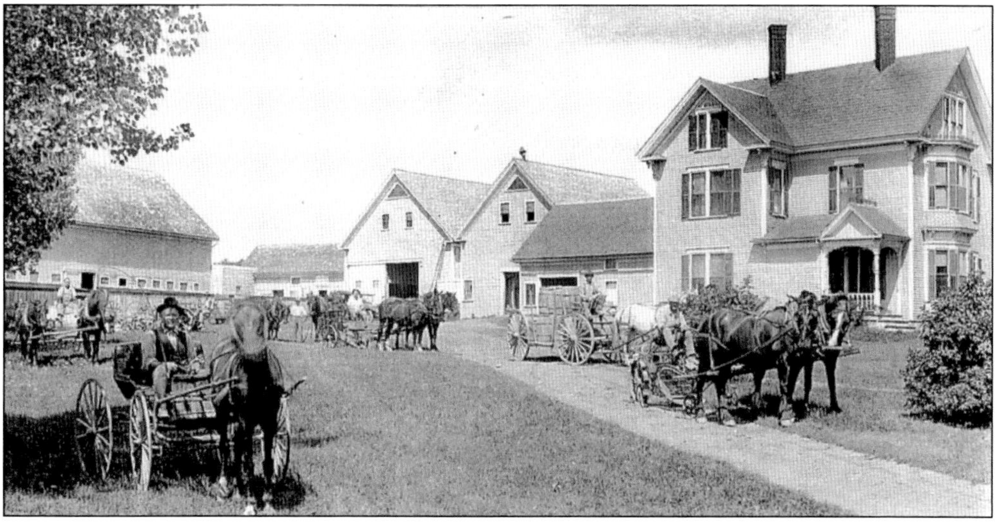

The Rackliffe Farm, a Local Showplace. Potato farmer Ralph Smith restored the beautiful Rackliffe farm to its original beauty in 1964. At one time, the farm had produced large amounts of seed potatoes. In 1907, the farm was sold to B.W. Sprague for the then enormous price of $20,000. The rich soil had raised 6,000 bushels of potatoes the previous year. Earlier in the farm's history, sheep were herded from Canada and all points in Maine to a slaughterhouse on the property by the Shaker Road and Route 7. Hosea Rackliffe shipped dressed lambs to the Boston market. He purchased the Corinna Center townhouse (built in 1839) *c.* 1897 and used it for wool storage.

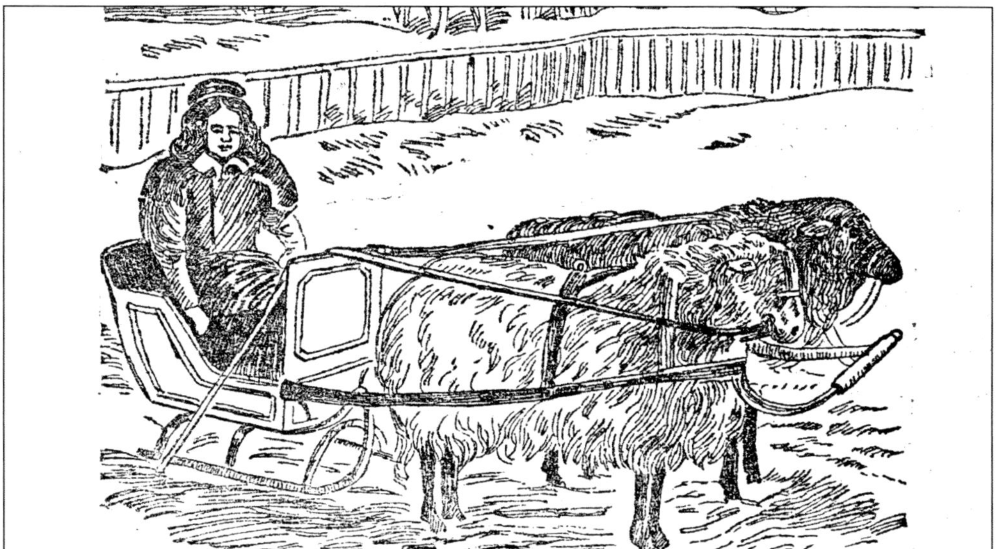

Miss Clementine Rackliffe Hitches up Pet Lambs. "New York papers has seized upon the item going the rounds some time ago about the novel team of pet lambs driven by Miss Clementine Rackliffe, the 13-year-old daughter of H.B. Rackliffe of Corinna. The Evening World of recent date contains the above picture and a short description. The well-trained little animals who mind Miss Clementine's lines are but little more than a year old. They appear to have quite as much fun as does their driver." (From a clipping in the Ellie Hurd scrapbook.) This sketch dates from *c.* 1898.

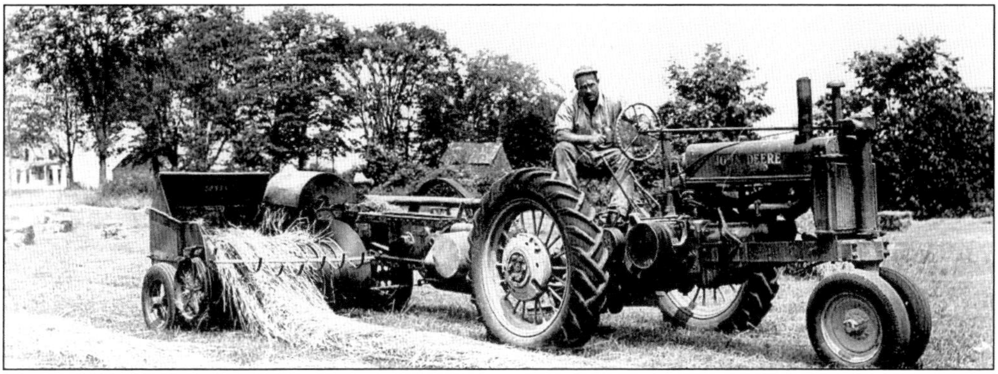

Maple View Farm Transitions into Maview Farm and Moves to North Carolina. Charles L. Jones, the original Maple View Farm owner, was a recognized authority on all dairy matters. His 38 head of purebred Holstein cattle was one of the first in Maine. A 300-tree apple orchard and an 8-acre patch of old-fashioned yellow corn supplemented his milk income. Fred J. Nutter married Jones's daughter Ruth and moved to a farm nearby with his eight head and Ruth's heifer. Ruth's cow proved to be a great foundation cow for the future herd. In 1920, a new barn went up, and the first testing of milk and artificial insemination in Maine was initiated. By 1949, Fred was the national director of the U.S. Holstein-Fresian Association. In 1963, Fred and his son Robert sold the herd except the calves and moved to North Carolina, where Robert now has a 620-acre dairy farm with 336 animals. The Maple View name was changed to Maview in the 1940s. The current farm also processes milk and sells ice cream locally. Shown *c.* the 1950s is Maview Farm with a new baler.

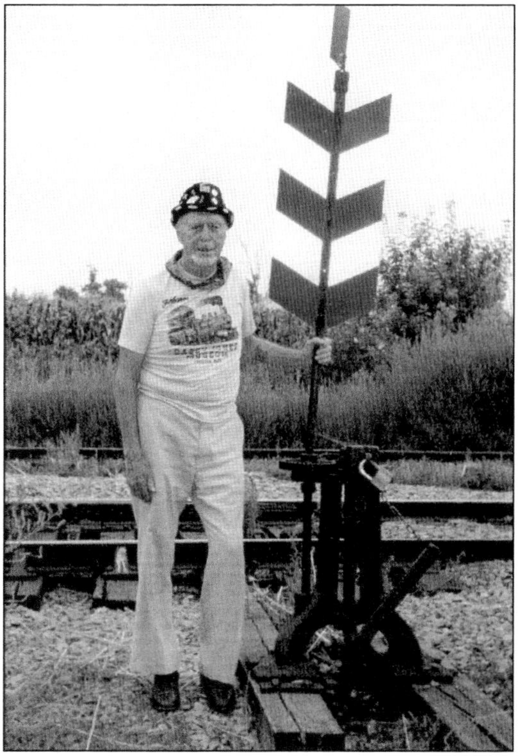

Irving "Fishbones" Stevens Still Riding the Rails Today. Irving L. Stevens, born in Surry, Maine, left the state and spent years traveling all over the nation riding the rails. At one time, he was elected "king of the hobos." He was also the inventor of Irving's Fly Dope, which was a big seller all over black fly country. The Environmental Protection Agency discovered it, and with excess paperwork and fees, eventually discouraged him from continuing the 20-year business. When he died in 1999, his ashes were shipped to Chicago, and a friend, "Ad Man," graciously spread his ashes in various boxcars, so Hobo Stevens is still riding the rails with his many friends to this day. Ad Man also delivered some ashes to Hobo Jungle in Britt, Iowa. As he "came in on the fly," he distributed some ashes, but the police spotted him and he was arrested for trespassing on a boxcar and given a $50 fine. Even so, he said "it was worth it for his old friend."

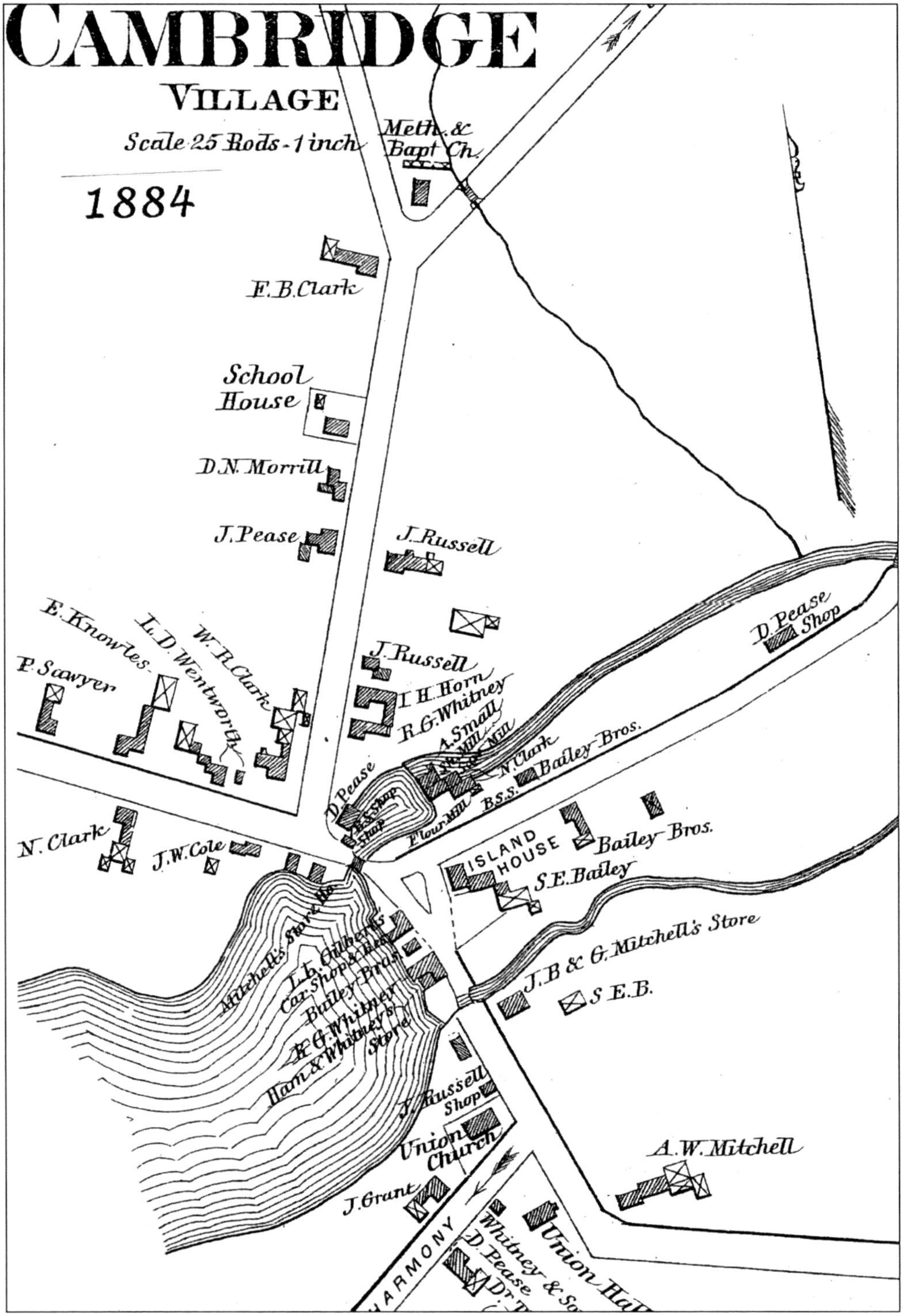

A Map of Intown Cambridge, 1884. Cambridge at this time had two physicians, one lawyer, three constables, five justices, and one hotel. There were also 10 merchants and 13 manufacturers.

Three

CAMBRIDGE

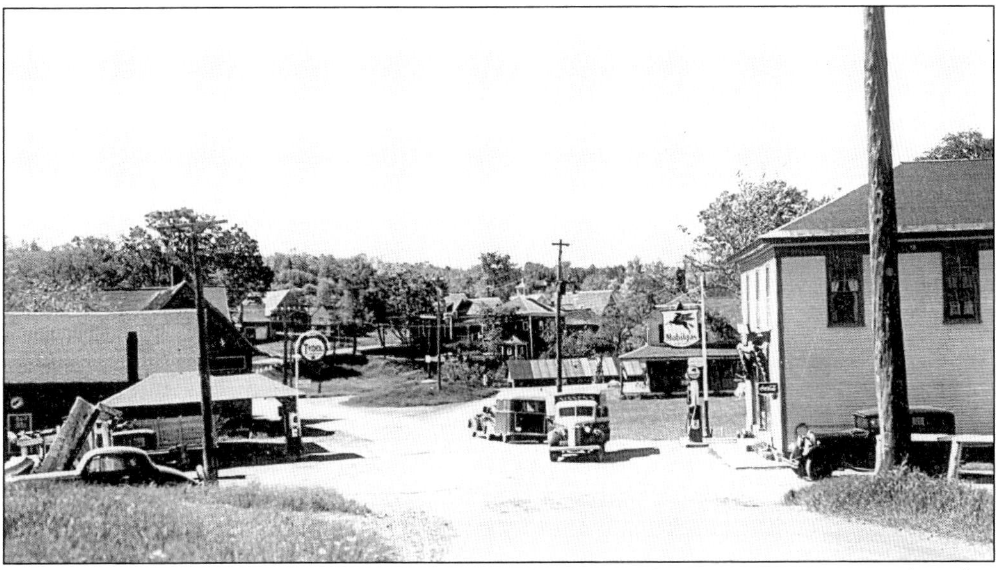

MAIN STREET, CAMBRIDGE, MAINE, C. 1935. The first settlers in 1804 were Joseph Tyler, Noah Littlefield, Jacob Hatch, and Mr. Kimball. The town was split with Ripley and was incorporated in 1834. Cambridge's population in 1840 was 461. In 1860, it rose to the highest ever, 516. The lowest population came in 1970 with only 281. In 1990, the count was 490. In 2000, 492 people called Cambridge home.

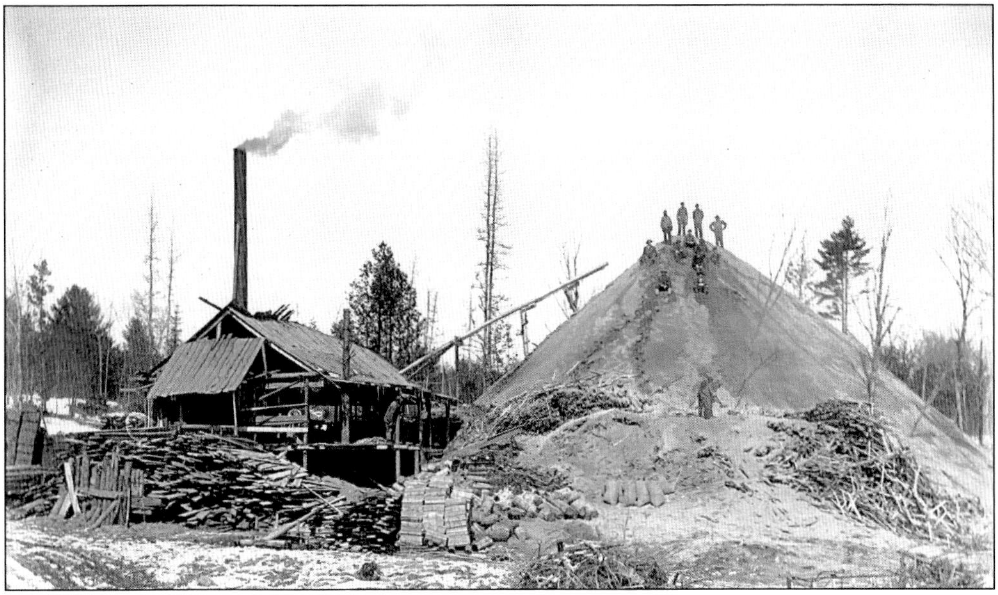

Local Sawmills Crank out Large Volumes of Lumber. The sawmill operation pictured was probably in the northwest part of the township near Pease Bog c. 1900. The earliest mills in existence were water-powered affairs closer to town. In town was a sawmill that was probably operational for the longest stretch. In 1968, the Bubar brothers operated the mill for a short time, but it was then removed from the site. A steam-powered sawmill on the lower side of the bridge was in operation for a short period of time in the early 1900s. At one time, a shingle mill was located on the Ripley Road near Glen Ring's farm.

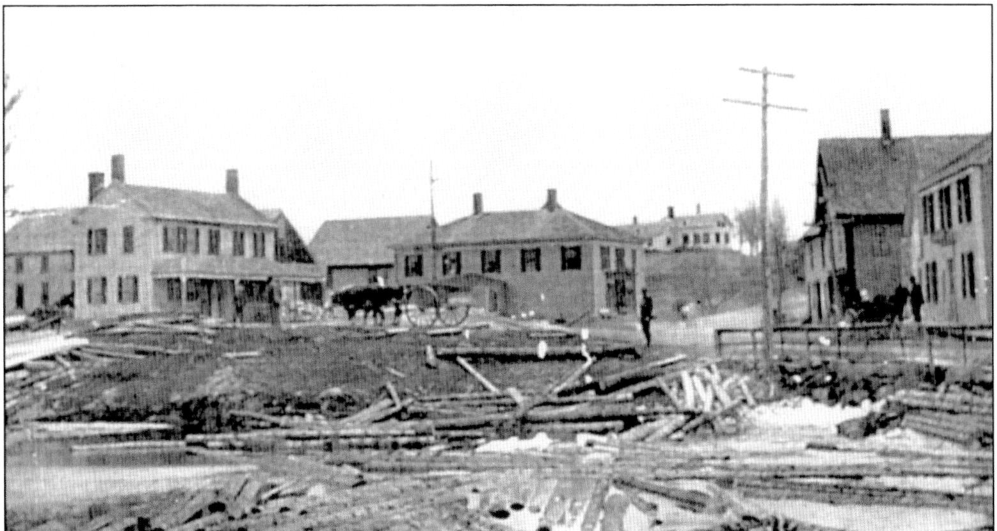

Lots of Activity on Main Street. The Island House Hotel was open for business. The Masons met in their hall. The Grange rebuilt the old church and, by 1911, had 200 members. The millpond was full of logs waiting to be sawed. The first sawmill and gristmill was built on this water privilege by Nathan Clark and David Bailey. In the 1960s, I helped owner Glen Carle saw my logs in his water-powered mill. The charge was $15 per 1,000 feet provided I helped "take away" from the saw and load the lumber on my truck.

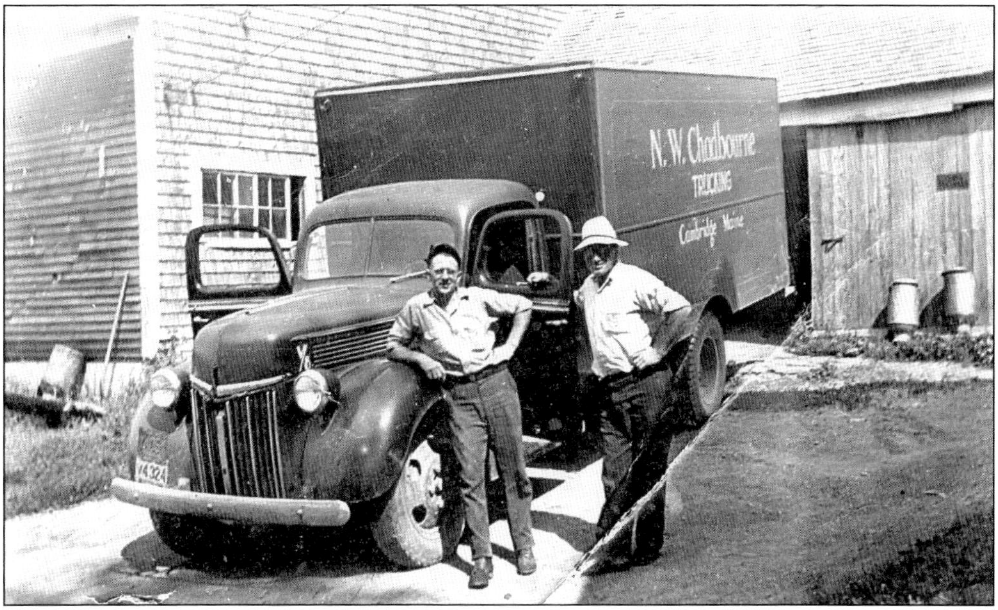

Norman Chadbourne, Enterprising Businessman. Norman Chadbourne (left) had a milk route in addition to his construction work. Raymond and Don Bailey used to haul milk for him. One of the first hay balers in town belonged to Norman. Paul Noble baled for him. One time *c.* 1960 it rained all summer, and Mike Folsom had to hire Norman's bulldozer in order to pull our baler through the wet, muddy fields. Around that time, I worked with Don Bailey picking up milk cans and hauling them to Newport. On the way home, we dumped the empty cans in the farmer's dooryard. We had to know each farmer's number and the right amount of cans to drop off. Shown on the right is Ralph Bailey, Norman's father-in-law.

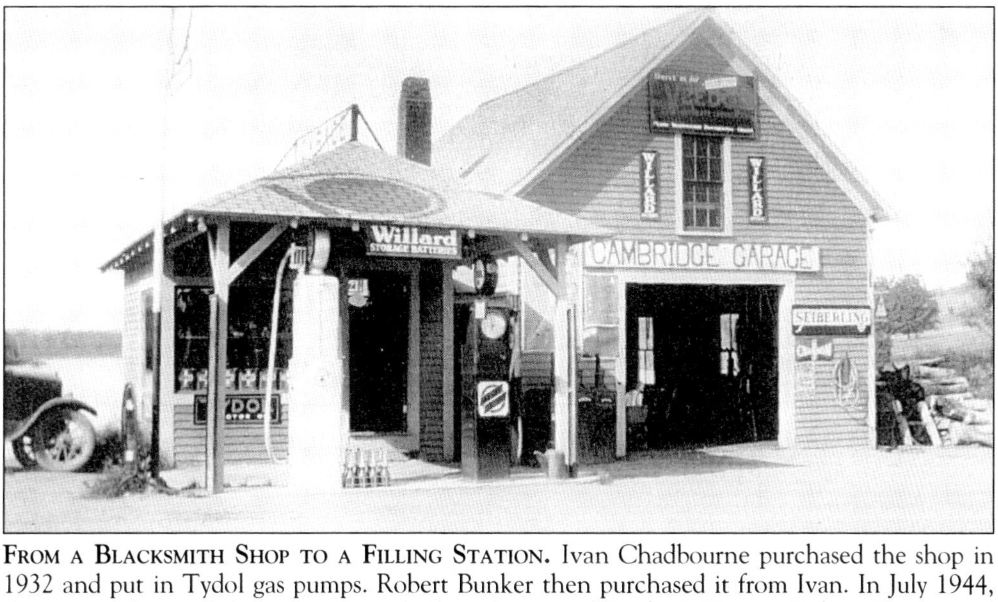

From a Blacksmith Shop to a Filling Station. Ivan Chadbourne purchased the shop in 1932 and put in Tydol gas pumps. Robert Bunker then purchased it from Ivan. In July 1944, there was a fire, and the garage was rebuilt and renamed Bunker's Garage. Robert Sr. operated the garage until 1972, when his son Robert Jr. took over. Robert Jr.'s sons, Mark and Adrian, operate the garage today.

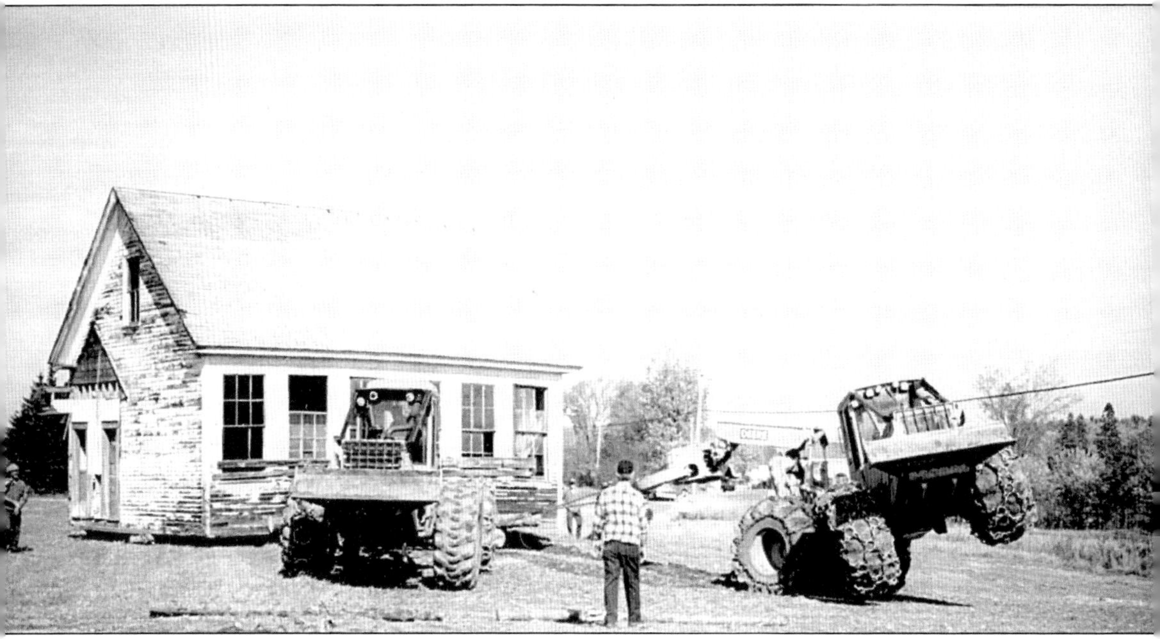

FLAT SCHOOLHOUSE MOVING DAY. The school was built in 1929 and closed in 1956. It was moved on October 14, 2000, pulled across the road by two skidders. One of the spruce skids broke on the way, so Jimmy Folsom went into the woods and cut another one. Roland Herrick had to cut part of the roof off the farm's corn crib to make a turn out of the barnyard. Another skid broke as the school crossed the road on a row of tires and rolls. The school was set on posts on a concrete pad and is being renovated by the Cambridge Historical Society. Skidders were provided by the Wynn Herrick Construction Company; Ralph Bailey and Zach Herrick were driving. Roland Herrick is pictured between the skidders directing traffic.

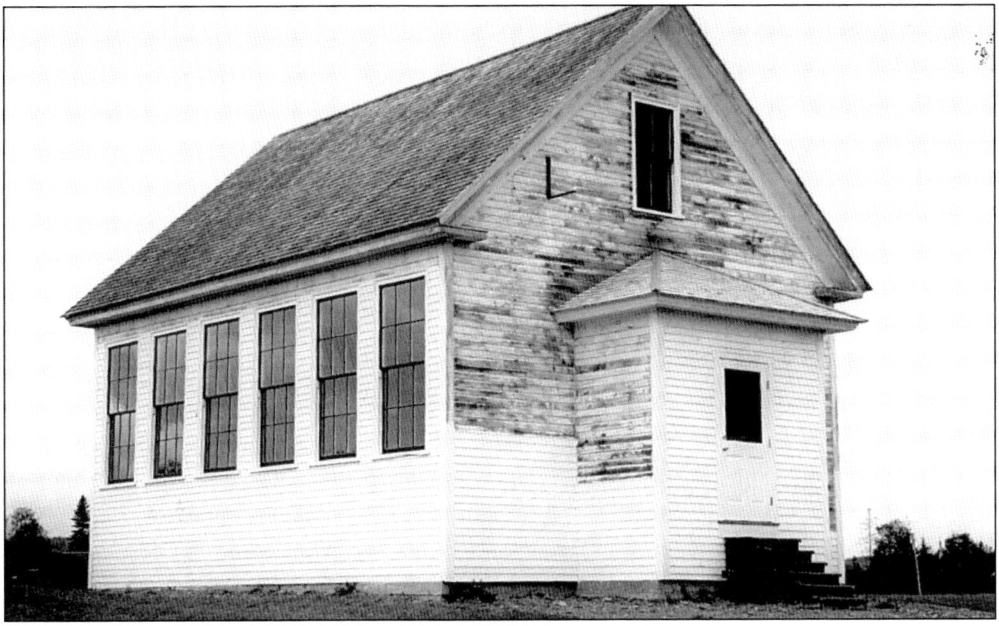

THE CAMBRIDGE HISTORICAL SOCIETY'S CROWNING ACHIEVEMENT. Citizens of Cambridge are proud of the recent achievement by their fledgling historical society. The whole town came together and supported the project to move and begin renovations to restore to original condition a one-room schoolhouse that had fallen into disrepair. The photograph shows the partially painted school in place at the new location on Goose Flat.

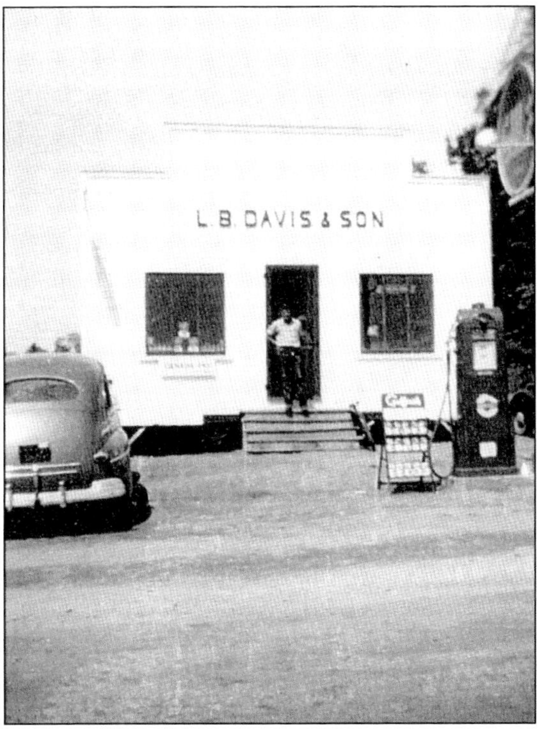

BUSTER'S STORE, A FINE ADDITION TO TOWN BUSINESS. Lindsey Davis opened a general store in 1951 on Route 150. The store sold general merchandise, and out back was a barber chair where Carolyn Davis Dubay would cut customers' hair. Junior Davis (in the doorway) planted four white pine trees out front that are still there today. One day, a salesman for the T.R. Savage Company came in. Carolyn called her dad, who was home milking, and said, "That savage man is here!" There was an immediate reply from the salesman. "Carol, I'm not a savage man; I wouldn't hurt anyone." The store has been moved and fitted up for a home; it is now owned by Jeff and Cathy Farrar.

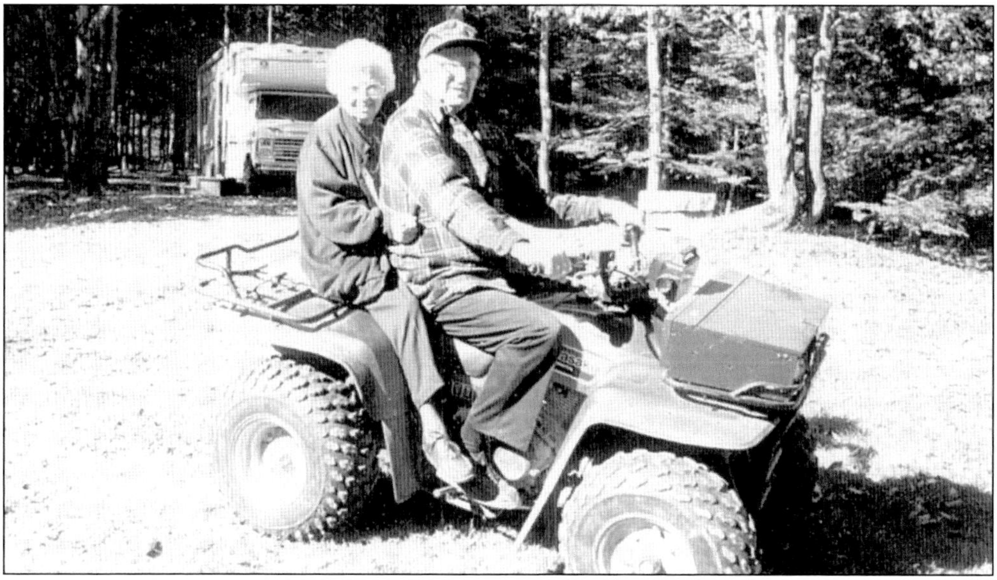

Bob and Lulu Heading out to the Cuddy Road. Bob and Lulu have lived in the old inn in the village since 1936. It had originally been called the Island House and became the Valley Inn when the canal was filled. The old barn, which housed 29 ponies and 25 dogs while owned by the Bunkers, was torn down in 1968. The horse stalls were marked with the identical metal numbers used to mark the hotel rooms. Bob and Lulu spend much of their time nowadays camping on their woodlot on the Cuddy Road.

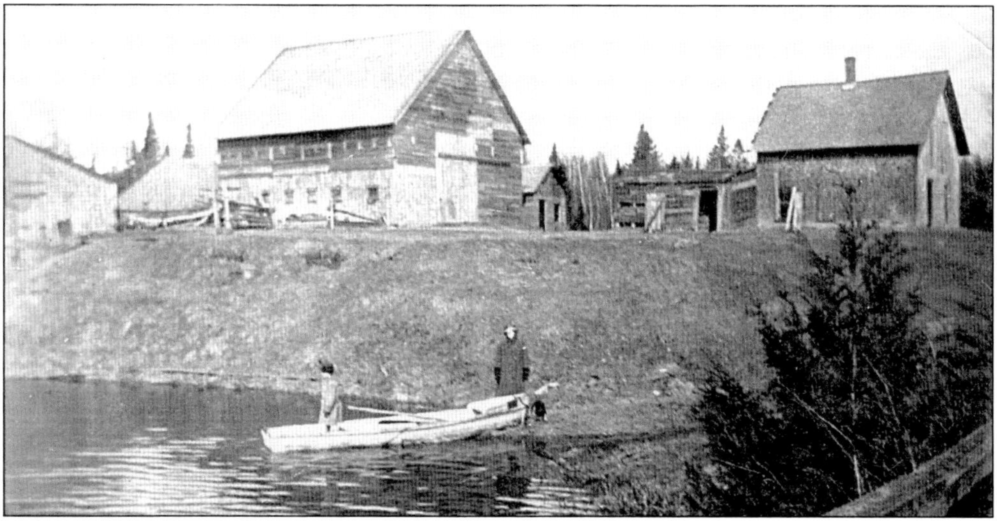

Main Stream Farm, the Scene of End-of-the-World Baptisms. In 1911, the *East Somerset County Register* reported, "In the spring of 1843 a great religious revival swept over the town, an opinion being prevalent that the world was soon coming to an end. Meetings were held in the different houses, and many were baptized, two, it is said by candle-light in the Main Stream." This photograph shows the farm buildings along Main Stream owned by Charles Henry and Abbie Moulton Folsom. Abbie's father was the previous owner. For refrigeration the family used a well across the road, where they kept a five-gallon can of milk suspended. William Earl and Almond H. were their sons. Neighbors remember Earl and Almond paddling up and downstream on a log and not falling off.

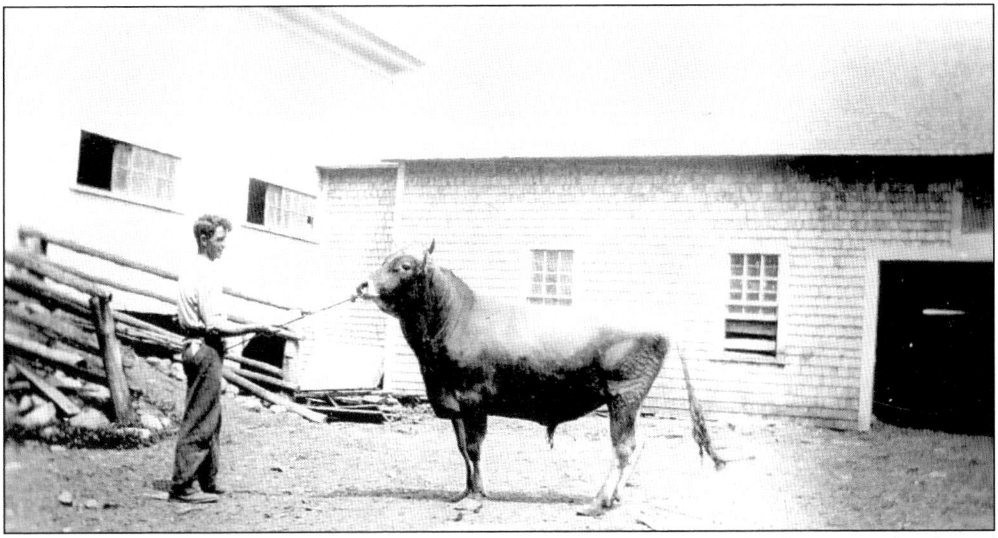

Elwin Folsom Shows Off His Prize Bull. "Elwin Folsom of Cambridge, recently elected superintendent of schools, is no doubt the youngest man to fill such a position, Mr. Folsom was 21 years old Nov. 13, 1912. He is a graduate of Coburn Classical Institute of Waterville, a member of Cambridge Grange and is interested in farming, also in automobiles." (From an undated newspaper clipping.) Elwin had a diversified farming operation milking cows and raising potatoes, beans, hogs, and poultry.

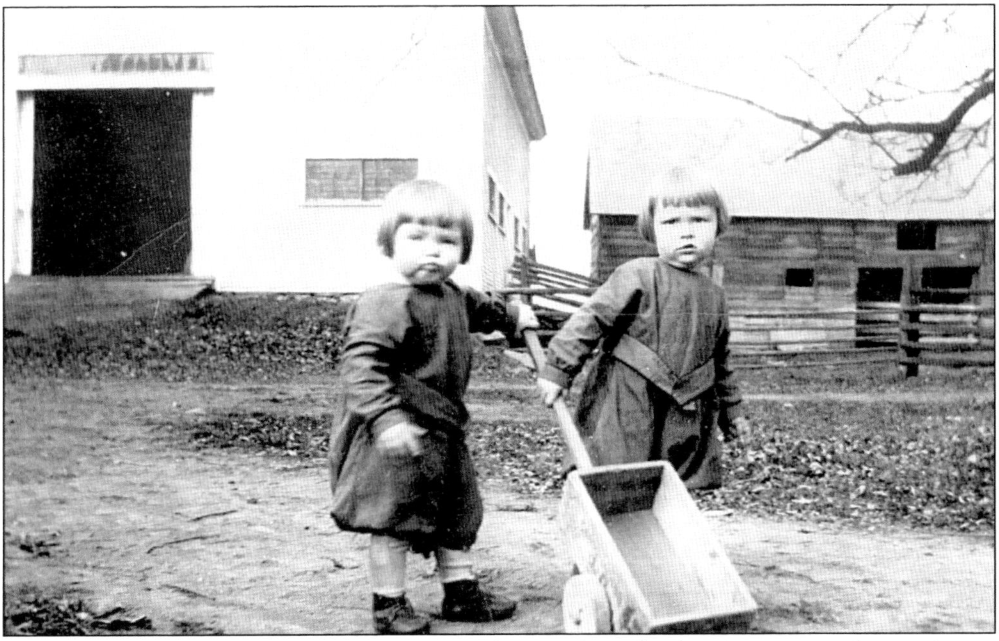

Twins Thelma and Elmer at Goose Flat. Elwin and Pearl Folsom's twins are shown playing in the yard at their farm. Thelma Folsom Camburn (left) learned early to "go get the cows." She later used the dump rake during haying to gather "scatterings." Elmer started milking at age 13 and farmed many years, becoming a teacher later on. Goose Flat apparently got its name because all the farmers along that road raised geese.

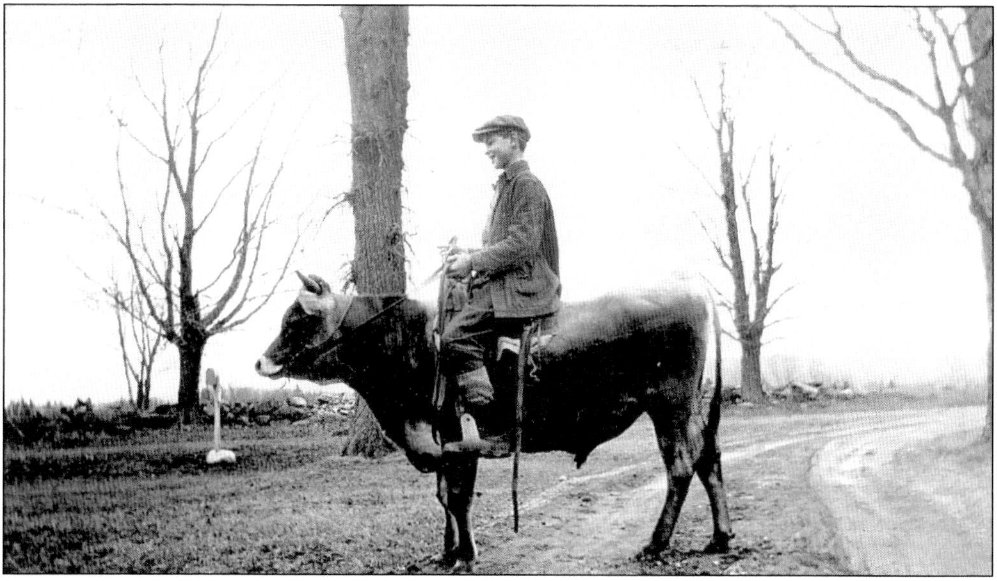

Bread and Butter Better Than an ATV. "We didn't have a four-wheeler back then, but this was still a lot of fun," Elmer Folsom recalls. "The bull didn't jog very well; he mostly walked. We didn't own a bike. We had lots of fun with the animals; teaching calves to lead and picking out a good pair to yoking them up and teach to pull."

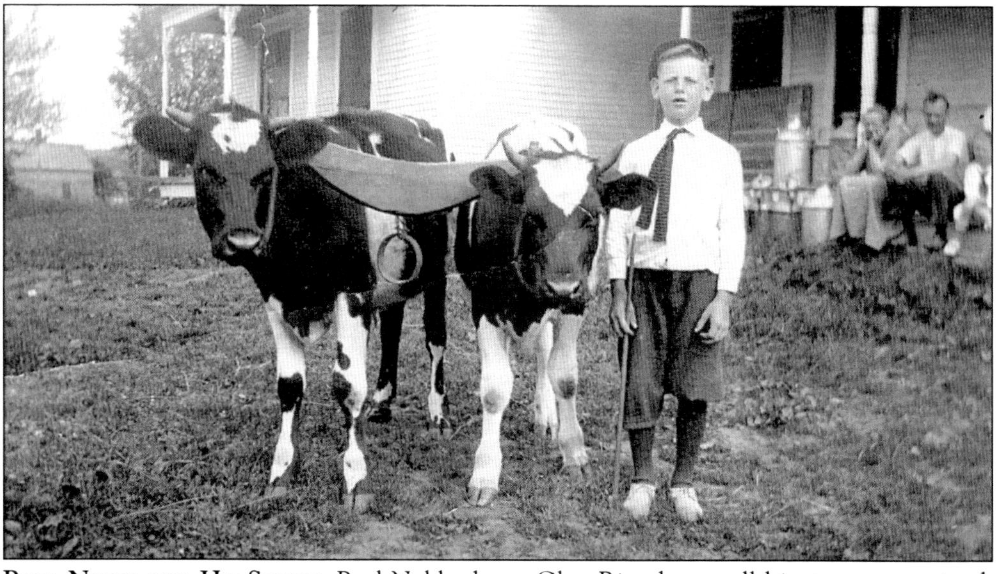

Paul Noble and His Steers. Paul Noble shows Glen Ring how well his steers are trained. When Paul was in grammar school, he would ride his pony to school, turn it loose, and it would go back home. At the end of school, his father would send the pony back to school for Paul to ride home. Paul loved horses and for years went to all the fairs and various horse-pulling events around the state.

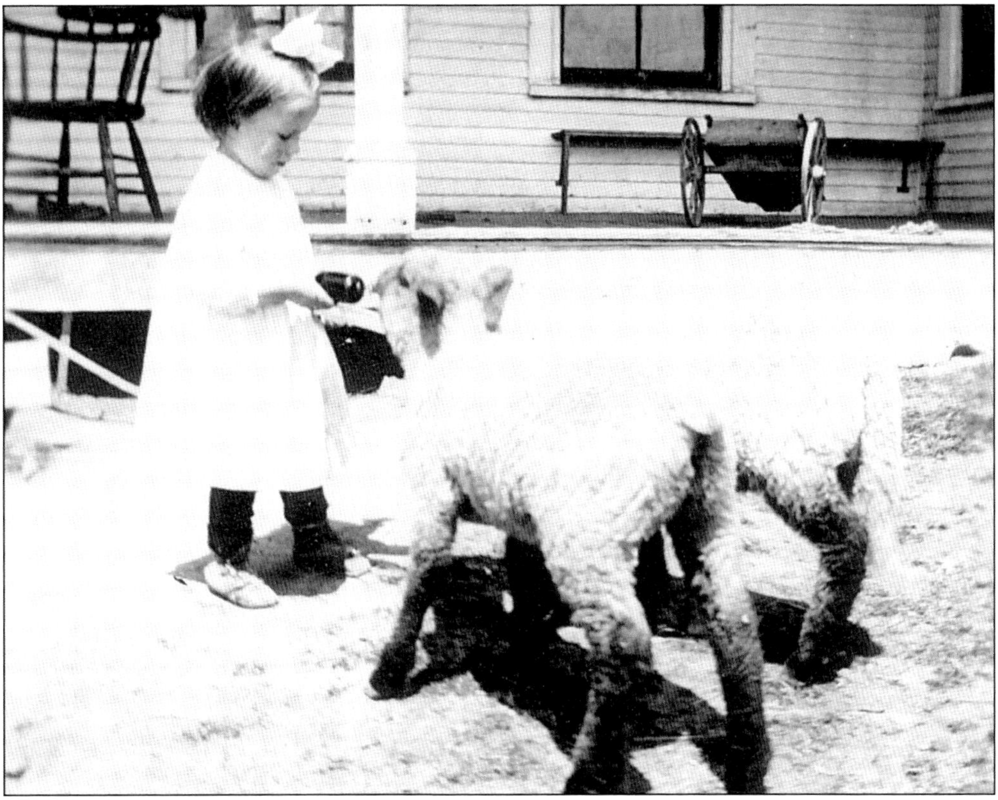

Rachel Ham Feeding Her Lambs, George and Daizy. Ivan Ham's daughter learned early the value of having animals and taking good care of them. Rachel was an avid reader at an early age and became very knowledgeable on many subjects. Her mother, Nora, was a caring midwife, and many women living in Cambridge had her at their side when they gave birth.

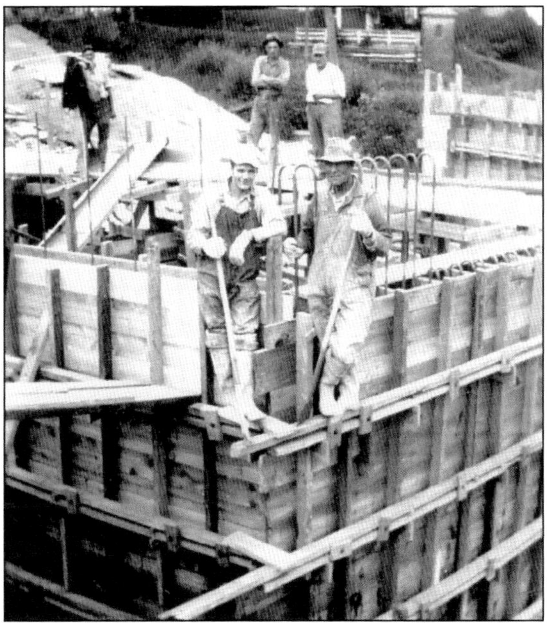

Building Cambridge Bridge. The concrete bridge that replaced the old one in the village was built in 1929 with local help. Pictured, from left to right, are the following: (front row) Buster Davis and Ray Austin; (back row) unidentified, Joe Morrill, and David Morrill. Buster worked for the state constructing many bridges; the next one done was on the Dexter Road at Dale Burdins's house. He was a practical joker, and it was always fun to have him on a job. Pete recalls milking cows by hand with his dad; Buster milked 12 in the time it took Pete to milk 6.

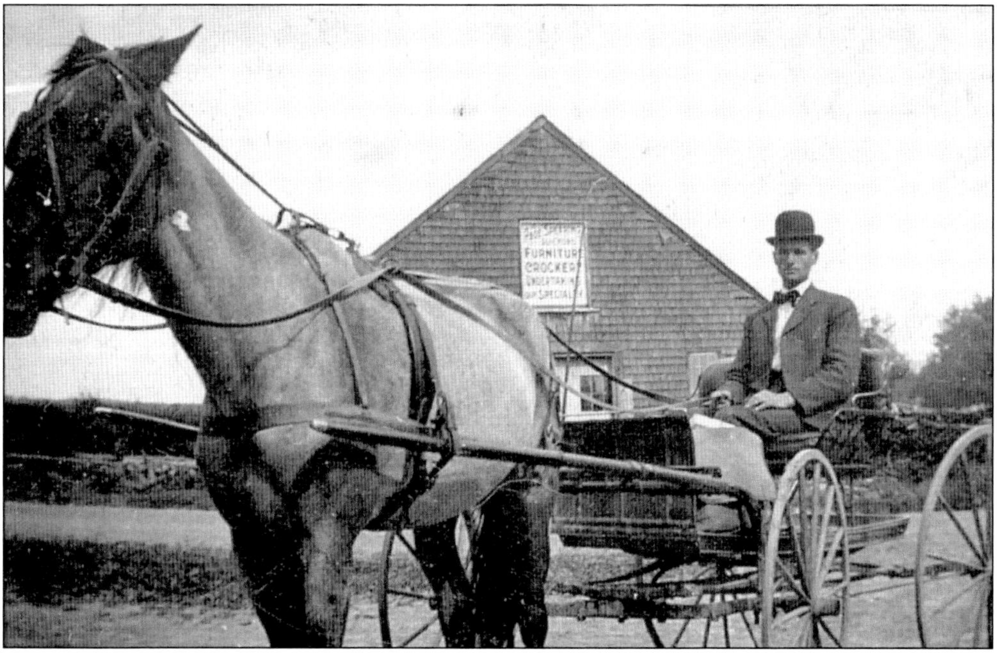

DELIVERING MAIL IN RURAL CAMBRIDGE. Tom Folsom is shown in the mail wagon about to make a delivery in Cambridge. At times he had to go all the way to Dexter to get the mail before delivering it. Pete Davis remembers helping Tom to hoe corn by hand. Pete would ask, "Is it time for dinner?" Tom would say, "Do one more row down and back." This went on and on until Pete finally stopped asking.

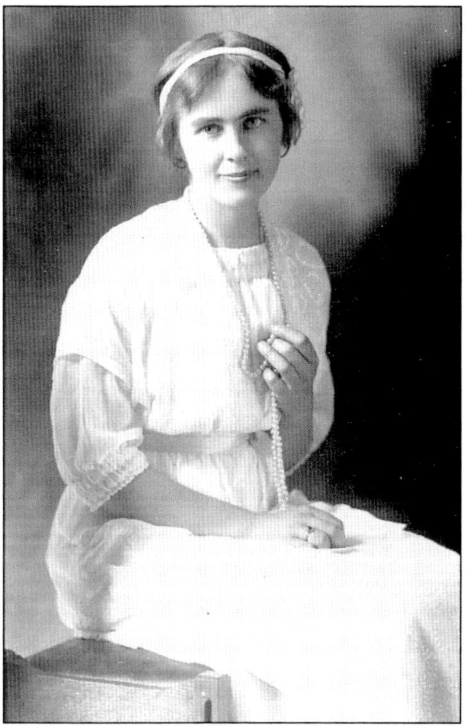

CARRIE MAY HOLT MARRIES WALTER GLENWOOD RING. "People said she was the closest thing to a saint," commented Carrie Ring's grandson Roger Carr. Carrie taught Roger to read when he was three years old, and he attributes that to his getting an education and becoming a teacher, recently retiring after 31 years. "I had asthma and Grandma Carrie was dying of cancer. We were both semi-invalids at the time, but reading was one thing we both could do," he said. Carrie's daughter "Jerry" also inherited her mother's gentle, quiet ways.

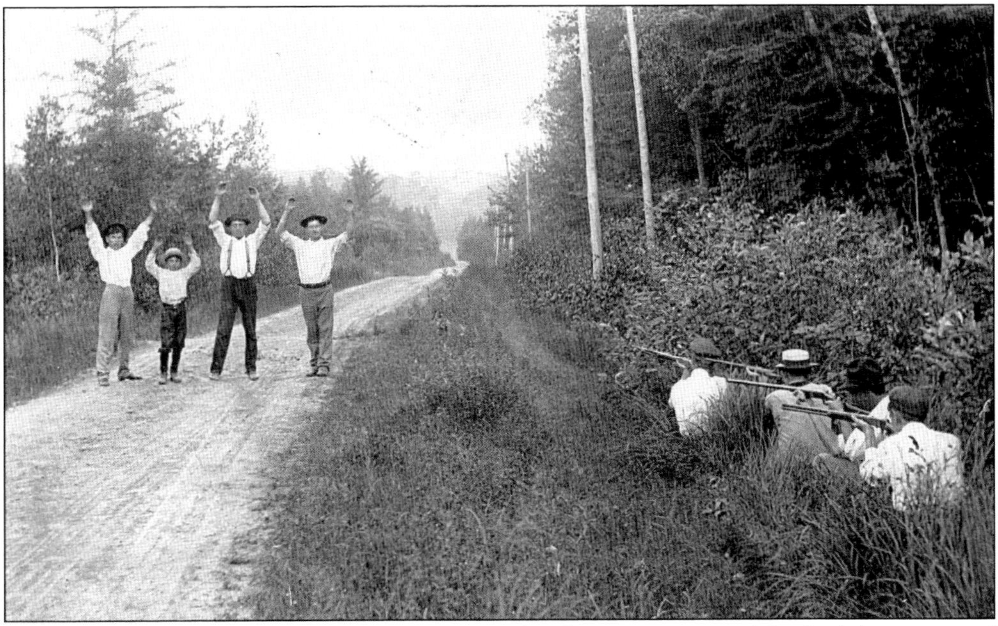

The Highway Men of Goose Flat, c. 1900. Is this the reenactment of the feud that separated the township into Ripley and Cambridge some years ago?

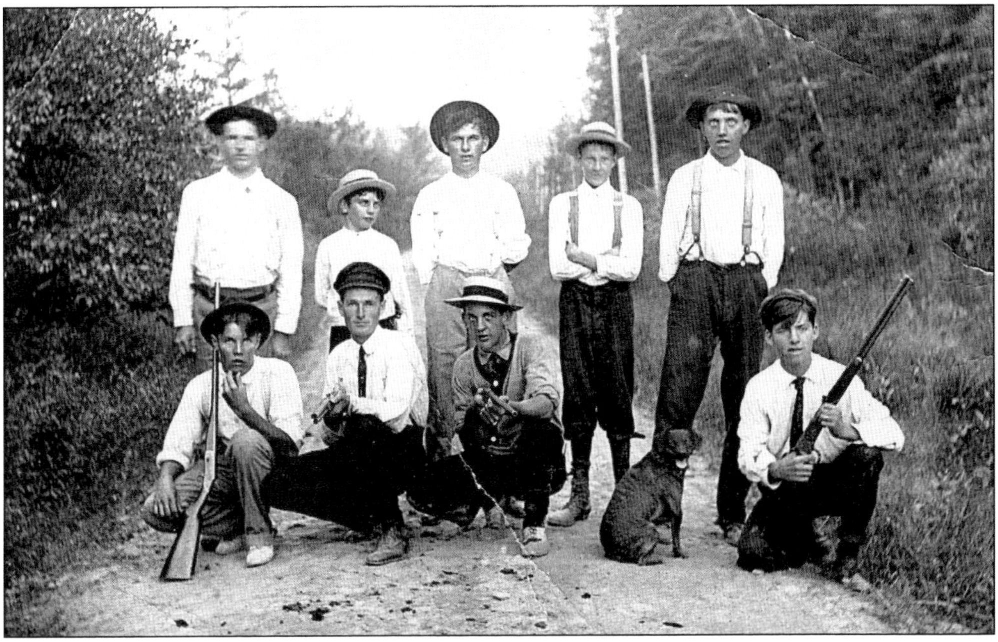

The Goose Flat Gang. This photograph was probably taken along Goose Flat leading to Main Stream. Pictured, from left to right, are the following: (front row) Glen Ring, Tom Folsom, Othie Sawyer, and unidentified; (back row) Dana Noble, three unidentified people, and Clair Sawyer.

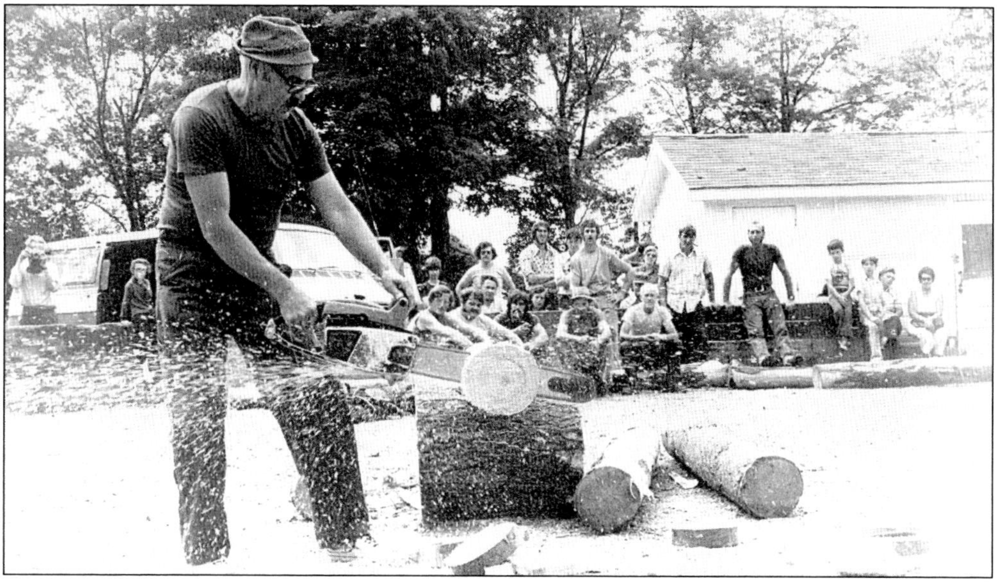

THE FIVE BURDIN BROTHERS AND THEIR DAD, SKILLED LOGGERS. Jesse Edmund Burdin attended school in Harmony and from there he went right into the woods. He and Marguerite Price Burdin raised 12 children, and he trained the five boys in woods work as they grew up. He and his boys were well known at the logging competitions all over Maine. Jesse had the reputation as being one of the more skilled bucksaw and chainsaw filers in the area. He was working in the woods the day he died on January 15, 1989, at age 74. In this photograph, Jesse is sawing "for time-cutting off three disks" at the Dexter Skating Rink in a logging competition 28 years ago.

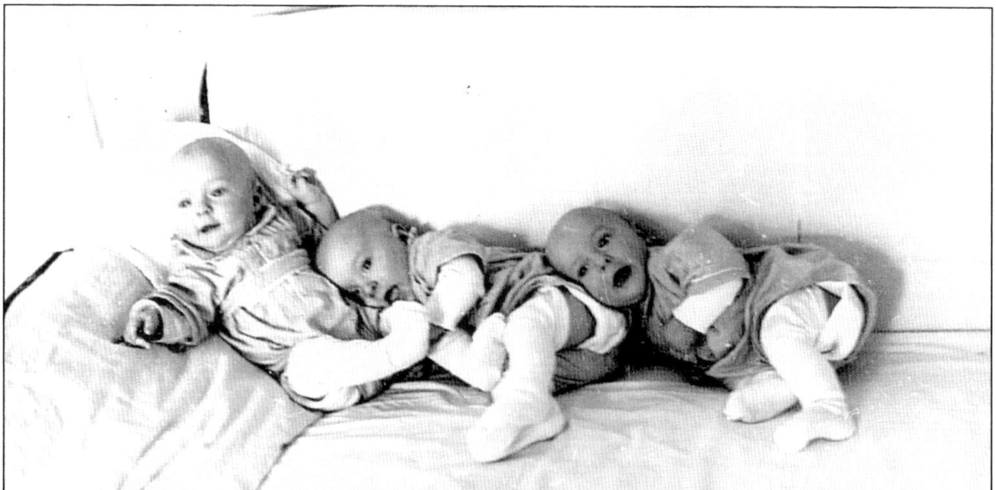

THE WATSON TRIPLETS AND THEIR MOTHER SURVIVE AN AUTO-TRAIN CRASH. Clinton (left), Clarence (center), and Chester (right) Watson were born on May 10, 1947, and were probably the only triplets ever born in Cambridge. When they were just five years old, a train hit their grandfather's car at a Pittsfield railroad crossing. Just before the accident, their mother, Hazel, "jumped up in the front seat and turned around to push her 3 sons, riding in the rear, to the floor of the car." (From the *Pittsfield Advertiser*, January 17, 1952.) Glass flew all over, but no one was injured.

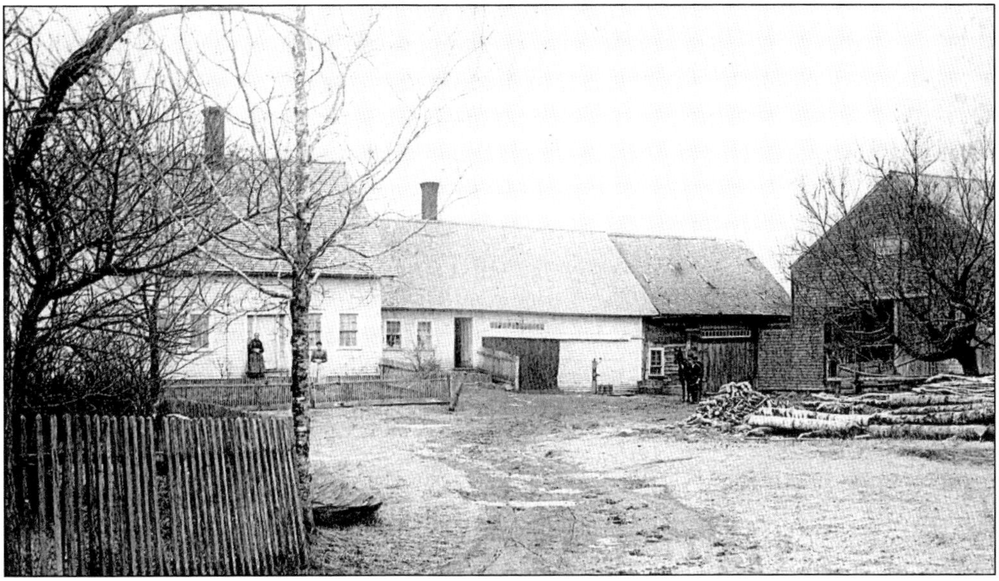

THE FOLSOM FARM. Dr. Josiah Folsom and his wife, Clarissa P., raised seven children here. Two families lived in the house. The barn on the far right was replaced in 1902. Elmer recalls his grandfather in his later years taking care of the horses, hens, pigs, and the garden. The firewood pile in the photograph was his job too. Grandmother made quilts and helped in the house. The children raised animals and learned solid values from their work. Everyone was needed and wanted.

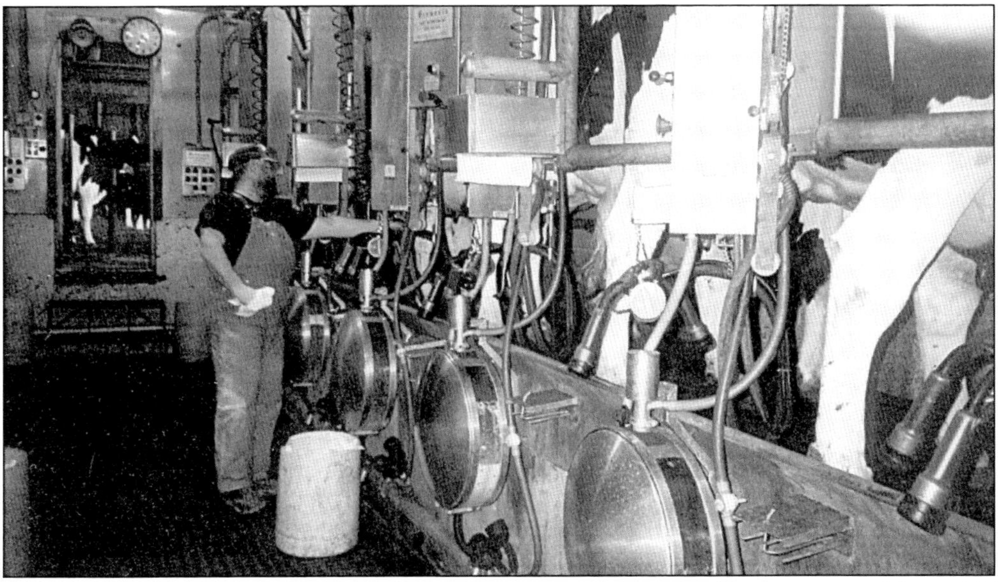

CAMBRIDGE FARMS TODAY. Jim Folsom and Ron Hartford now milk 190 cows and have 135 young stock. They farm 400 acres of hay and 400 acres of corn silage. Ron is preparing cows in their double-eight herringbone milking parlor with automatic takeoff and in-place washing unit. One man can milk 50 cows per hour with this system. When they started years ago, they used Jim's father's three-stall parlor before it was remodeled. Elmer, Jim's father, is still there daily raising calves and feeding up like he did as a youngster, and in the very same barn.

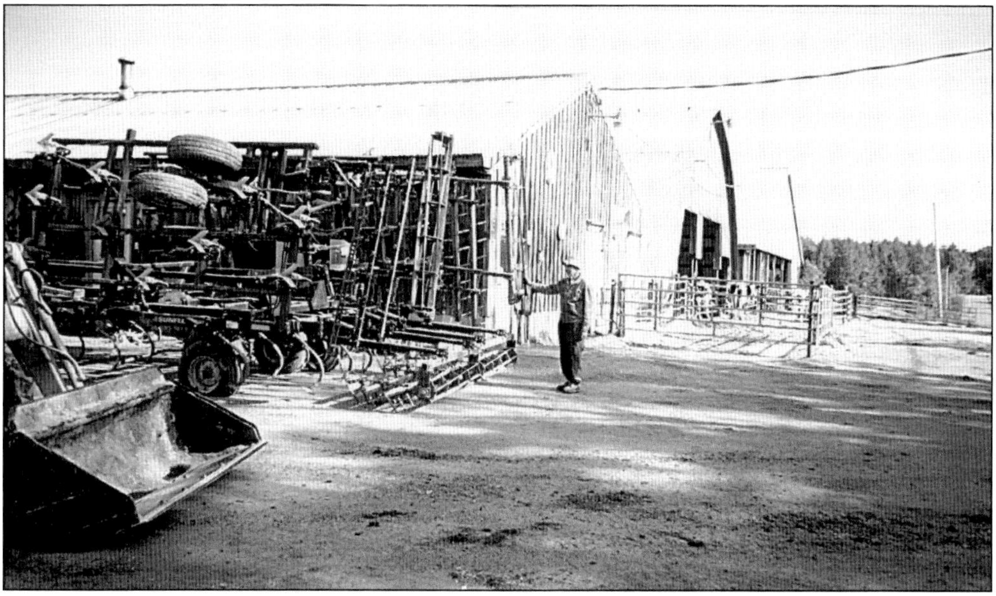

A GIANT HARROW NEEDED TO FARM TODAY. Elmer is standing in front of a giant soil finisher, or Vibra-Shank, used to till corn ground and smooth it out in one operation. This single farm has replaced 15 local farms that milked about 12 cows each 50 years ago. Today Cambridge Farms does it with just six people. The farm of the past probably had 8 to 10 workers contributing to its productivity, all living meaningful lives. The current milk prices are at 1978 levels. Are we really better off today?

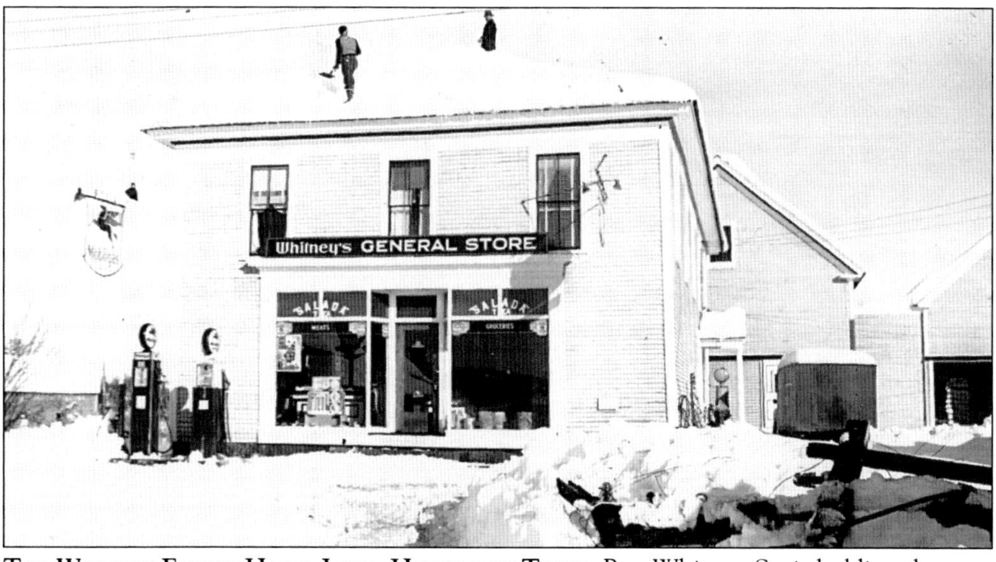

THE WHITNEY FAMILY HAS A LONG HISTORY IN TOWN. Ray Whitney Sr. is holding the rope tied around Harry Perkins while Harry shovels off the roof *c.* the 1930s. Besides this general store, the family ran a gristmill using a hammer mill to grind up grain for local farmers. It was run with a Pontiac automobile engine. Corn and oats were ground up and mixed with cotton seed. Upstairs in the storage bins was a basketball hoop where the local lads used to play.

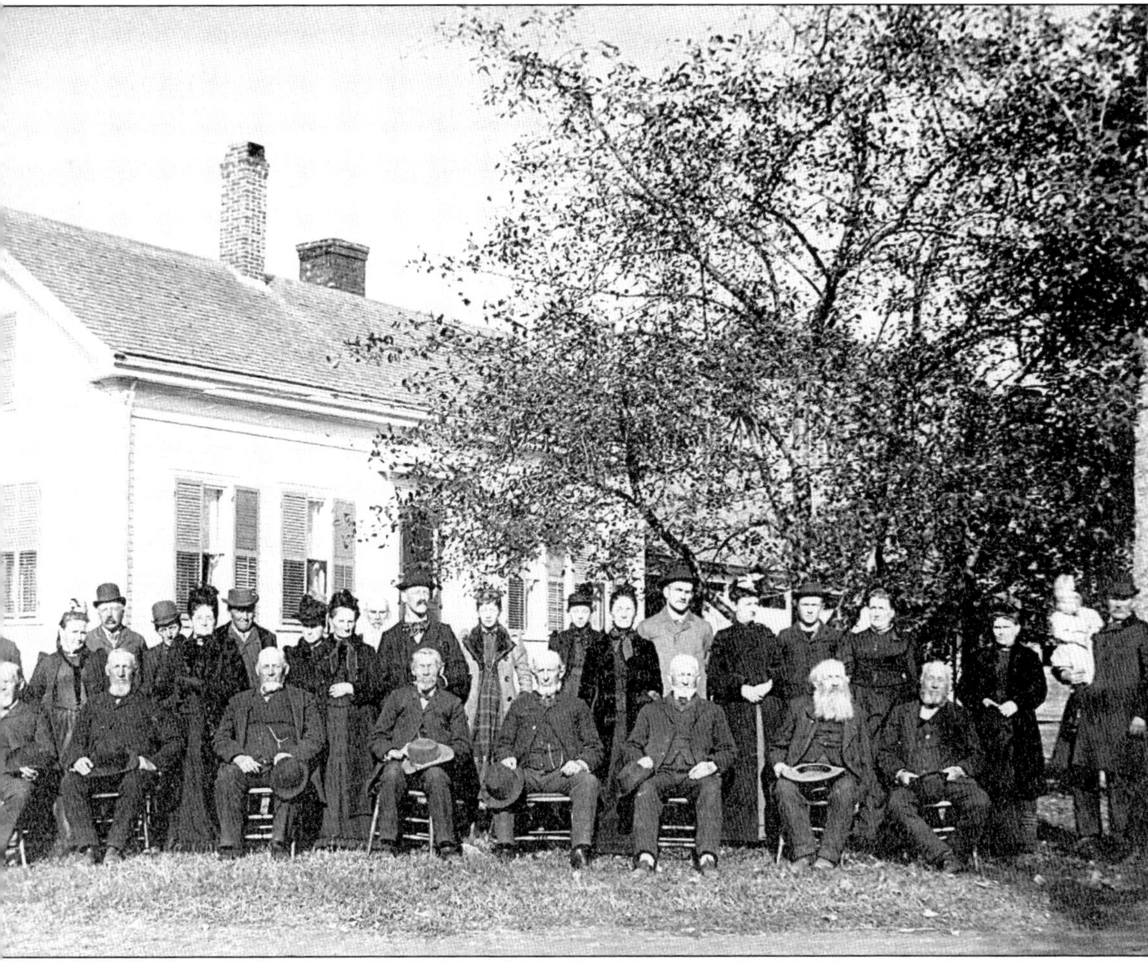

NINE MITCHELL BROTHERS IN CAMBRIDGE BY 1834. Joseph and Mercy Buzzell Mitchell came to Cambridge from Norway, Maine, in 1834. They had previously lived in New Hampshire. Joseph had been to sea at the age of 12 and had served in the War of 1812. They had eight children upon moving here, and a ninth one, Alva W., was born in 1834. Alva eventually farmed in Harmony and developed the Harmony Beauty variety of potato. This photograph shows eight of the nine Mitchell brothers in front of the home where they were raised on the Ripley Road.

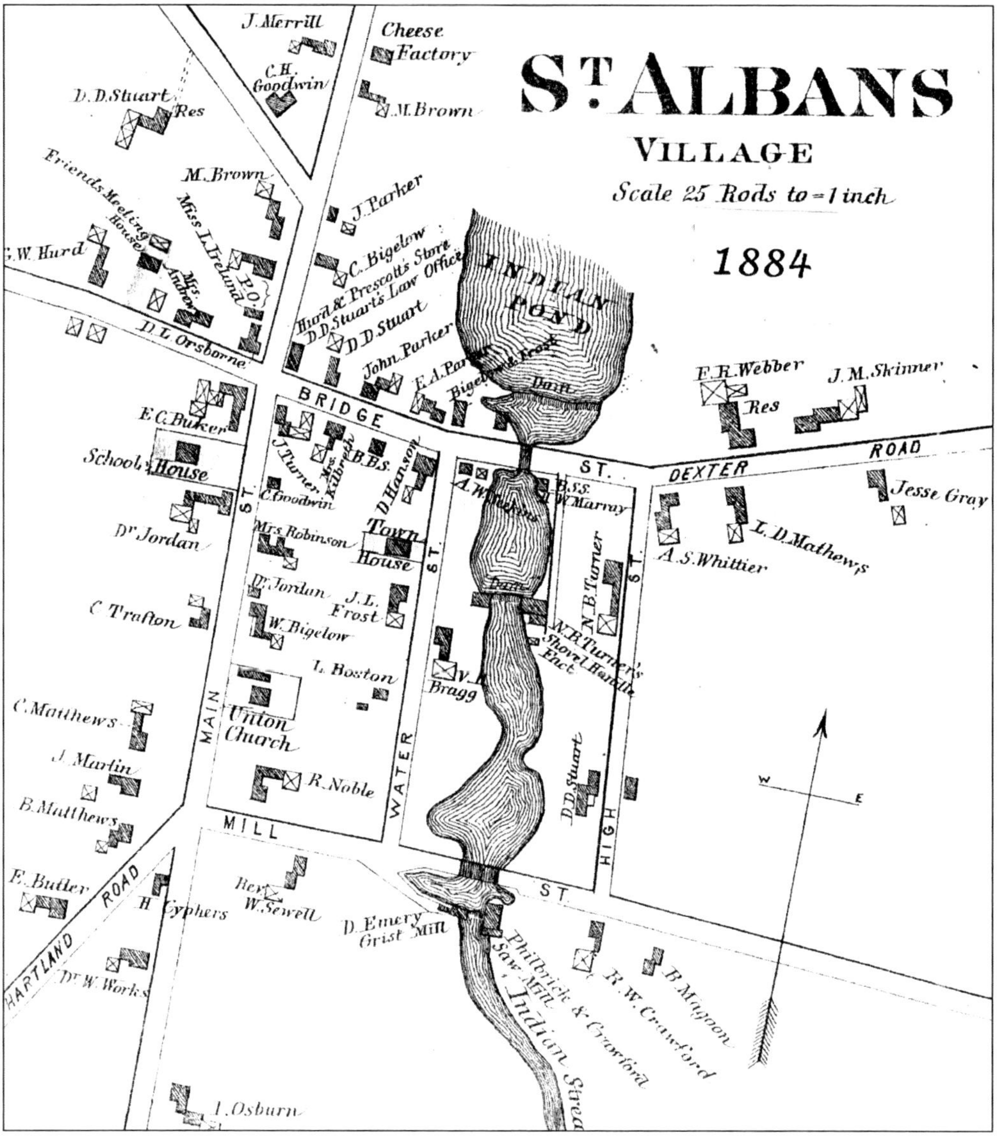

A Map of Intown St. Albans, 1884. At this time, St. Albans had a lawyer, a constable, 7 justices, 4 merchants, and 11 manufacturers.

Four

St. Albans

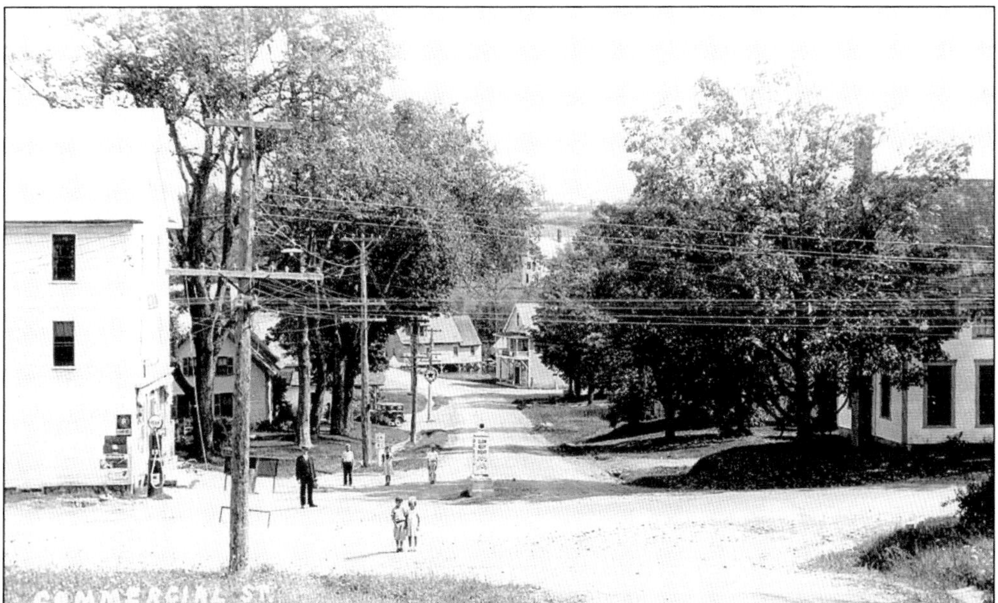

Main Street, St. Albans, Maine. The first settler of St. Albans was Judah Hackett in 1800. First called Berlin, then Fair Haven, it was incorporated in 1813. In 1846, the Hartland and St. Albans boundary line was changed, and in 1862, a part of Ripley was annexed to St. Albans. Its population in 1820 was 371; in 1860, 808; in 1940, 950. In 2000, the population had risen to 1,836.

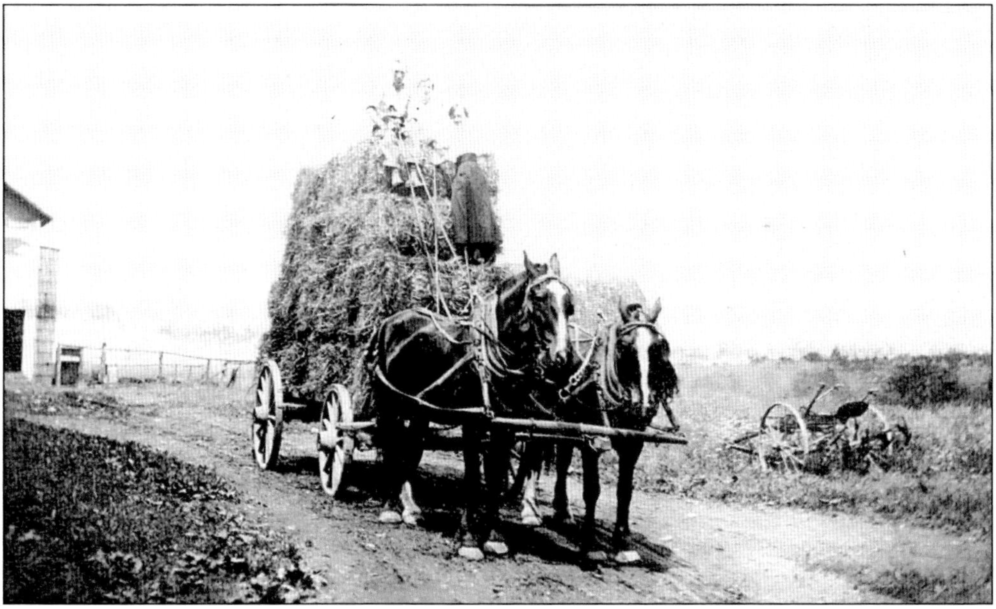

Earl Patten Taking a Load of Pressed Hay to Market. Earl was a cattle dealer for a good part of his life. I worked for Albert "Mike" Folsom on Chandler Hill in Ripley when he purchased an older, "clever" cow from Earl one time. When I tried to put the milker on her, she nearly kicked me and the milking machine through the barn wall. Albert thought she must have come from Quebec and never saw a milking machine before. We called her "the French cow." After a few days trying to use the machine, we gave up and Albert called Earl to take her back. Earl agreed to bring another to replace her, but it would cost Albert more. We always wondered how many times that French cow got sold to unsuspecting farmers around here. Shown, from left to right, are Earl (driving), Vera Hanson, and Clara Chase.

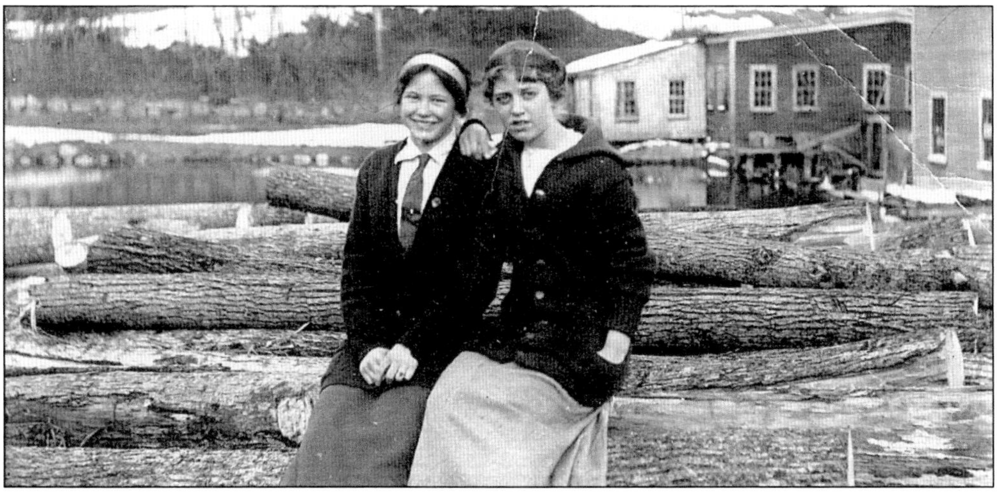

The Last Mill a Thriving St. Albans Business. The last factory on the stream leading from Big Indian Pond was formerly an old carding mill, shingle mill, repair shop, and factory. After George and James Martin owned it for nearly 20 years, C.A. Batchelder purchased it from Calvin Southard and W.H. Watson in 1905 and rebuilt it into a last factory (making lasts, shoe trees, artificial limbs, mannequins, and novelties). Young ladies pose on a pile of basswood logs in the mill yard ready to be moved inside for sawing.

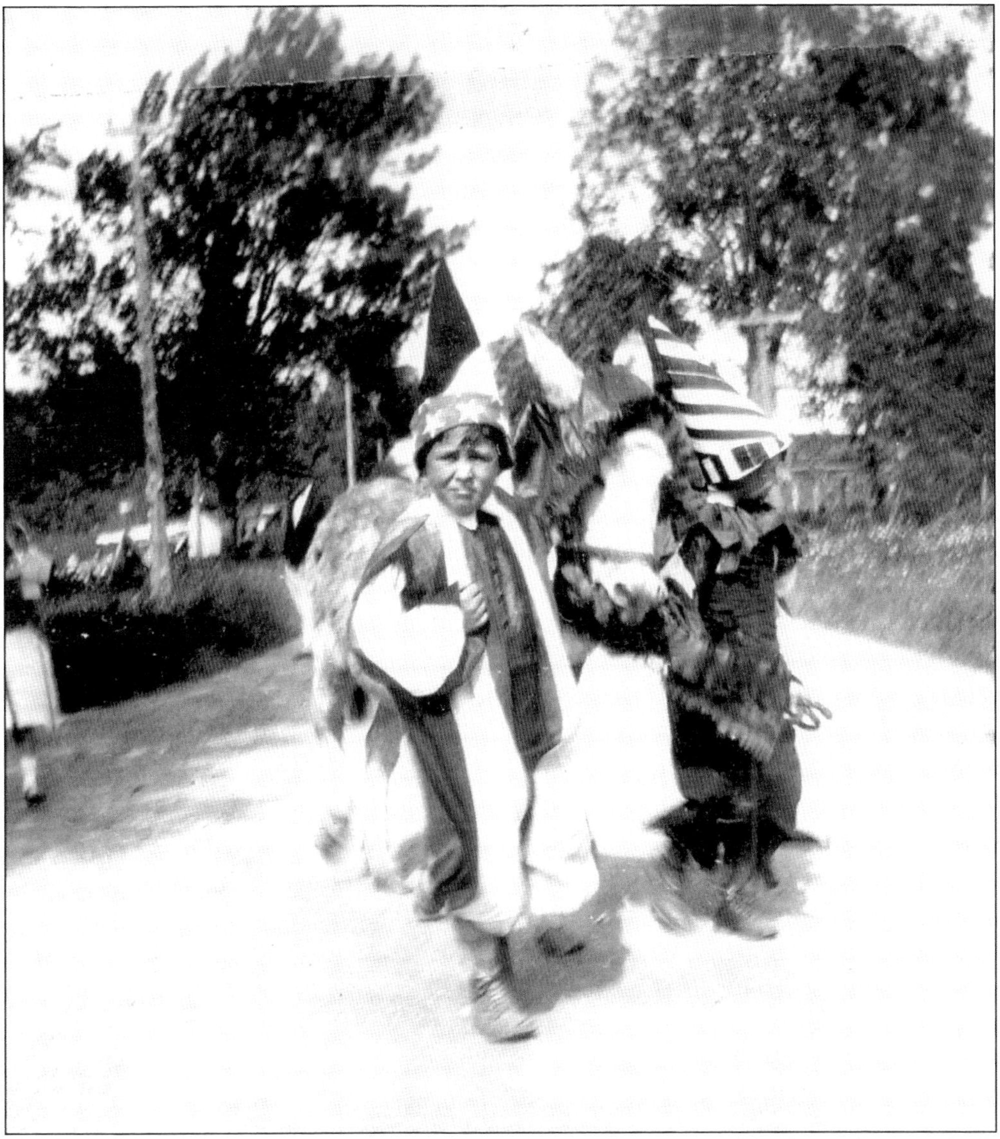

The St. Albans Parade. Ed Patten recalls the scene: "Al Tracy, the blind man from Garland, sold the mule to Dad [Earl Patten] and he got Carroll Hunt to ride it to St. Albans. Lois Worthen, Dad's housekeeper, dressed us kids up. Mom had died when I was five years old. We paraded on the Corinna Road near the old M & M Dance Hall and where Victor Springer lives now. I was about eight years old. That's my brother Leon on the right. It's about 1928."

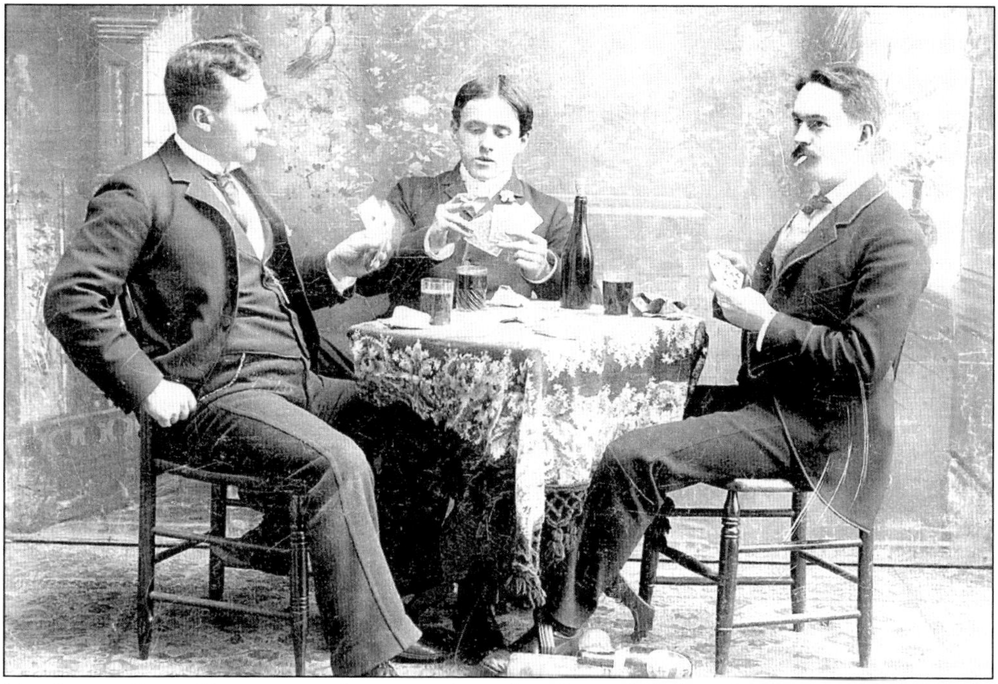

The Lower Store Proprietor. Posing on the right is Samuel Wilson Green. Sam was originally from Scottish royalty, the Stewart clan. He landed in New York and moved to a farm in Albion, Maine. He and his wife, Sadie, moved to St. Albans and purchased the Lower General Store. After he died, she ran it for many years. Their daughter Marjorie married Dana Martin, who had Jersey cows and used to bottle milk including chocolate and strawberry in pint and half-pint bottles. He made a lot of his sales at the Hartland Tannery.

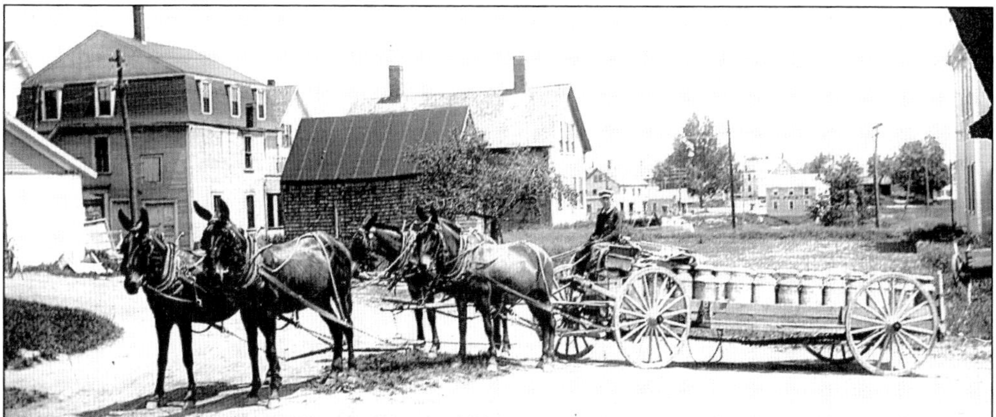

Mules Hauling Milk to Newport. Earl Patten worked for Elmer Johnson and was hauling milk to the Borden's plant in Newport. You did not see many truckers with mules in those days. Earl hauled wood and hayed for Glen Hanson. One day while haying, Glen refused Earl a break to get a drink of water, so Earl quit and went to work rebuilding the dam at the lake. Soon after that, Earl was drafted into the army. After World War II, he farmed on the Bigelow Road and went into the cattle and meat delivery business with Ralph Hanson. He traded cattle all over central Maine, making frequent trips to Canada to replenish his supply.

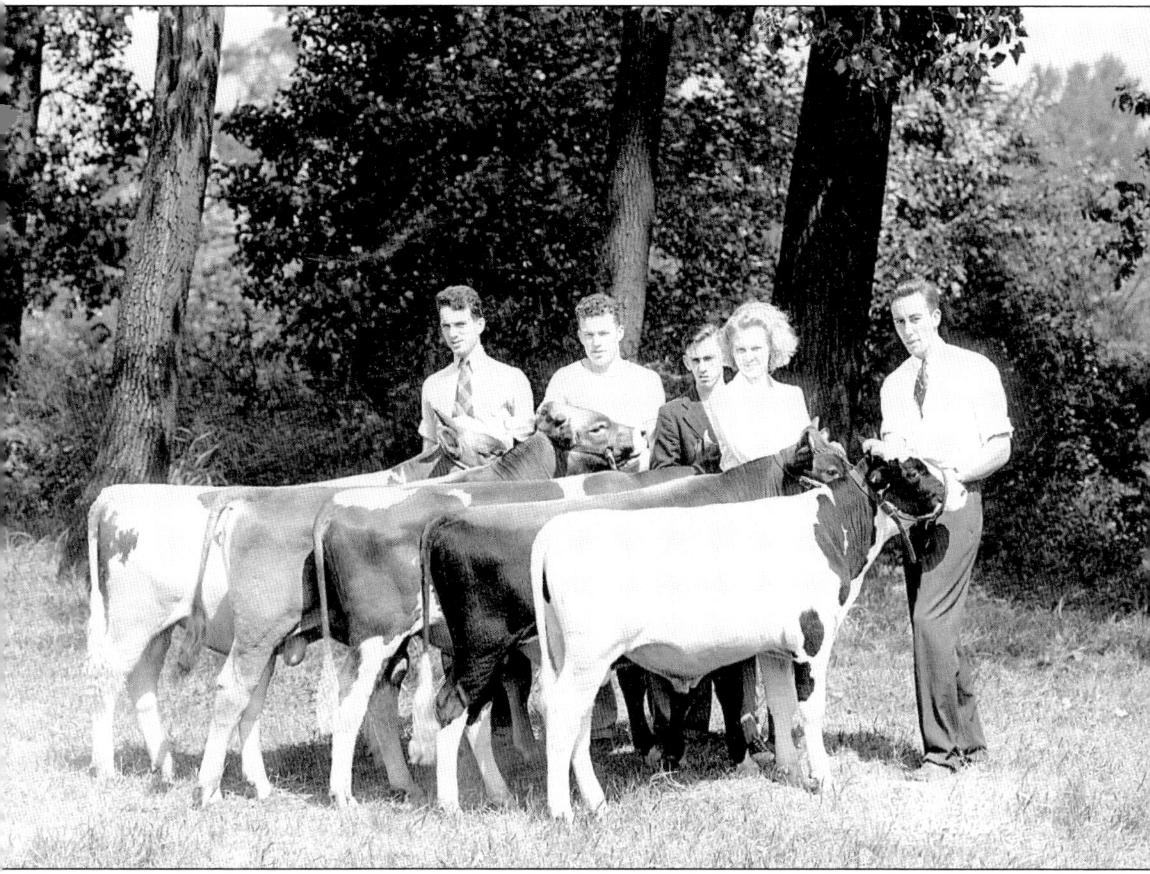

Barbara Patten's Bull Wins a National Championship. "The Jersey is the All-Star breed, more cow to milk, less cow to feed. More stream-lined for better cream line. Less cost, more profit, is our creed." Barbara Martin Patten could not be more proud. She had entered the State Jersey Cattle Club jingle contest and had won. The prize was a Jersey bull calf. But this was not the first time. Previously she entered the national contest and won first place with an essay. She also raised a bull calf then, won at all the local Maine events, and made it to nationals, where she won grand champion. Barbara is pictured fourth from the left.

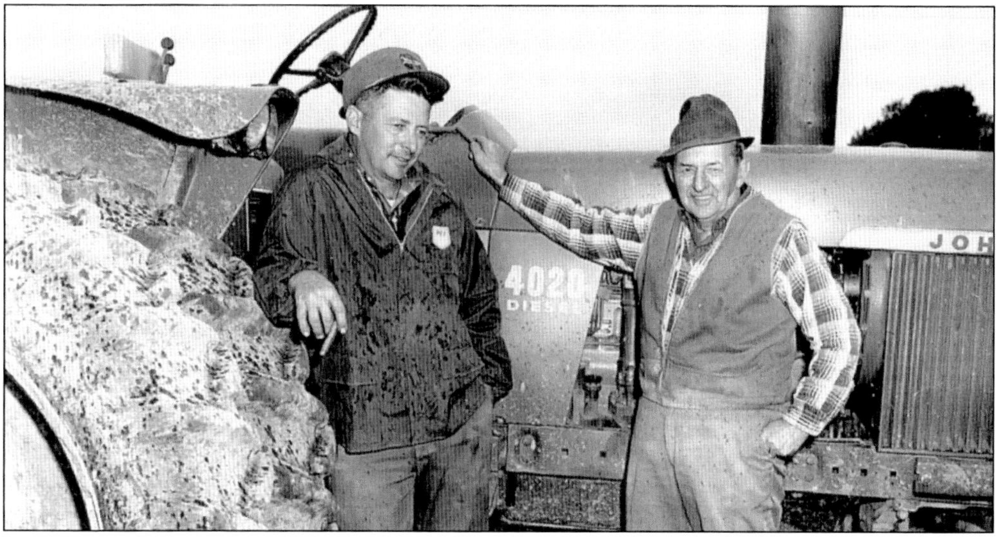

THE CHAMBERS DAIRY OPERATION, THE LARGEST IN ST. ALBANS IN THE 1960S. Elmer and Luella Chambers moved to St. Albans in 1932 with their two sons. By 1944, Elmer and his son Kenneth became partners and started to enlarge the operation. They eventually developed free-stall cow and milking parlor operations all under one roof. The milking herd grew to 225 cows, the largest in the area. Artificial breeding is used extensively with Dairy Herd Improvement Association records that track milk production and various other records. In the early 1960s, I attended an open house along with many other farmers to view this modern dairy business and Bruce Ballard's new free-stall barn.

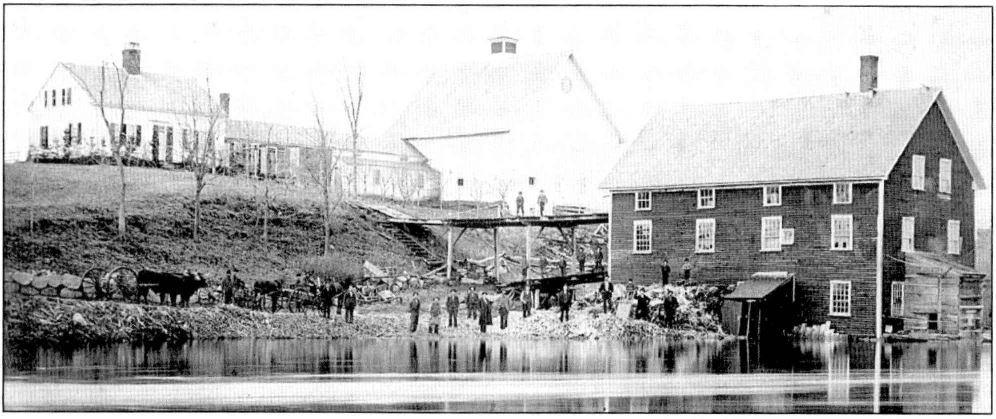

THE NAPOLEON BONAPARTE TURNER MILL. In 1854, N.B. Turner bought out Holman Johnson, who had started a shovel factory on the banks of the mill stream. He operated it until 1896, when N.B. Turner Jr. took it over, owning it until 1903. In 1947, the larger building was destroyed by fire. Harold and Kenneth Bishop bought the original shovel-handle factory and manufactured snow fencing. Selwell Products owned the building when it burned in 1967. In the late 1950s, I brought apples to be pressed by Harold Bishop in a former blacksmith shop on the east side of the stream near the Corinna Road. He charged $5 for the rum barrel and 10¢ a gallon to press. It took about 10 bags of apples of various varieties to press out 50 gallons of good-tasting cider. We helped Harold along with the process and had a good time. When we got home we added 10 pounds of sugar to the barrel and waited. One year I brought over a quart from last year's press and passed it around. The old-timers there judged my cider-making ability. "Son, that's goood cidah." I was so proud!

A Native Inventor Runs for President. "St. Albans has been the home of 25 or more Picture Makers. The Wing family being the most prominent among them, as 5 brothers and 1 sister all worked at this same trade. Simon Wing, born in 1826, commenced making daguerreotypes in 1846 locally before moving to Waterville and then to Boston in 1861." (From *The 1913 Centennial Celebration: A History of St. Albans.*) Wing's invention *c.* 1860 of the Wing Multiplying Camera was known all over the world and completely revolutionized the making of pictures. This *c.* 1900 photograph shows his Ajax Camera. Wing (right) was very studious and inventive, having predicted air flight by humans 50 years before it became a reality. He helped organize the Labor Party and was its first candidate running for president against Grover Cleveland in 1892.

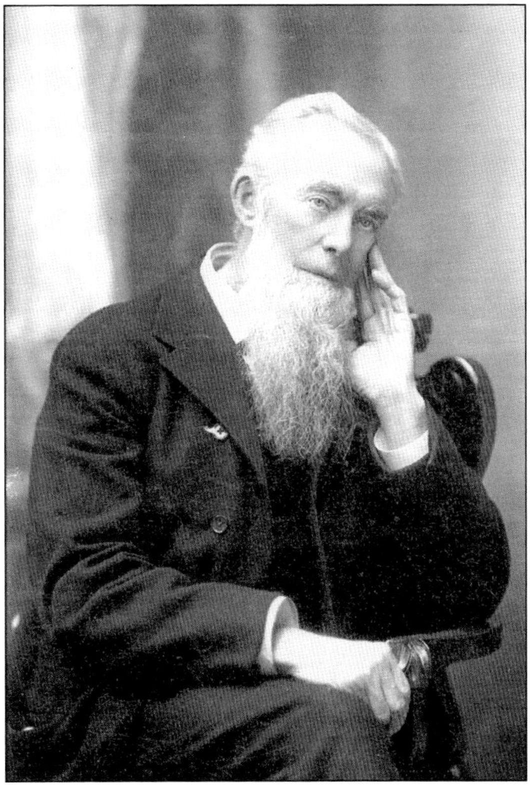

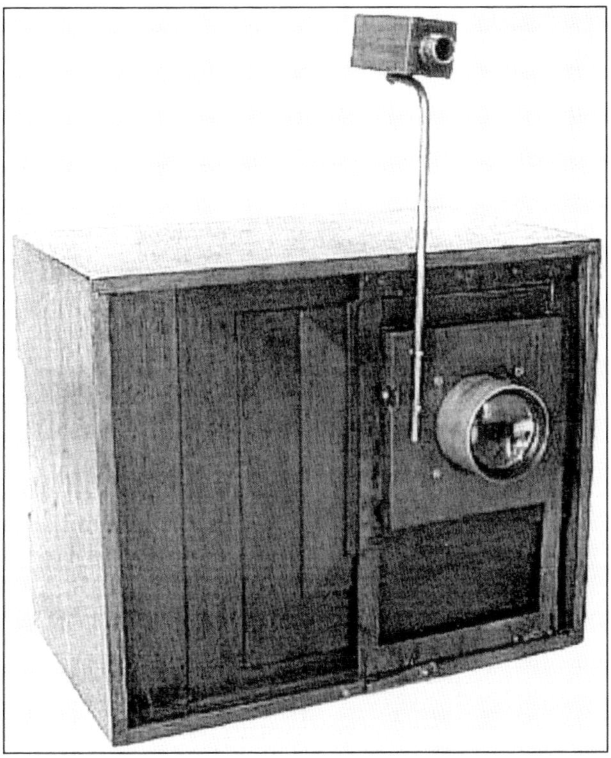

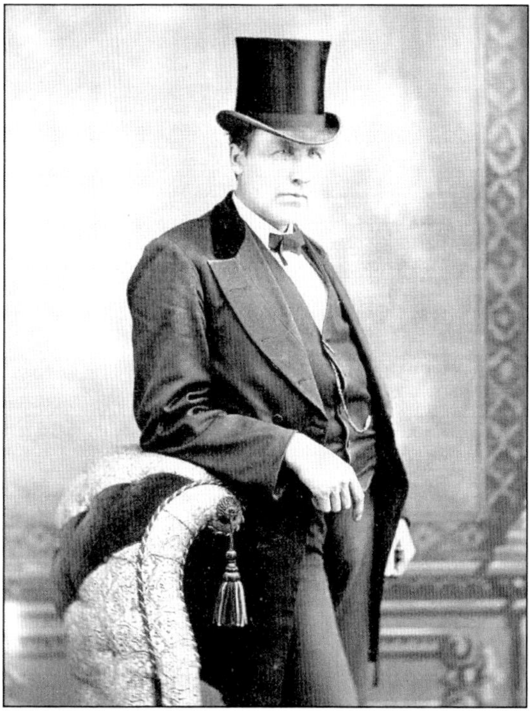

The Wealthiest Man in Maine Practices Law in St. Albans. Lawyer David D. Stewart was rumored to be the richest man in Maine in 1910, when he inherited his brother's wealth. The will ordered D.D. to "dispose of the estate where it will do the most good." And that he did, giving millions of dollars to various Maine institutions, including the new town hall. D.D. Stewart wrote a letter to his brother Levi on January 14, 1876, while on vacation in the South. "I found the country past Washington DC here far poorer than I had any idea of—almost an unbroken swamp with the exception of a patch of land just big enough to build a dirty village on, now and then. The whole country's poor—not worth rebelling for and not worth a tenth part of what it cost us to put the rebellion down—and how they continued to fight so long and so well, I don't see."

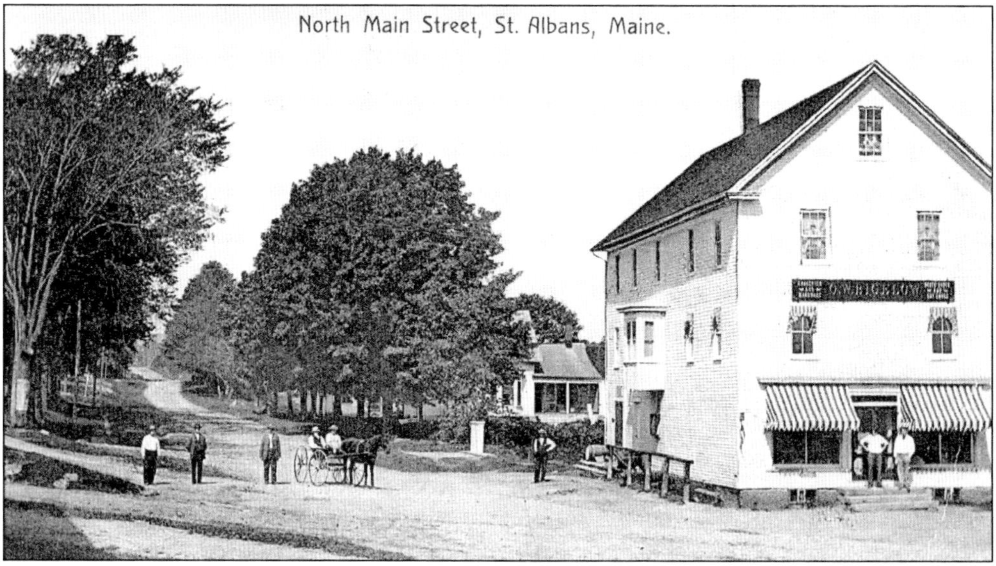

D.D. Stewart's Office above the General Store across from Croquet Court. The Hansons ran the store for years when D.D. was upstairs practicing law. In 1994, Vera Hanson recalled, "D.D. was her husband's great-uncle and he was waited on by the Hanson family not only because he was rich but also because he had a great intellect and a great knowledge of the law." He at times argued cases before the Supreme Court in addition to handling local cases. In my research I found him retained by the Town of Corinna in the C.C. Libby tax collection case of 1881; he received $500 for services in the Downing suit in Ripley in 1873 and $300 for services in the cost of a suit against the Town of Hebron. In 1888, Ripley hired him to collect a bill against the Town of Levant. In 1898, D.D. charged Ripley $39 for legal services.

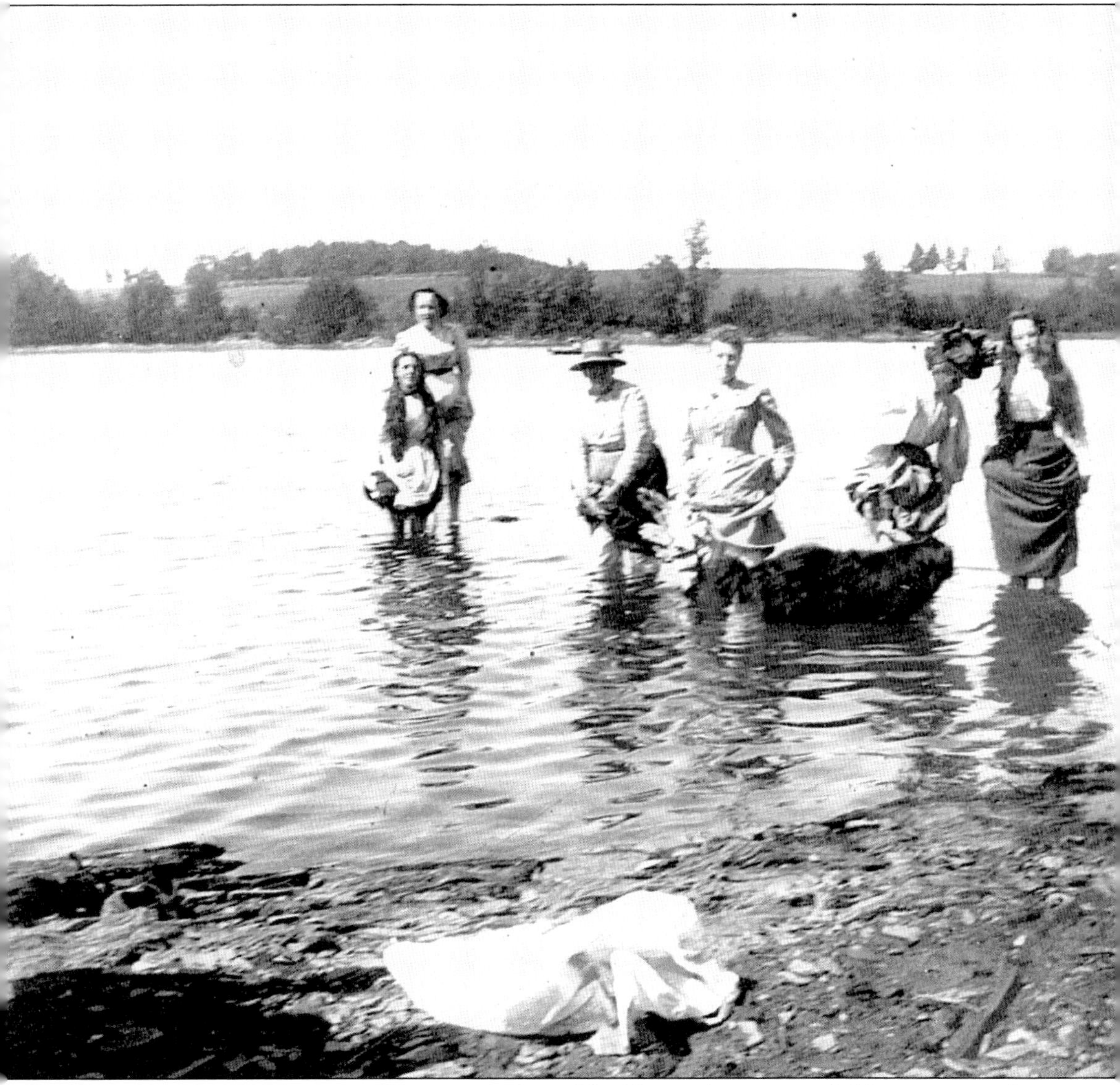

BIG INDIAN POND, A FAVORITE RECREATION SPOT. The Native Americans of old were supposed to have an encampment between Big Indian Lake and Little Indian Lake. There was not much of a lake until the white settlers came and put in a dam. Elmer and Newell Philbrick used to cut ice all winter every year on the pond. Newell made a saw rig to increase volume to keep up with the demand. The local boys would clear a place on the ice to skate, and when they came back the next day, the Philbricks would be cutting ice out of their skating place. Earl Badger owned Birch Island, and one winter he was going across the ice to cut some wood and one of his horses went through. Help arrived, put a rope around the horse's neck, and pulled him to safety. In 1964, a rod and gun club was formed. It became the Big Indian Fish and Game Association in 1967. The club developed a public boat landing and helped to get the lake stocked with trout. At one time, Camp Albans for girls was located on the lake near the Ballard Road.

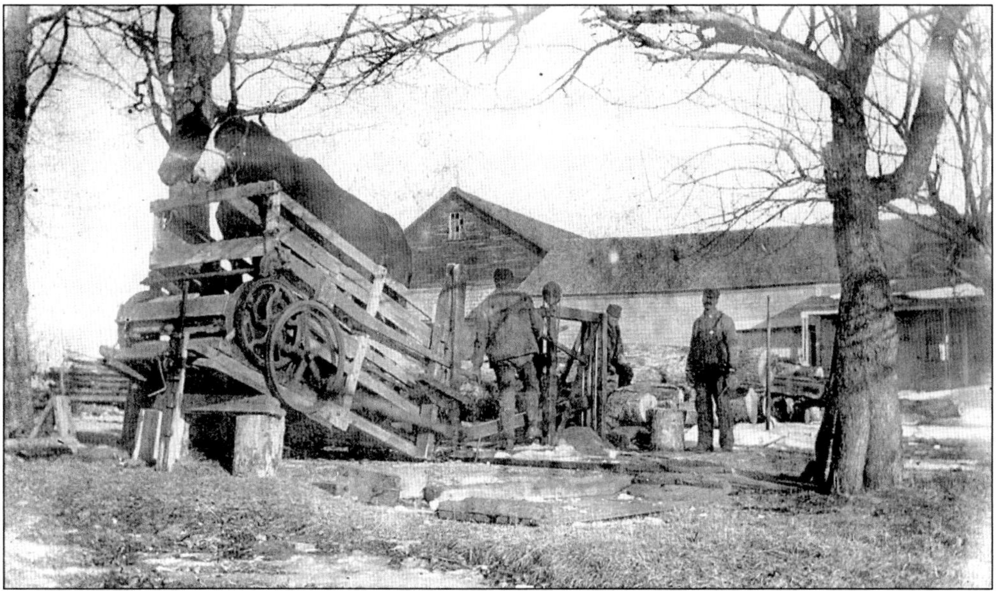

Sawing Wood the Easy Way at Mower Farm. Sid Mower was an easy-going man who had a successful, diversified farm. His brother Charles bought 1,200 acres of Main Stream Lumber Company land and had crews and trucks cutting and hauling logs to his sawmill in town.

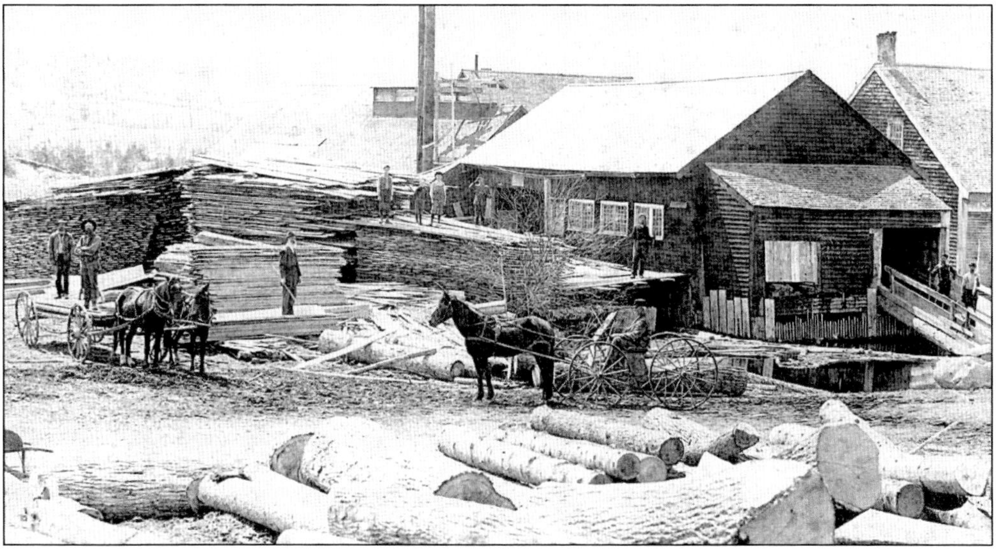

Waterpower Dominates in 1869. "At this time St. Albans had 8 water powers on various streams and ponds in town. Number 1 was at the outlet of Indian pond, no machinery upon it. Second dam, shovel-handle, carriage shop, sash and door, and shingle machinery. Third dam, grist and saw mills. Fourth at Lothrop's Mills; saw and grist mill, and tannery. Fifth, shingle mill in north part of town on a stream fed by Rogers' pond in Ripley. Sixth, on the east branch of the stream; shingle mill fed by a small pond. Seventh, on a branch of Footman Brook, unoccupied at present. Eighth, on another branch of Footman Brook, unoccupied. Manufactures for St. Albans are 200,000 shingles, 400,000 feet boards and timber, 8,000 dozen shovel handles, and 75 to 100 tons of leather." (From *The Water-Power of Maine*, by Walter Wells, 1869.) Shown here is a steam-driven sawmill possibly near the lower dam.

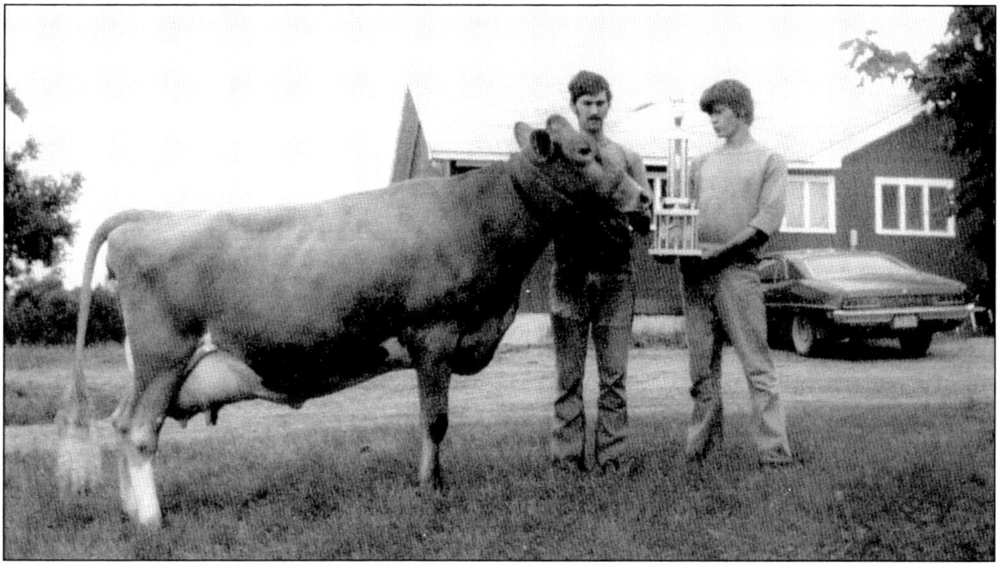

THE BUBARS' 1980 GUERNSEY GRAND CHAMPION TWO-YEAR-OLD. David Bubar holds Maple Row Freida, and Stephen Bubar has the trophy. Freida was judged the best two-year-old in the Guernsey Futurity at the Bangor Fair. Steve Bubar moved to St. Albans from Linneus in 1919. The farm was passed to Corey Bubar, then Wendall Bubar, and is now owned by the fourth generation. The Bubar family was a pioneer in artificial breeding in 1937, helping to organize the Coop in East Newport with some other local farmers. They are now milking 40 head of cattle.

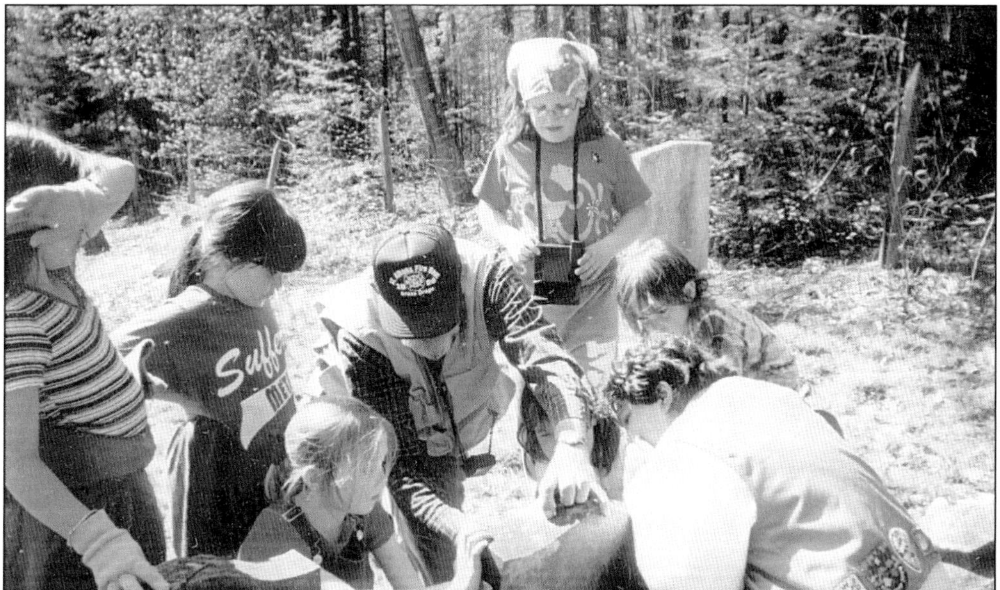

THE GIRL SCOUTS LEARN TO DO GRAVE RUBBINGS. Ron Russell enjoyed showing the girls how to do gravestone rubbings. This photograph shows Brownie Troop 42 and Junior Girl Scout Troop 459 at the Wing Cemetery in 2002. Pictured, from left to right, are Whitney Martin, Charlotte Cazzassa, Courtlyn Clark, Ron Russell, Jessica Russell, Samantha Beatham, and Ariel Humphrey.

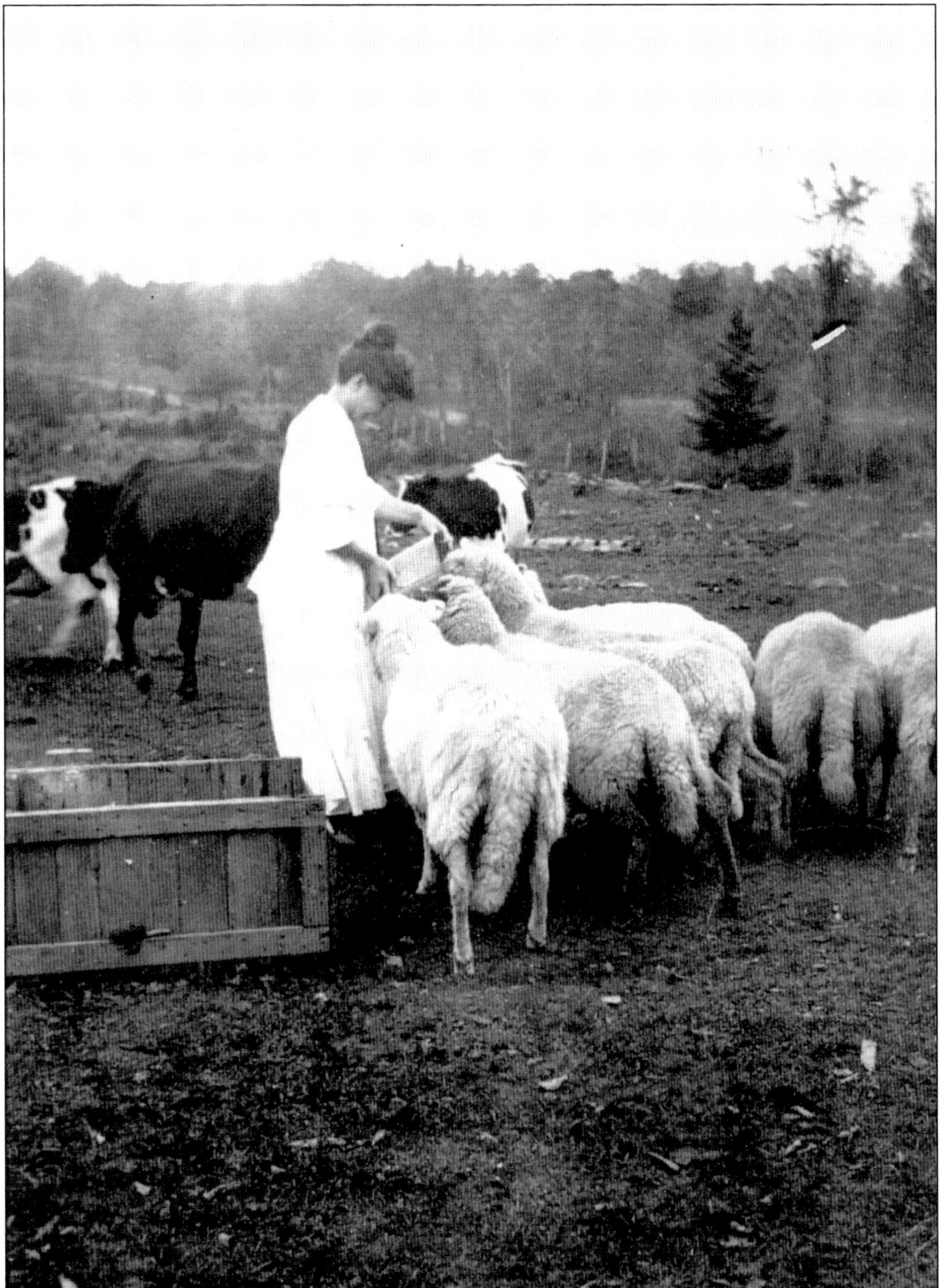

LIBRARIAN NETTIE MOWER FEEDING HER SHEEP. The first library was in East St. Albans. It started in 1898 out of the Crocker house on the Dexter Road. A library association was formed with a membership of 75 patrons and 125 books from the Women's Christian Temperance Union. In 1909, the old Crocker homestead was moved across the road and fitted up for a library and reading room. By 1913, it had 700 books.

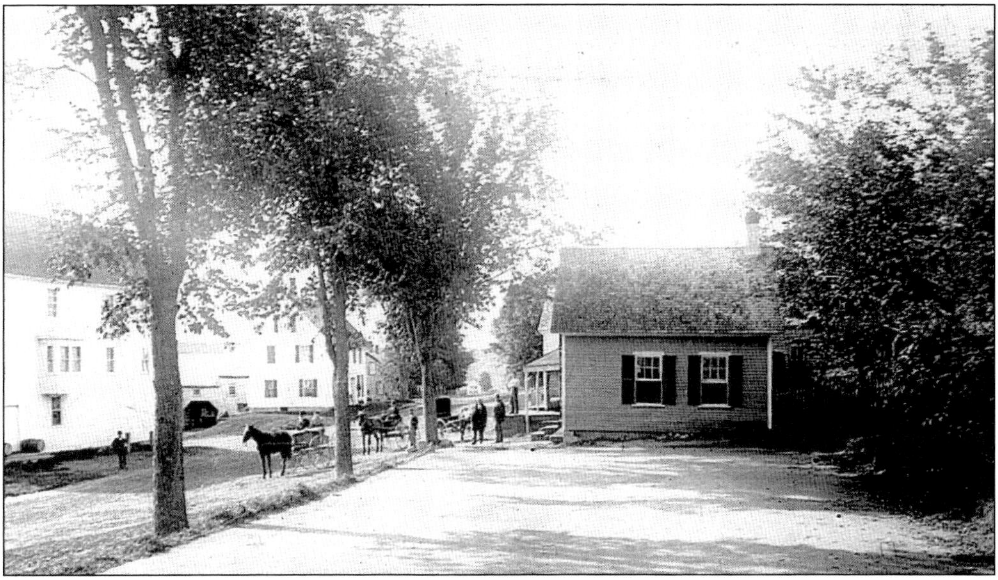

ST. ALBANS A HOT BED FOR CROQUET. Croquet is believed to have been first played by 13th-century French peasants who used crudely fashioned mallets to whack wooden balls through hoops made from willow branches. The modern game has been traced back to Ireland c. 1852. It was introduced to England, and by 1870, croquet had reached all of the British colonies and America. Pictured is the croquet court set up in the heart of St. Albans Village, as the game caught on here in a big way.

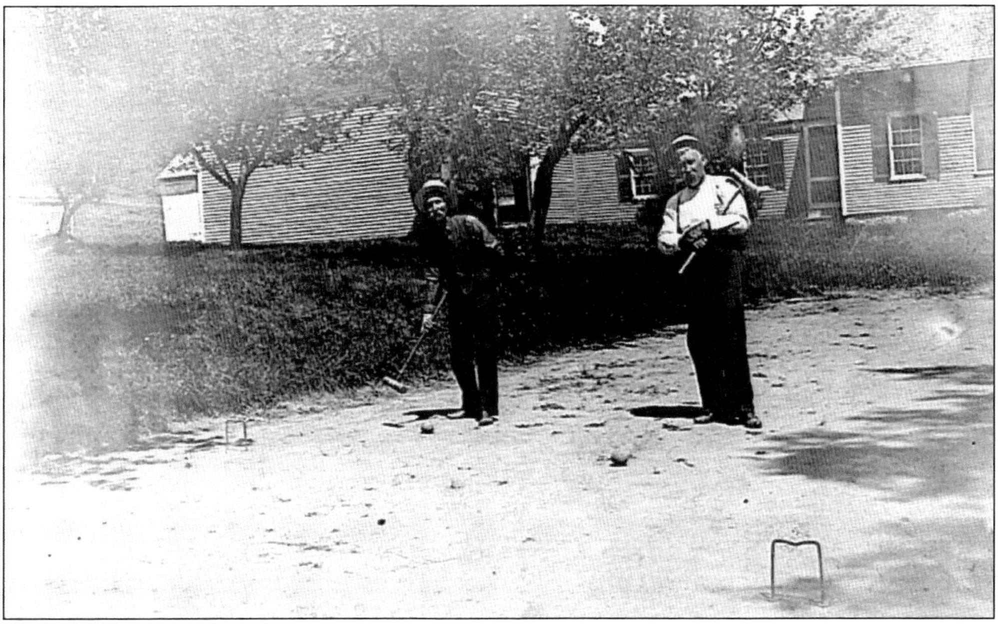

LOCALS ENJOY A GAME OF CROQUET AT NOON. Croquet became one of the primary social and recreational activities of the British leisure class and rapidly spread around the world. Just how and who got it started in St. Albans, Maine, is anyone's guess. Lawyer D.D. Stewart, whose office was just across the road above Hanson's General Store, was a regular noontime player. One of the men pictured above is Daniel Frost, the local postmaster.

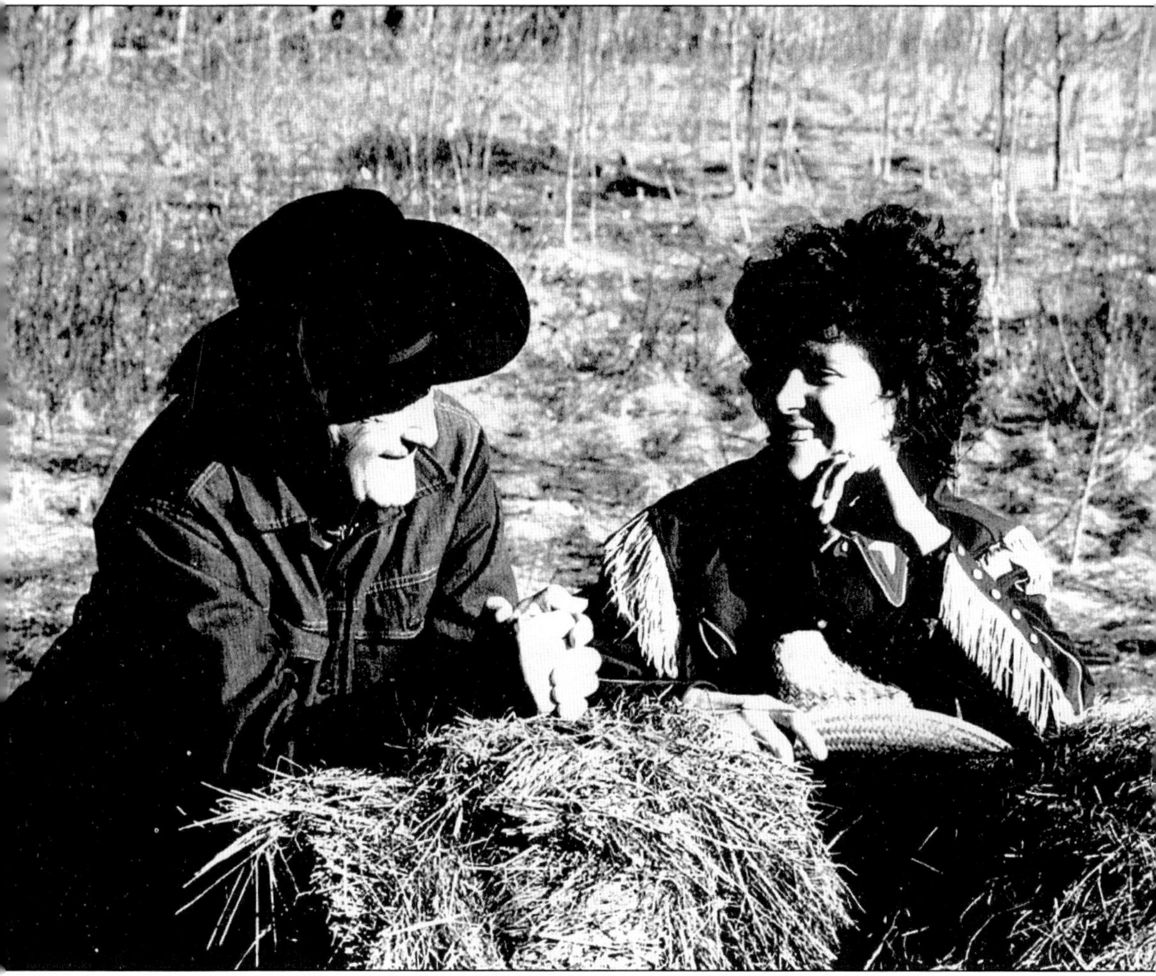

Slim and Kathleen Clark. "Slim and I met at a talent show in Hartland. I was one of the talents. He invited me up to his mountain home to 'see' his etchings. Within months we became engaged, and were married on February 20, 1982," said Kathleen Clark. The Mountain Road ranch house would frequently ring out with music as he sang duets with Kathleen, a chiropractor in Hartland. Raymond Leroy "Slim" Clark had an interest in country music at an early age and decided by age seven or eight to be a country singer. Slim was eventually making $25 a night—real good wages for the Depression era. He started recording in 1946 in New York City, but in the fall and spring, he would just disappear. Slim would go hunting and fishing when the season came. One of his favorite records, made for children, was called "The Cat Came Back." His music awards are too many to list here, but the crowning achievement was in 1996, when he was inducted into Nashville's Walkway of Stars in the Country Music Hall of Fame. He became the third entertainer from New England to have been chosen to join the elite 272 performers memorialized. He also had a reputation as a painter of outdoor, wildlife, hunting, and fishing scenes.

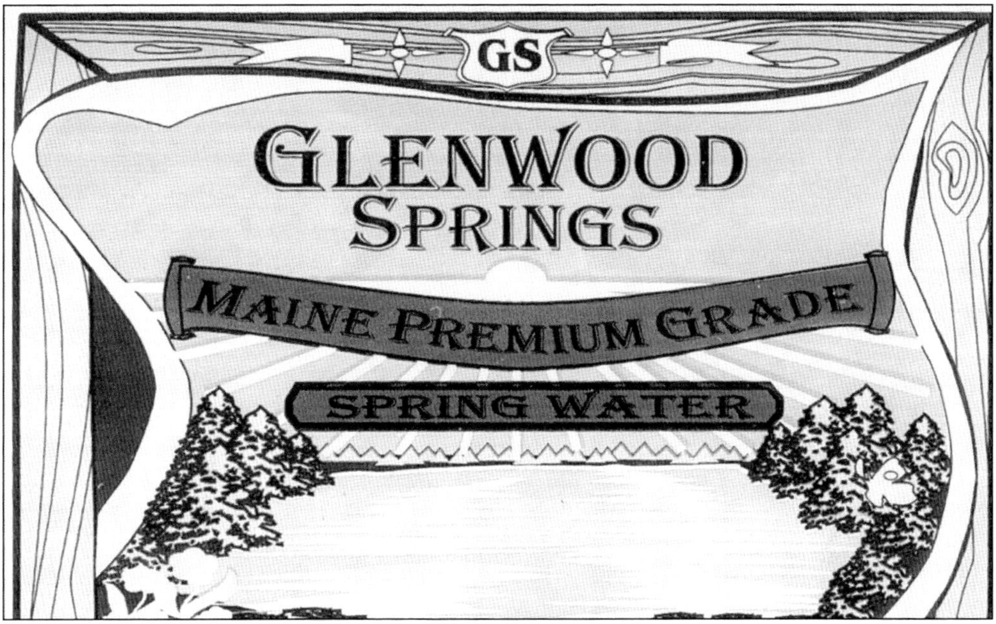

GLENWOOD SPRINGS RUNNING STRONG AFTER 100 YEARS. Henry Shaw of New Hampshire saw the possibilities. Bottled water is in demand in our modern society. In 1993, he purchased the Jennie Springer farm. The spring was used only locally in the past few decades, but Mose Wilkins had a permit from the state in the 1930s to bottle and sell it. The spring had first been popularized by Dr. Moulton in the 1890s as a "medicinal water and nature's remedy for many ills." Today it is known as Glenwood Spring, Premium Grade Pure Natural Spring Water with no mention of mineral content. The water is pumped to a water depot building, where it is bottled or fills large tank trucks.

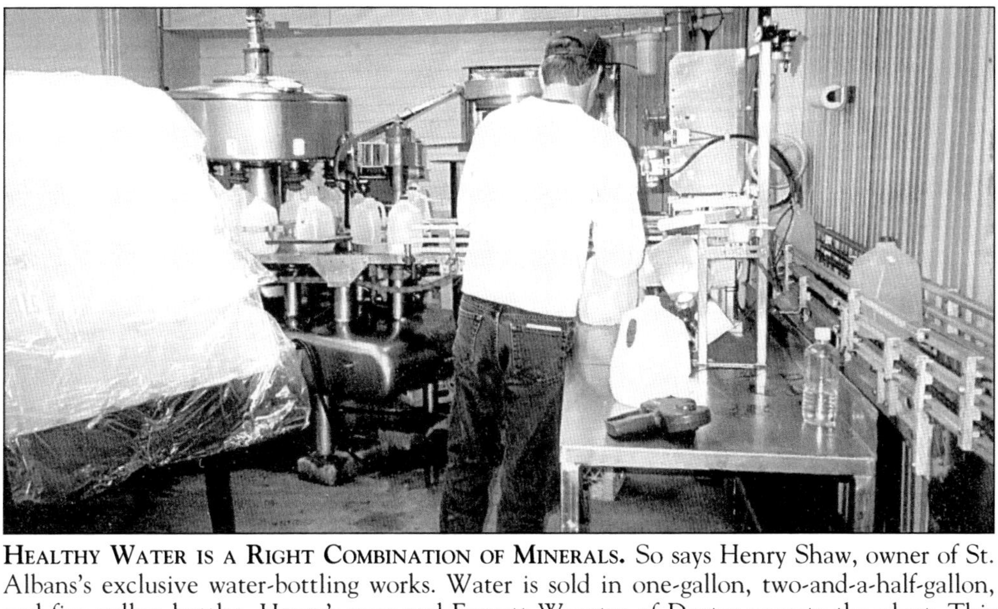

HEALTHY WATER IS A RIGHT COMBINATION OF MINERALS. So says Henry Shaw, owner of St. Albans's exclusive water-bottling works. Water is sold in one-gallon, two-and-a-half-gallon, and five-gallon bottles. Henry's sons and Everett Wooster of Dexter operate the plant. This photograph depicts the filling line for one-gallon bottles that will be distributed in stores under the Glenwood Farms label and other private labels.

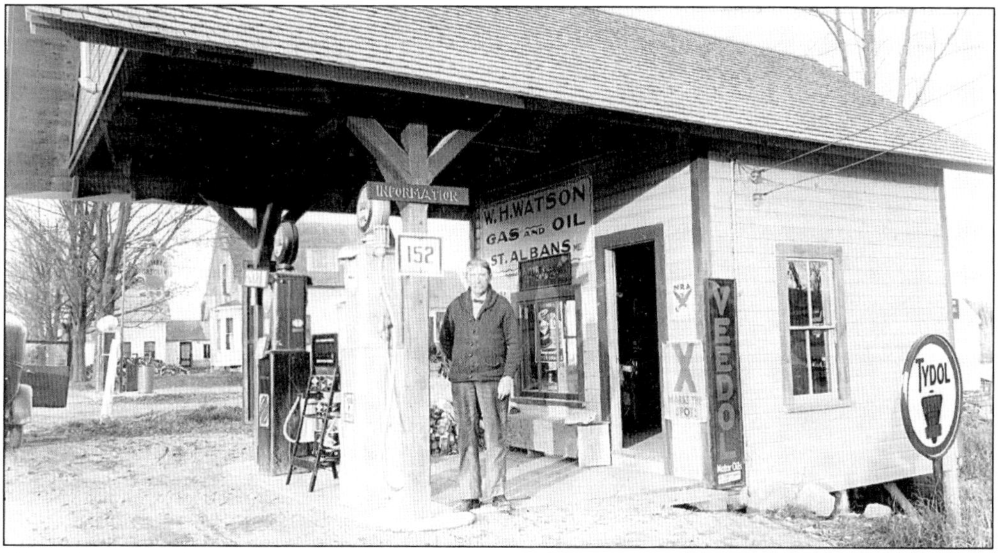

W.H. Watson, Gas and Oil on Route 152. Albert Burton from Hartland was a gas and oil distributor and set up small filling stations all around the area. Shown here is Billy D. Wolf tending the pumps. The station was located on Route 152 just beyond the Upper General Store on the road to Todd's Corner. Just beyond Watson's was the George Libby Gulf Station and Feed Store. George helped the local farmers during the Depression by extending credit for grain. After he died the credit was called in and some farms were sold to pay for the grain in those hard times.

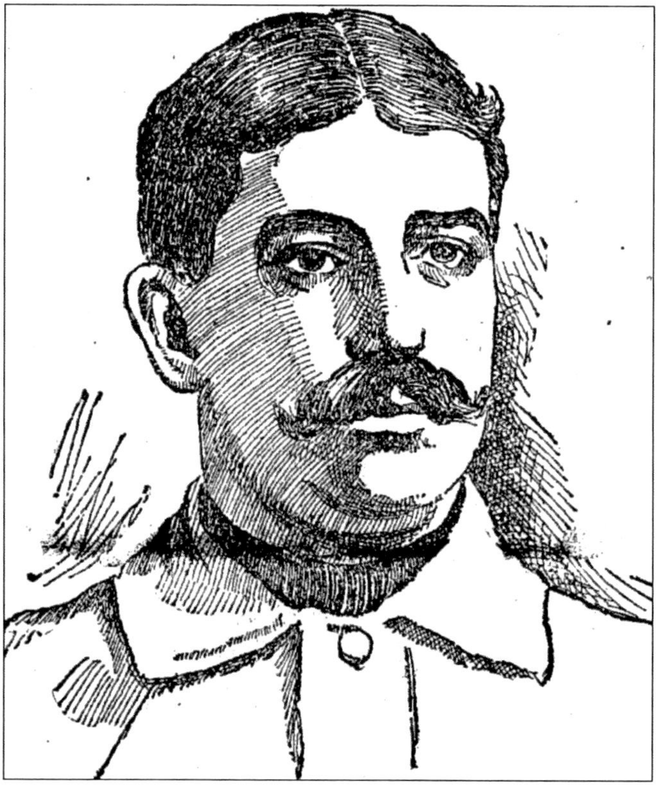

Topsy Magoon Makes It to the Major Leagues. This illustration hails from a September 24, 1898, *Sporting Life* magazine. "George H. Magoon is a clever young infielder playing for the Brooklyn Club of the National Baseball League." Born in St. Albans in 1875, George H. "Topsy" Magoon made it to the major leagues in 1898 and played for teams in Brooklyn, Cincinnati, and Chicago. He also had a long career in the minor leagues.

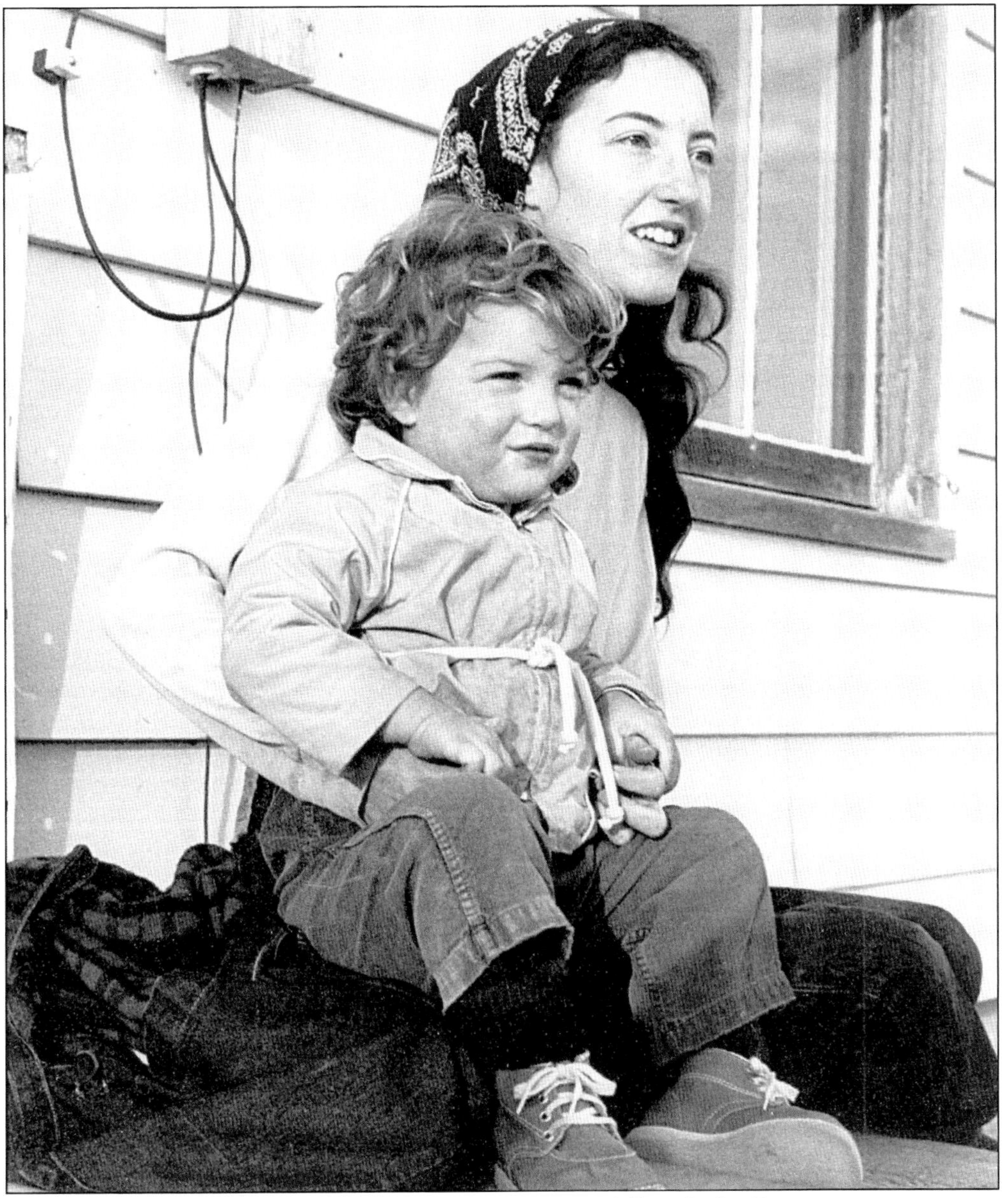

FROM ST. ALBANS TO HARVARD TO MAINE POLITICS. Yellow Light Breen, age two, sits on his mother's lap. Jill Breen has been a midwife serving the central Maine area since 1978. Yellow, who graduated *cum laude*, was selected to deliver the senior oration at the 1993 Harvard University commencement exercises before a crowd of 28,000. Yellow became a lawyer and went on to work in Maine government. In his speech, he said, "I come before you dressed in the uniform of a Harvard graduate, but in the civilian world, the world beyond these ivied walls, I am a resident of the tiny town of St. Albans, Maine. The people of St. Albans believe in growing things, building things, making things, not in talking about things. It is, in short, the academic's worst nightmare. In a time when much of the world is increasingly fragmented and atomized, the bonds and claims of neighborhood are still strong in St. Albans. America faces the task today of building a sense of community when we often lack a shared sense of place. What we can do is seek to make the places where we do live into real communities."

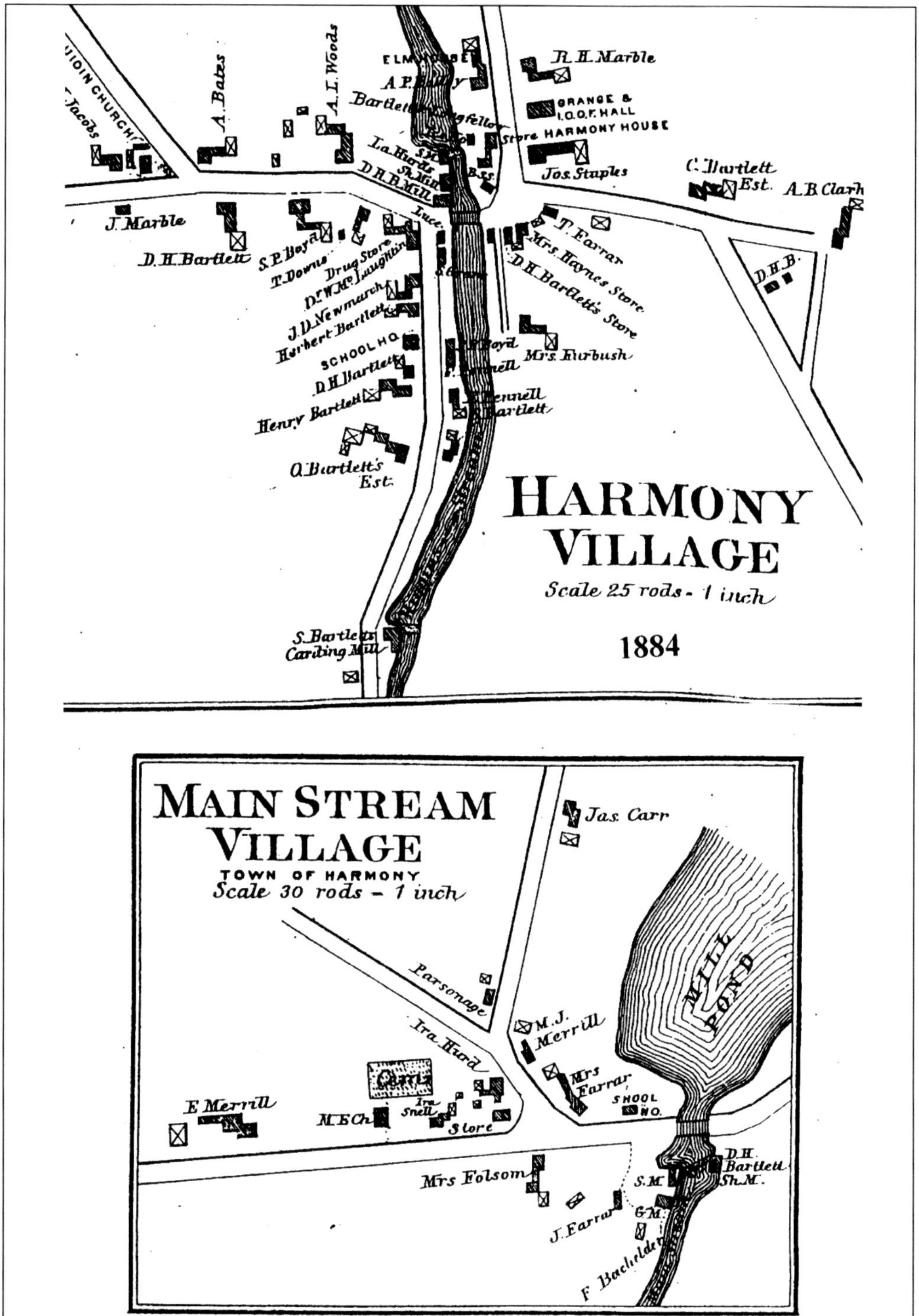

A Map of Intown Harmony and Main Stream Village, 1884. At this time, Harmony had one physician, two lawyers, one constable, six justices, six merchants, and one hotel. There were also 13 manufacturers.

Five

HARMONY

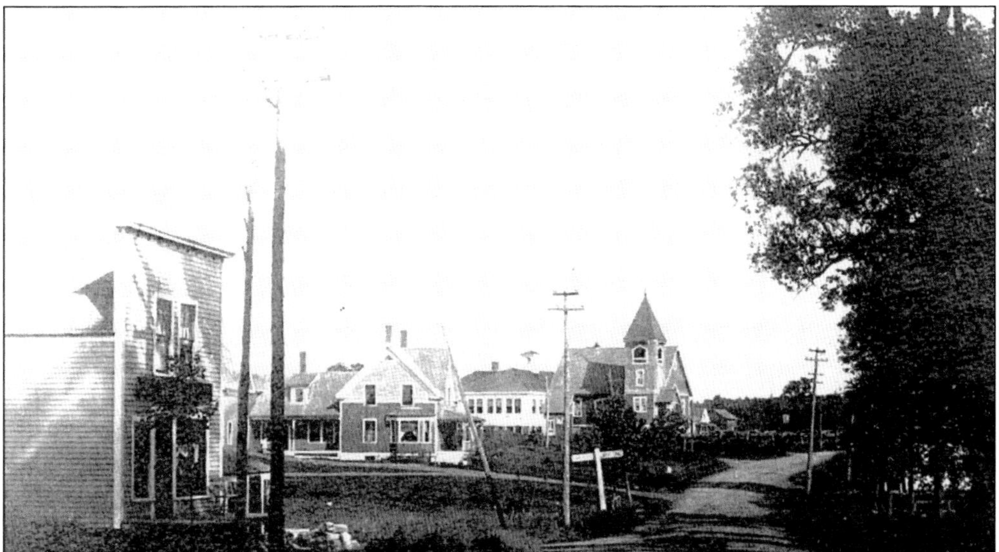

MAIN STREET, HARMONY, MAINE. Harmony—called Vaughnstown until 1803—was first surveyed by Samuel Weston in 1790. The first settler was Trustum Hurd in 1796, and Harmony was incorporated in 1803. Its population stood at 351 in 1810, 584 in 1820, and reached its peak of 1,107 in 1850. By 1900 the population had dropped to 571. In 2000, 954 people lived in Harmony. "In 1840 there were in the village 4 stores, a cooper's shop, a shovel handle factory, a hatter's, a tannery and a shoemaker's shop. A chair factory stood where the creamery once stood." (From *East Somerset County Register*, 1911.)

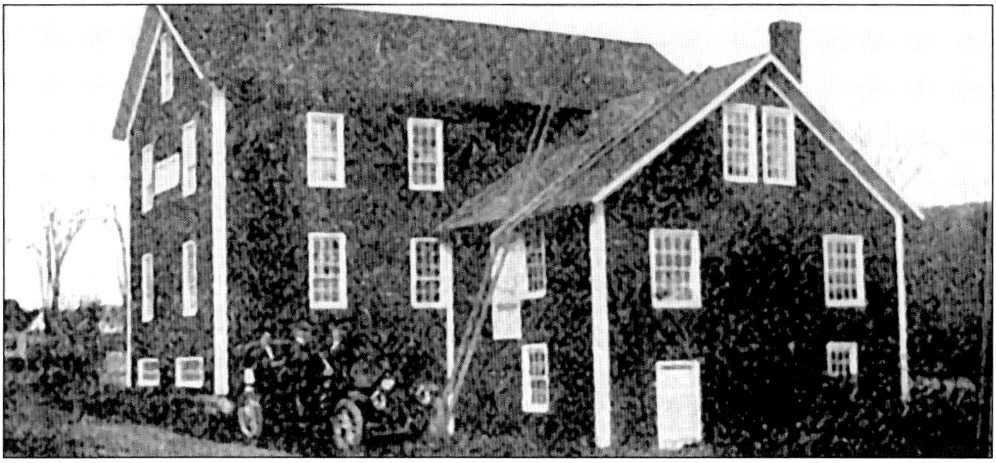

The Bartlett Mill, a Longtime Harmony Business. Started by Ozias Bartlett, the mill carded rolls and made woolen yarn and blankets. His son Stedman increased the business, and his son Herbert changed to the manufacture of yarn. Harry Bartlett then took over the mill at the age of 16 and enlarged the business throughout the central part of the state. The Bartletts' manufacture of yarn is well known for its excellence even to this day. Ozias's son Russell Bartlett invented a lathe for turning out shovel handles and then invented an apparatus for raising sunken vessels. He was lost at sea on a return trip from Europe. This photograph shows the mill before the fire of 1911.

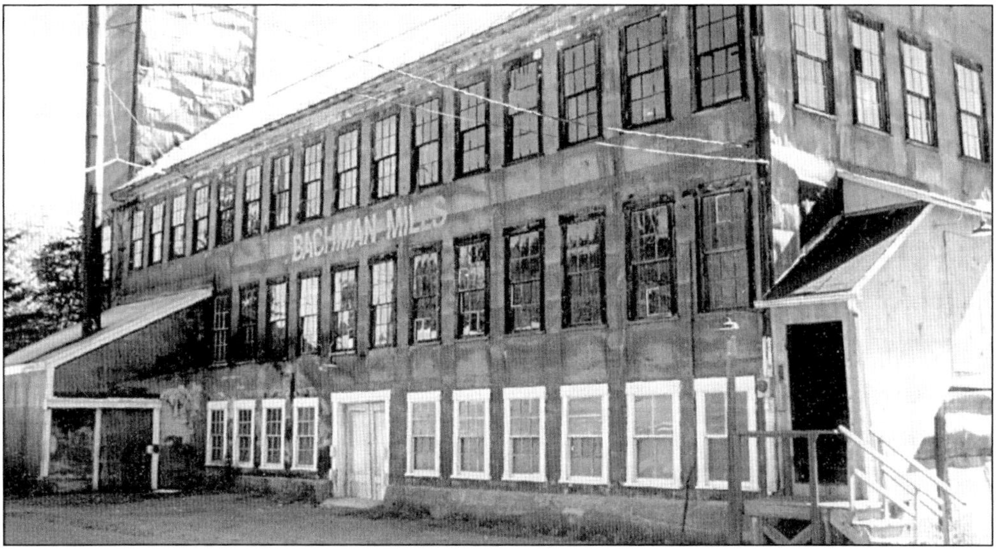

The Bachman Mills Management Finds a Mysterious Basement. The mill was built in 1897. No one remembers when the basement was last cleaned; it was mostly used for junk storage. On July 4, 1990, the mill's management decided it was time to tackle the project. That is when all the trouble began. They found biting rats as large as puppies, and then a subbasement was discovered through a trap door that was bolted closed from below. There was a box down there imprinted with the name "Elias Varney" and dated 1841. Hall and Warwick were killed going into the subbasement and Carmichael had his arm ripped off. They found rats 3 feet tall that had only two legs. Another worker was mysteriously sliced apart in a machine, all except for his boots. Don't worry, folks; it's only the Bartlett Mill, which was used as the fictional Bachman Mills for the Stephen King movie *Graveyard Shift*.

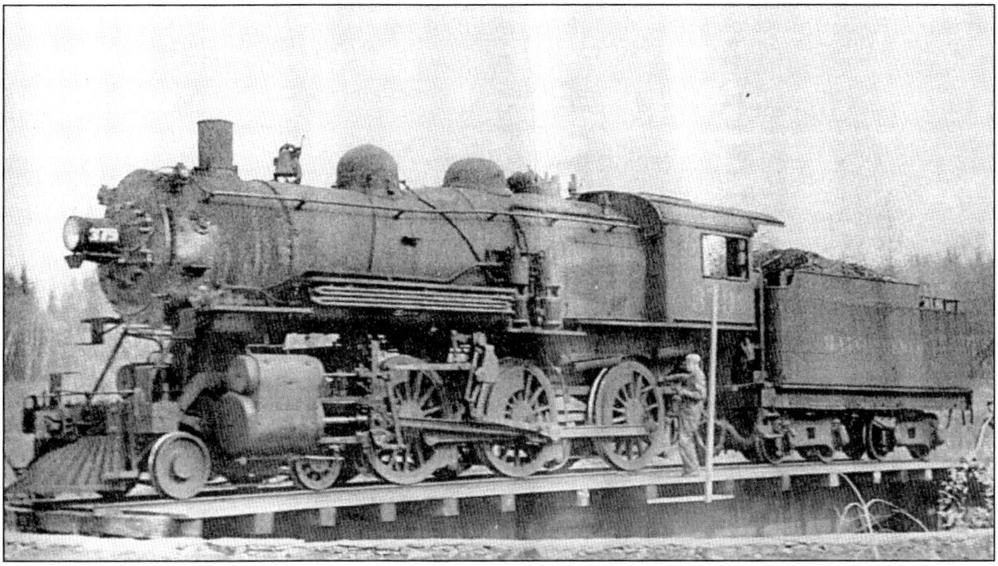

The Railroad Comes to Harmony. The Belfast and Moosehead Railroad came into Harmony from Main Stream on August 15, 1912. There was a terminal with a roundhouse and a turntable (shown in above photograph) for the train that came into town three times a day. The turntable and tracks were removed in 1966.

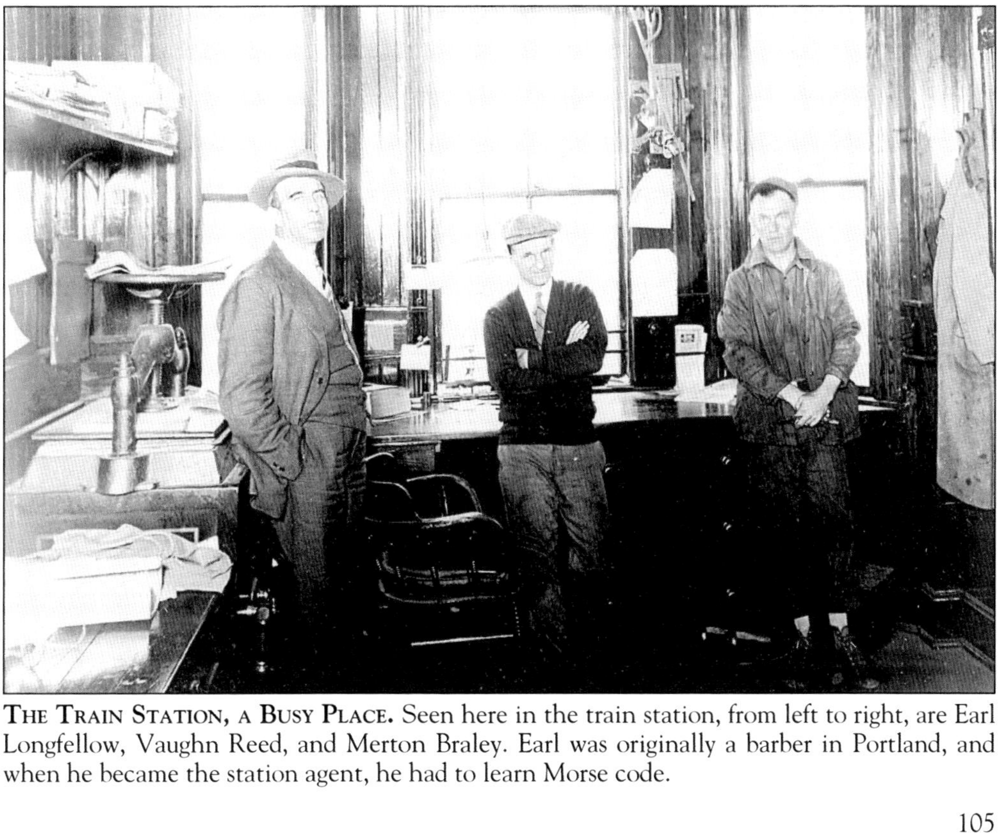

The Train Station, a Busy Place. Seen here in the train station, from left to right, are Earl Longfellow, Vaughn Reed, and Merton Braley. Earl was originally a barber in Portland, and when he became the station agent, he had to learn Morse code.

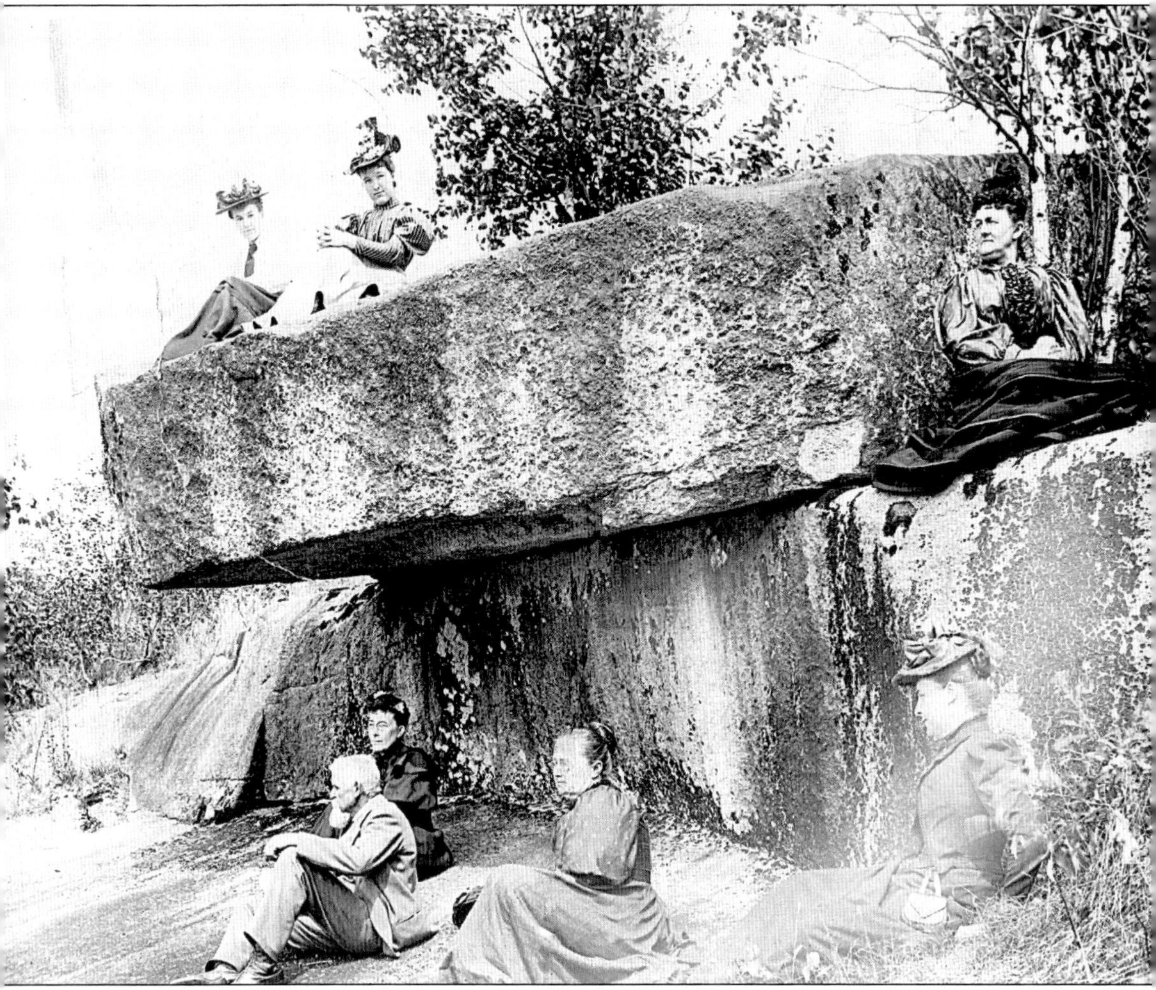

Three Devil's Head Murder Mysteries Still Unsolved. These are the facts we know. Isaac H. Dugan (age 44), Betsey Dugan (age 33), and George Dugan (age 11 months) are listed in the 1860 census. They lived on a road just below Devil's Head, with B. Reed's home nearby. Hunters in the area recall some old cellar holes in that vicinity. Clerk of Courts Seekins found Skowhegan court records dating back to 1856 stating that Mrs. George Dugan (Betsey Smith) entered a plea of not guilty to murdering Jane Dugan, a widow whom the state maintained she had beaten with a wooden club. Betsey was acquitted of this murder. Some years later, no one knows exactly when, Harmony lawyer Cleopas Boyd made a warrant out for her arrest when Betsey's husband was also found dead, supposedly with a bread spoon pushed down his throat. Betsey sought the services of lawyer D.D. Stewart of St. Albans, and again she was found innocent.

In this c. 1880 view, Dexter citizens are enjoying the view from Devil's Head. From left to right are the following: (front row) Mrs. Samuel Eldridge, Henry Dole, Georgia Dole, and Mary Ireland; (back row) Mabel Sawyer, unidentified, and Agnes Sawyer. Directly in front of them and a short distance down the mountain was the Dugan homestead, where the killings occurred.

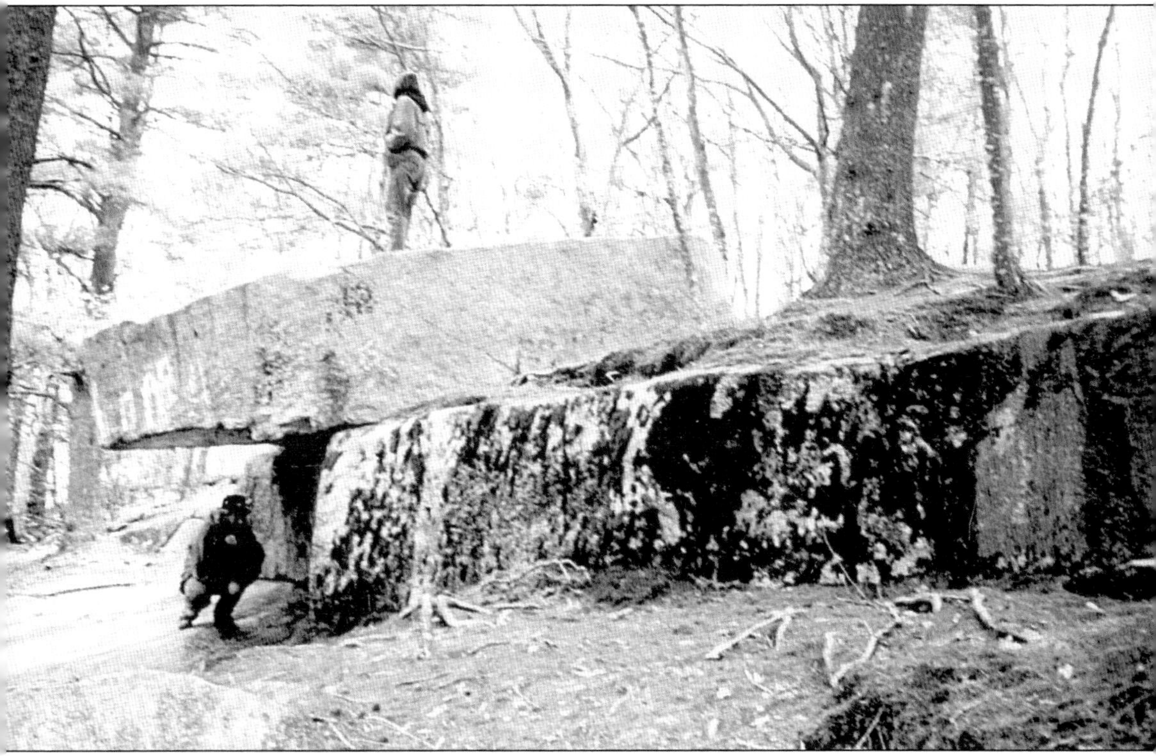

DEVIL'S HEAD TODAY. Then the Betsey Dugan story gets murkier. Two men were rumored to have stopped at Betsey's on the way to Bangor with some whiskey and cider. A William White had just sold his farm for $600 and had hired a neighbor to drive him to Bangor. The neighbor claimed that "he and White filled up at Betsey's and he did not come to life for most of 2 days and White meanwhile had disappeared." White was never located. It is not known whether he continued on his way when he sobered up or disappeared near Devil's Head. It was claimed that Betsey died in New Hampshire and was returned to Harmony to be buried on the farm beside her husband, under an apple tree where there are a few other graves. "It was said that she had money enough to meet all charges so was of no expense to the town." (From the Vertine E. Ellis personal notes, at the St. Albans Historical Society.) The photograph shows Robert Desmarais and Liz Breault looking over Devil's Head.

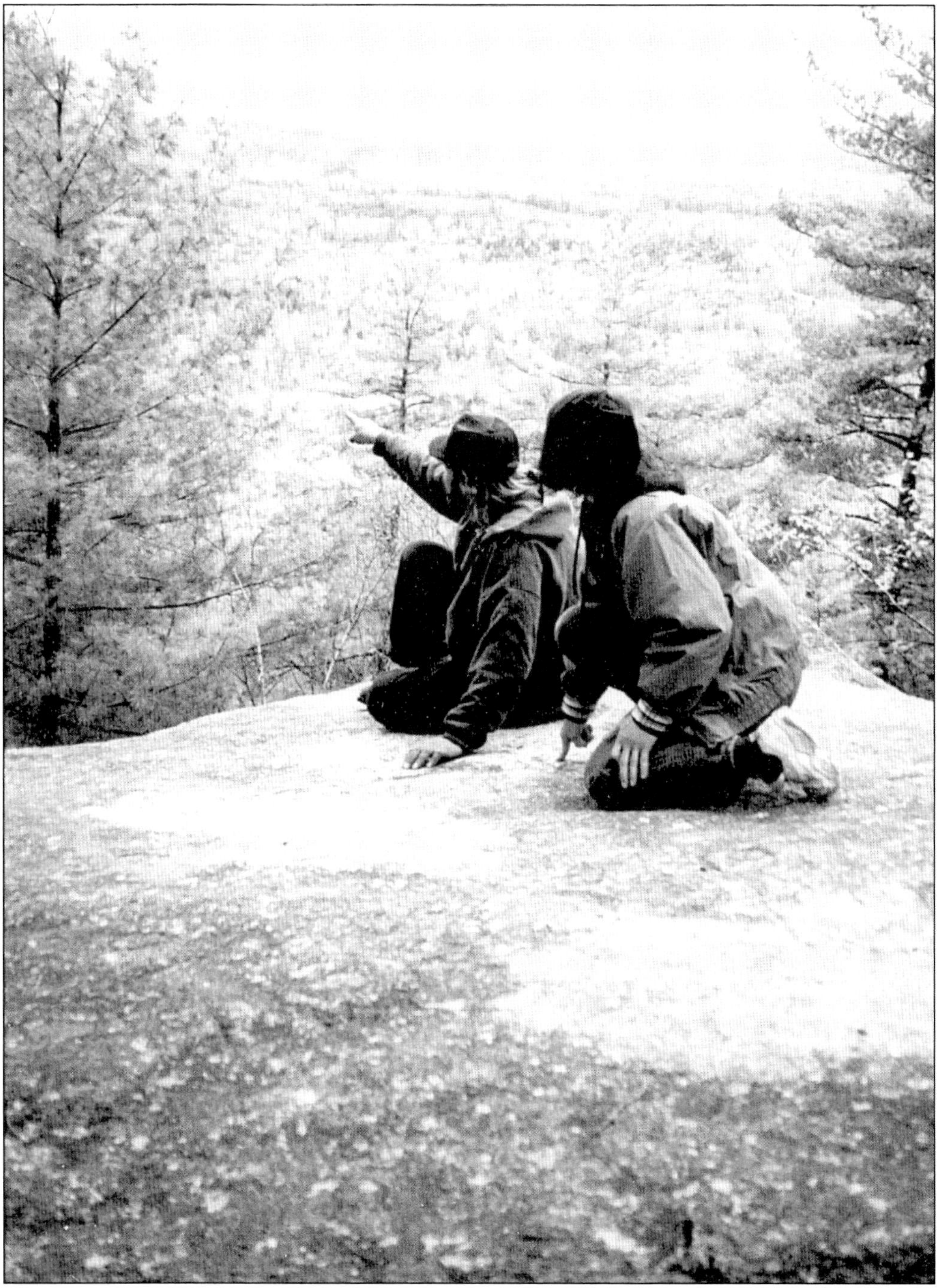

Prehistoric Man Used Devil's Head to Locate Other Landmarks. Archeologists have visited this rock formation from time to time, and some claim that the holes drilled in the top of the rock were used for holding sticks that would align with other high places across Moose Pond. Liz Breault has her finger near one of the holes, and Robert Desmarais is pointing to a distant mountaintop. A short distance from Devil's Head is a small cave that looks partially man-made.

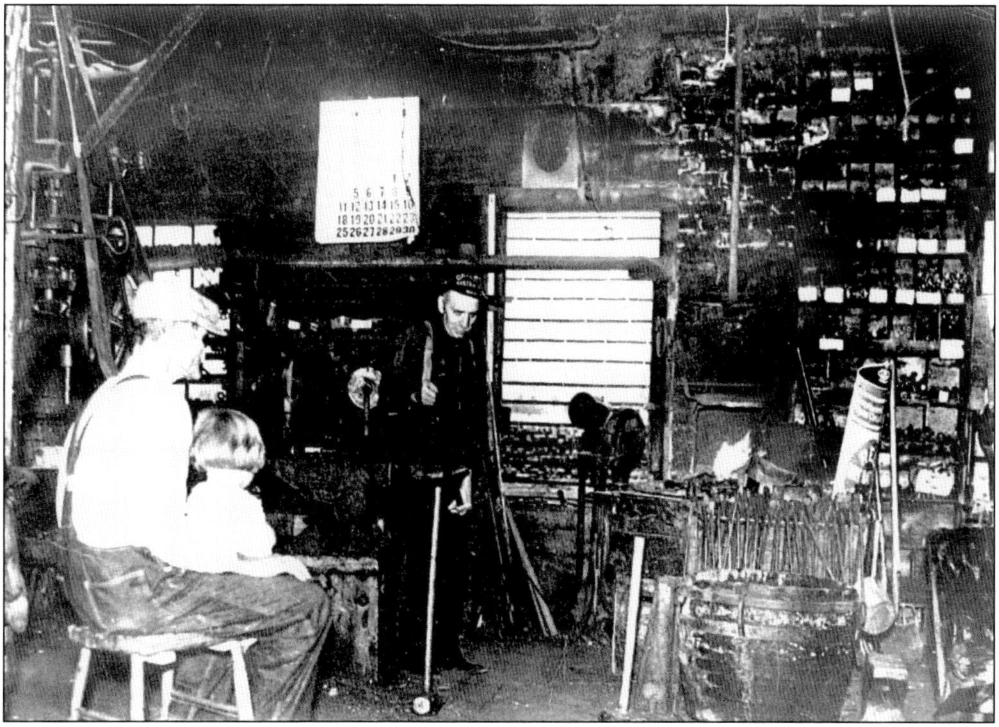

The Main Street Blacksmith Shop. The man working on the anvil is an unidentified Wellington blacksmith. At one time, Orrin Page, Richard Wilcox, and William Farrell did ironwork and horseshoeing. Ivan Chadbourne rebuilt the shop into a garage and added a house. Shirley S. Brown later ran the garage.

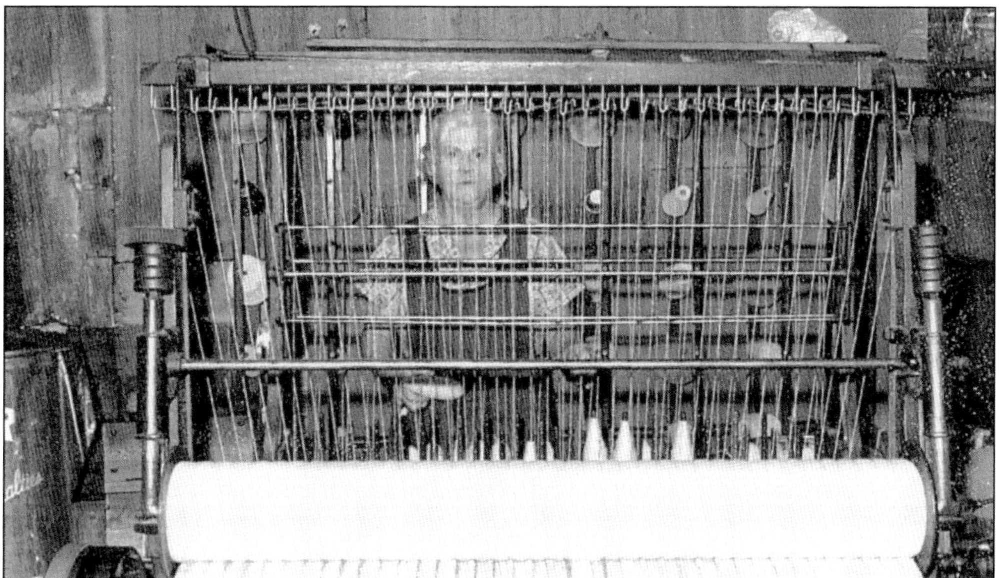

Bea Page Spooling at Bartlett's. One of Lucian Dube's best workers while he was foreman at Bartlett's was Bea Page, the wife of Clyde Page. Bea is pictured behind the spooling frame where the yarn from the bobbins is moved to a big roll.

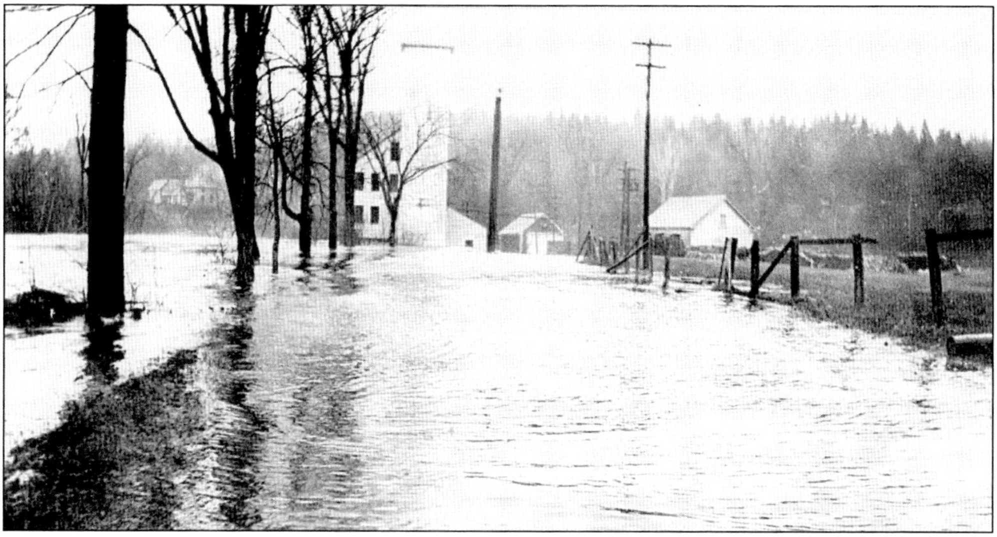

FLOODS DEVASTATE HARMONY. The first flood on record was in 1817, when three bridges on Higgins Stream were destroyed. The 1898 freshet caused some damage but not like what was to come three years later. On December 14, 1901, a thaw set in with a warm, drizzling rain followed by a heavy fog and then more rain. The Wellington and Collins dams had given way due to a vast amount of water accumulating from Scribner's Bog and Grant Brook. Ice piled up three layers high on the bridge, and the road beside the Bartlett Mill was washed out to a depth of 15 feet. This photograph shows the road to the Bartlett Mill from a more recent flood.

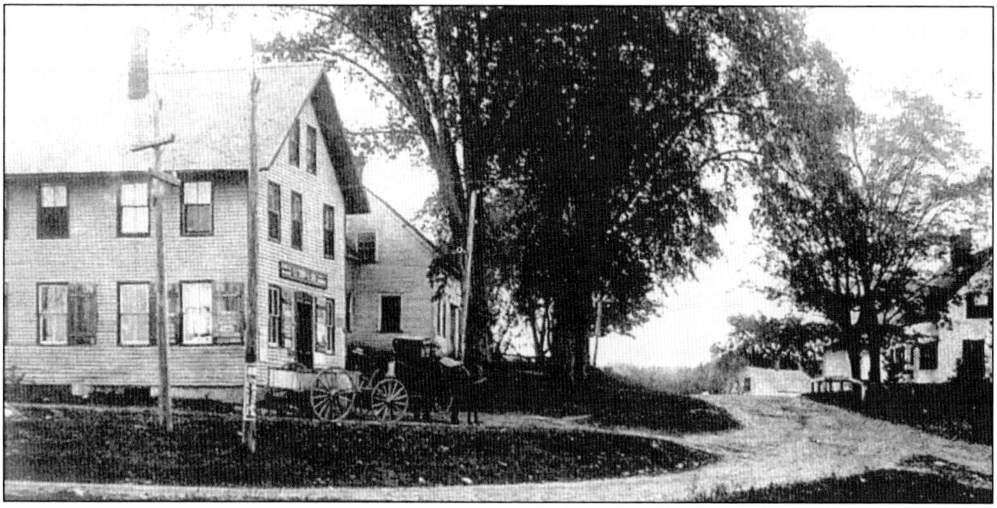

HURD FLIES INTO A RAGE, MURDERS HIS BROTHER. Just around the bend of the road in this view from Main Stream Village toward Harmony, the deadly deed happened. Howard and Eugene Hurd lived on adjoining farms. Howard lived in the home farm, and his brother Eugene had a contract to purchase from Howard the one in which he resided. The brothers had always quarreled. "Howard's colt was in the oats and Howard went over [to Eugene's] and drove him out. In about 15 minutes, the sharp report of a gun rang out in the still air. Mrs. Coston immediately called to her husband, 'Charles, Eugene has shot Howard, and I guess he has killed him, for he don't get up.' Eugene was sentenced to life imprisonment at hard labor, but was pardoned about 1925." (From *Harmony's History: Happenings, Habits, and Humor*, by Charles Carroll McGlaughlin.)

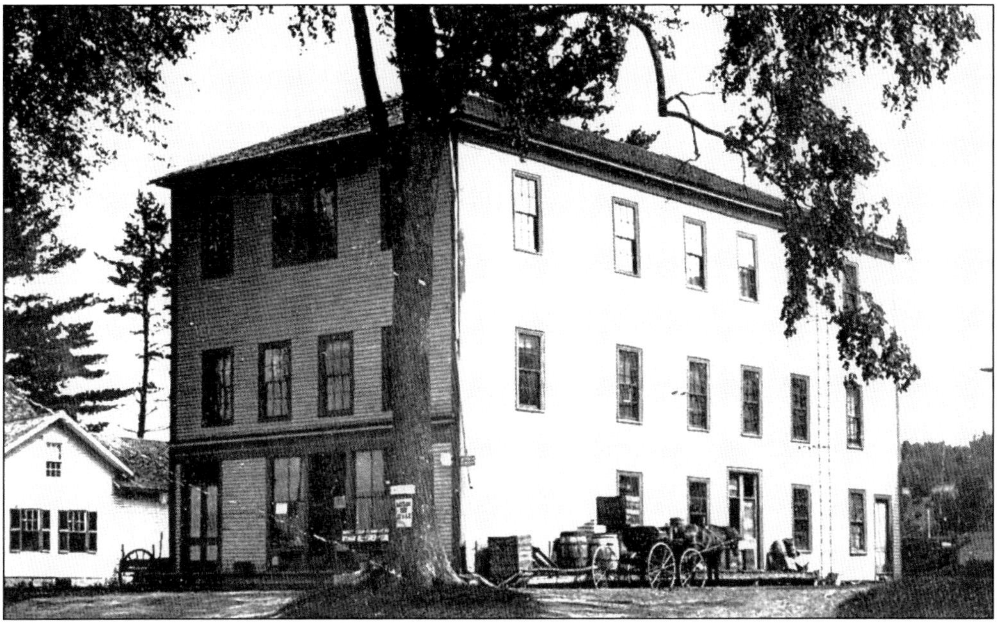

Yankee Storekeeper Offers a Good Trade at Odd Fellows Hall. "The best place to trade," says R.E. Gould, storeowner and author of *Yankee Storekeeper*. "When I took over the store at Harmony I figured the stock was a detriment and my chief asset was the location. Harmony is still a one-horse town as towns are graded by city people. All the surrounding towns had to come to Harmony to do business, and my store was a potential trading center for a huge territory."

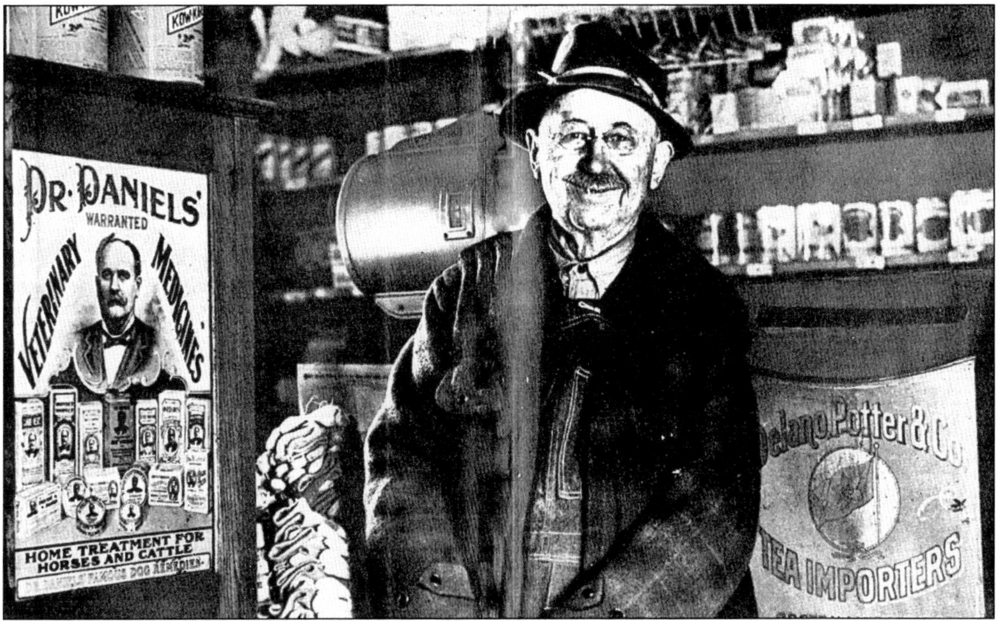

The Philosophy of Running a General Store. "The country storekeeper, if he is to be a successful merchant, must be able to deal with any and all, must buy a great many things—must know what to say and must sift a small amount of truth out of a vast pile of lies and must know values of nearly everything," R.E. Gould wrote in his 1946 book *Yankee Storekeeper*.

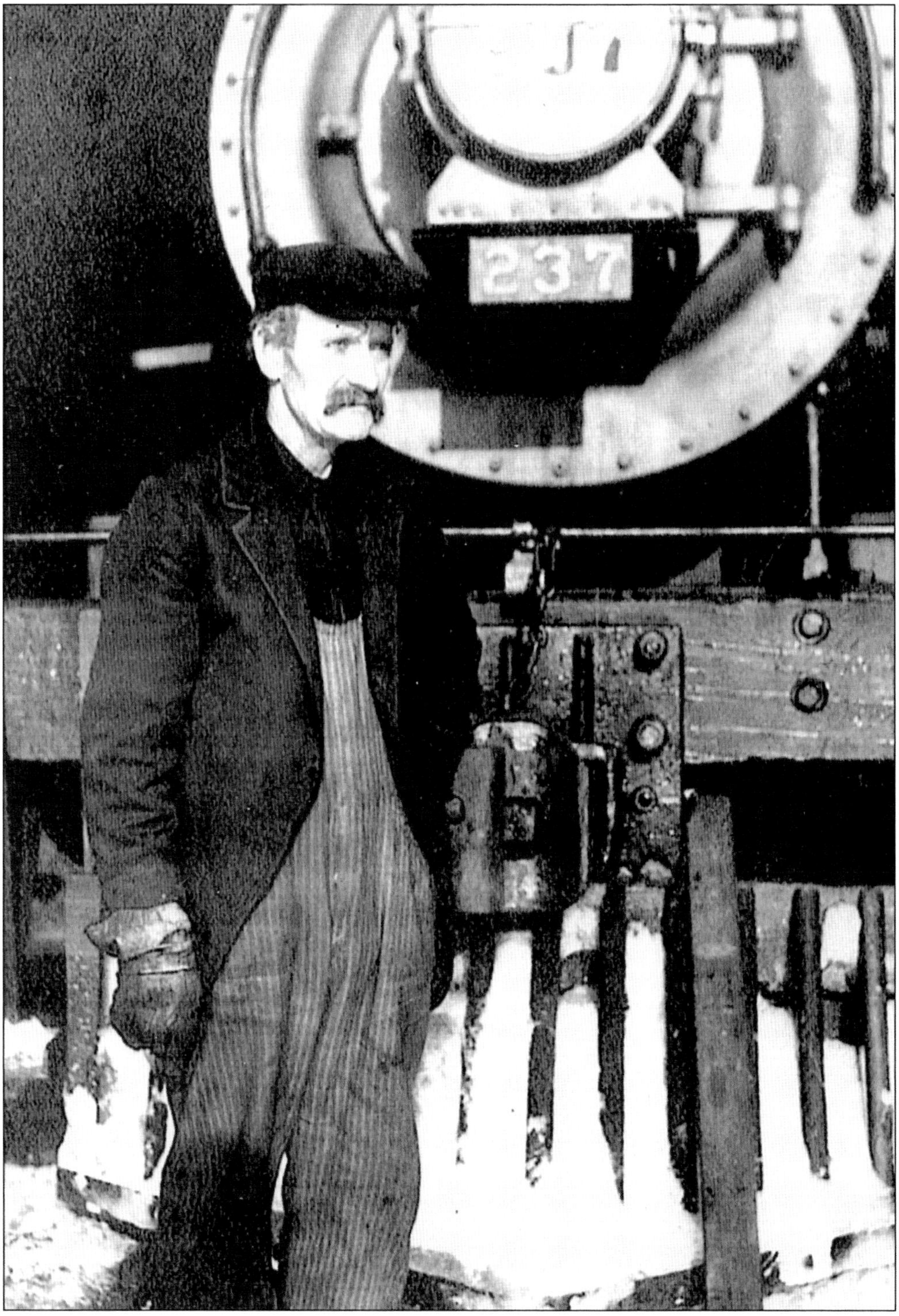

ORA WILLIS, NIGHT WATCHMAN. Ora is pictured in the engine house one cold winter night. He enjoyed working for the Maine Central Railroad and was an honest, faithful employee for many years.

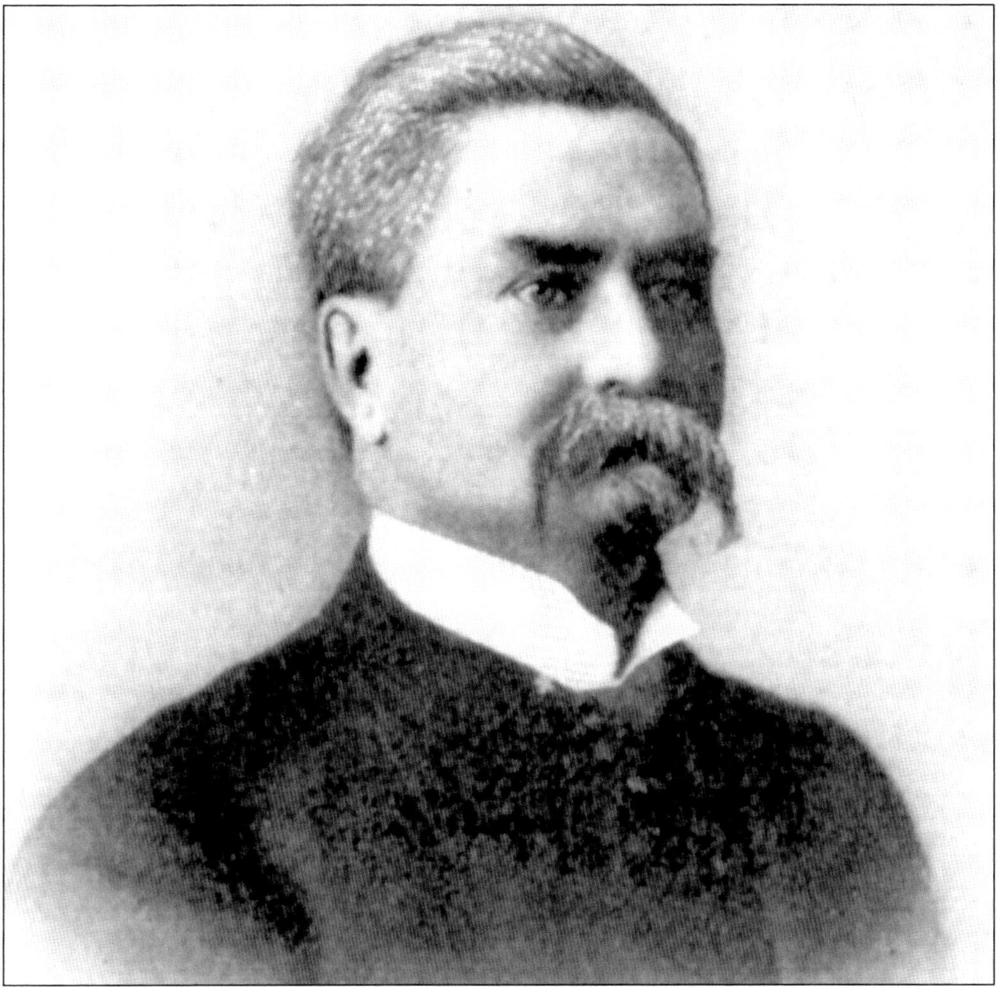

Bartlett Tripp, a President From Harmony . . . Almost. Bartlett Tripp started out as a schoolteacher at the age of 14 and paid his way through Waterville College. He went out West to Iowa and California to teach but returned to the East and graduated from Albany Law School, along with his classmate William McKinley. He went West again, settling in the Dakota Territories, where he became chief justice of the Dakota Supreme Court. William McKinley is rumored to have considered his college friend Bartlett to be his vice presidential candidate in 1898. Had Bartlett been chosen as running mate, he would have become Pres. Bartlett Tripp from Harmony, Maine, when McKinley was assassinated in 1901.

The Reverend William Tripp settled in Ripley and Harmony, but his sons had a broader vision as the country was developing. Enoch started out working for Plummer P. Todd and then Adonijah Webber at West Ripley in a mercantile business that failed. In 1845, he headed west across the Great Plains. He worked in the boot and shoe business, farmed, opened a tannery, operated a sawmill, and along the way became a Mormon. He was arrested at one time for unlawful cohabitation because he believed in multiple marriages and had 32 children. His brother William was a teacher and later became a lawyer in Wilton, Maine. He served in the Maine House and Senate, becoming president of the Senate in 1849. He moved to Iowa in 1852 and opened a law practice there, then moved to Yankton, South Dakota, to be a partner in his brother Bartlett's law practice. He was appointed surveyor general of Dakota and was city attorney when he died in 1878.

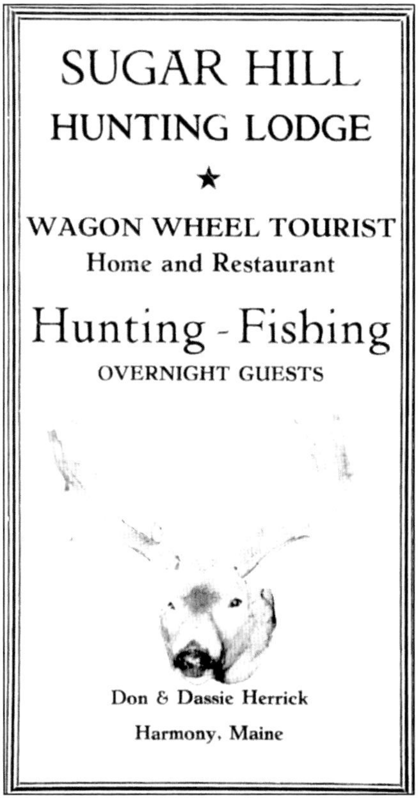

COME VISIT SUGAR HILL HUNTING LODGE. "We have about 1,000 acres of our own beautiful private hunting country. This is natural deer country. There is also a plentiful supply of partridge. You can hunt with or without a guide. Non-resident License fee is $20.25. You have a choice of staying at our tourist home or if you wish we have 3 log cabins and a farm house a short distance from town where you can stay. Special home-cooked meals are served at our Wagon Wheel restaurant." (From a Sugar Hill Hunting Lodge brochure.)

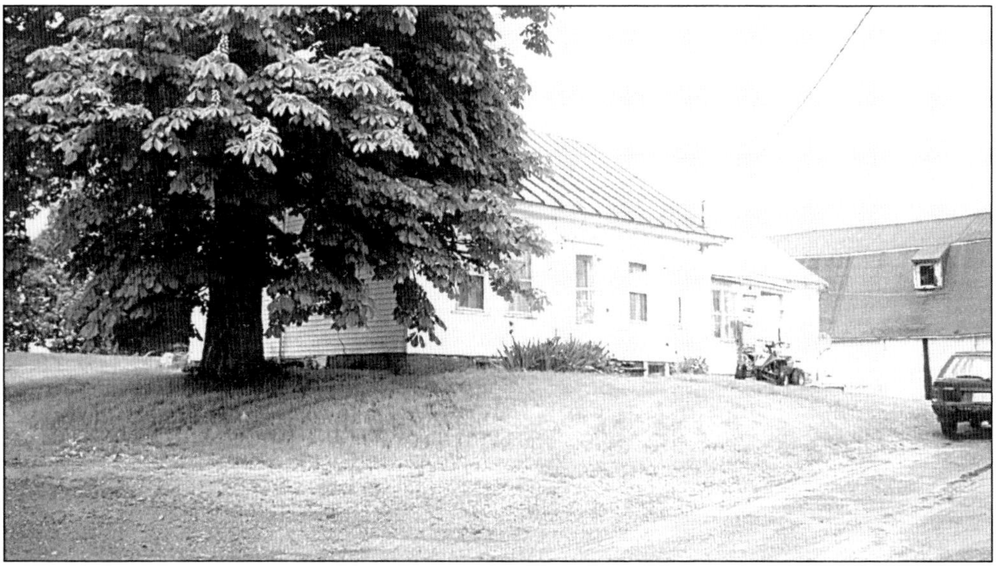

THE HARMONY BEAUTY POTATO DEVELOPED LOCALLY. The Harmony Beauty potato was a cross between the Russet and Vermont Green Mountain varieties. It was developed by Alva Mitchell, a Cambridge native who lived on the Preston Chadbourne farm (shown in present photograph) in the northeast corner of town c. 1880. Alva was born in Cambridge in 1834, one of nine boys in the large Mitchell family. His parents, Joseph and Mercy Buzzell Mitchell, were two of the early settlers of Cambridge.

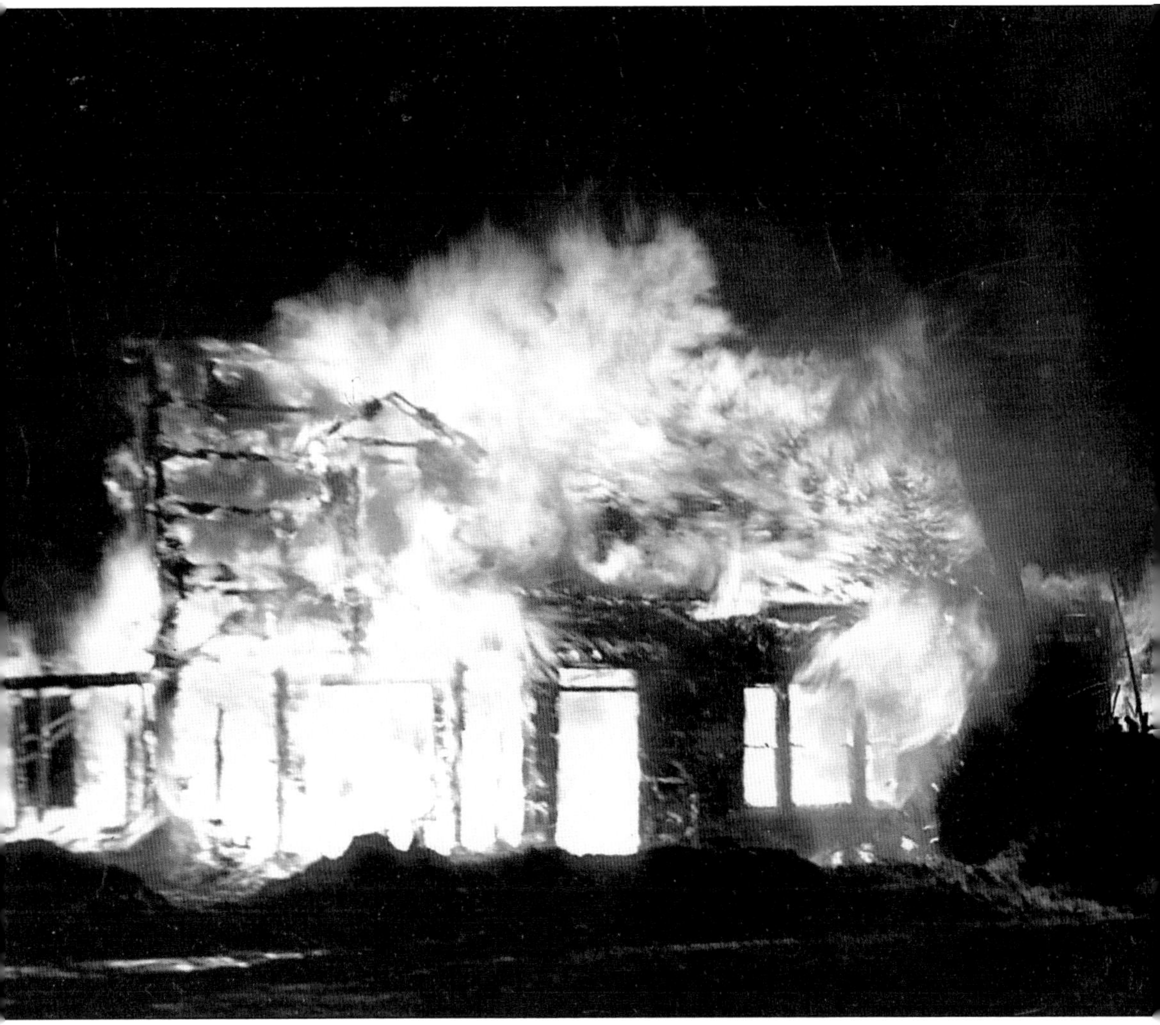

A Firebug Raises Havoc in Harmony; 13 Buildings Destroyed. Everyone was in a panic. Fires were breaking out everywhere. It started when five buildings burned in town. Then, about three or four weeks later, between September 20 and 26, 1886, eight more fires occurred. On September 25, three fires broke out at the same time. They happened in all directions of town; no one was safe. Alfred Hurd, a ward of the state, was accused but was never convicted. Theories surfaced about who was behind the fires. Some said Chicago anarchists were using Harmony as a practice ground. Others thought the Bangor and Piscataquis Railroad had sent an armed band of despoilers to burn the town. All of Harmony went under military guard. One farmer heard a noise outdoors one night and fired. "He found his old buck, which he had hitched to a tree in the orchard, lying dead, full of buckshot." The mysterious 1886 arsonist was never caught.

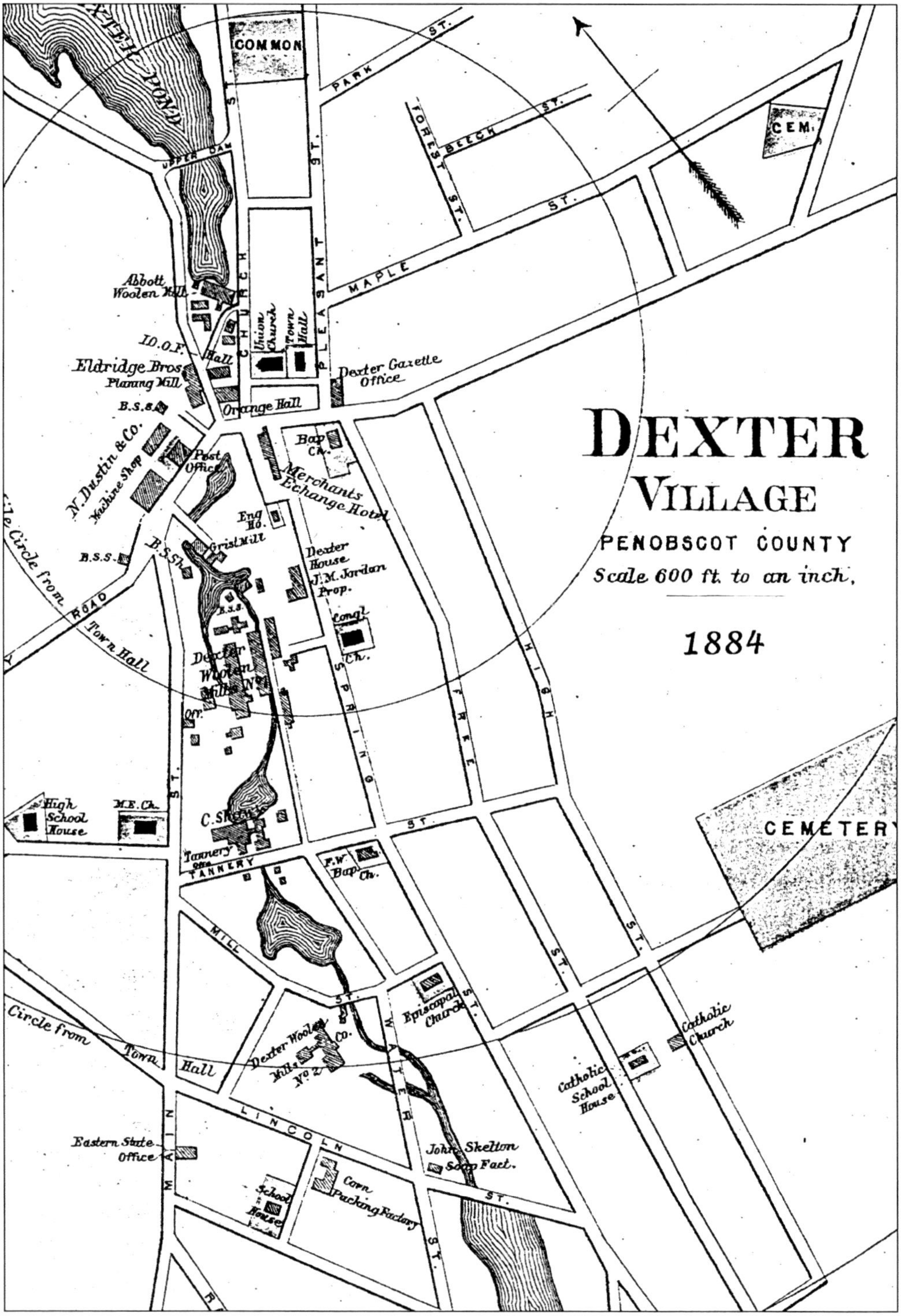

A Map of Intown Dexter, 1884. At this time, Dexter had six physicians, four lawyers, two dentists, eight constables, three livery stables, two insurance agents, two hotels, and one newspaper (the *Dexter Gazette*). There were also 10 justices, 51 merchants, and 50 manufacturers.

Six

DEXTER

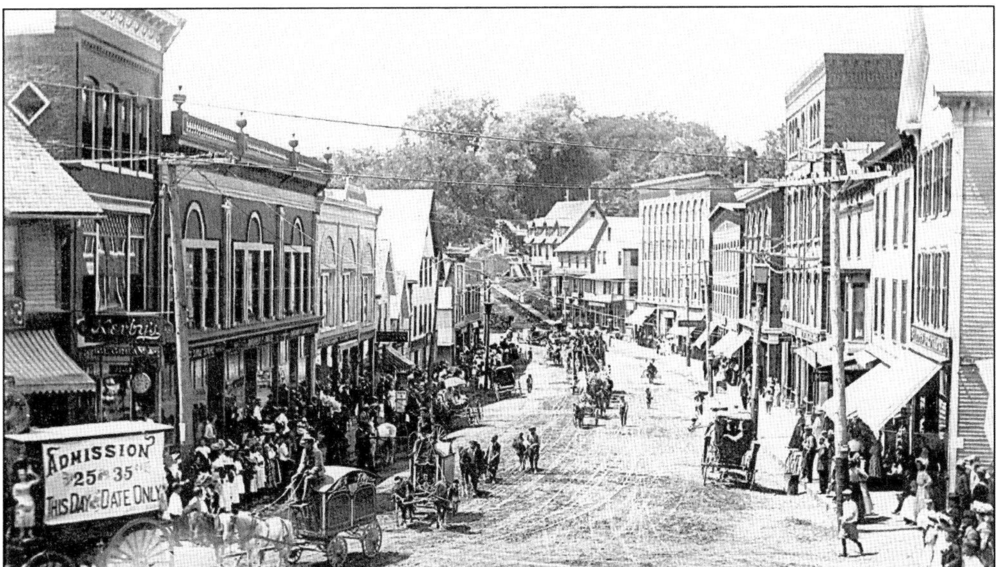

MAIN STREET, DEXTER, MAINE. Dexter's first settler was Ebenezer Small in 1801, and the town was incorporated in 1816. The population in 1820 was 461. From 1860 to 1870, the population grew by 512 to 2,875 but then dropped 312 by 1880. From 1900 to 1920, the population grew by 1,172 to 4,113 only to drop again in 1940 to 3,714. In 1970, the population was 3,725, growing to 4,419 in 1990 and dropping to 3,890 in 2000. In this photograph, the circus comes to town c. 1910.

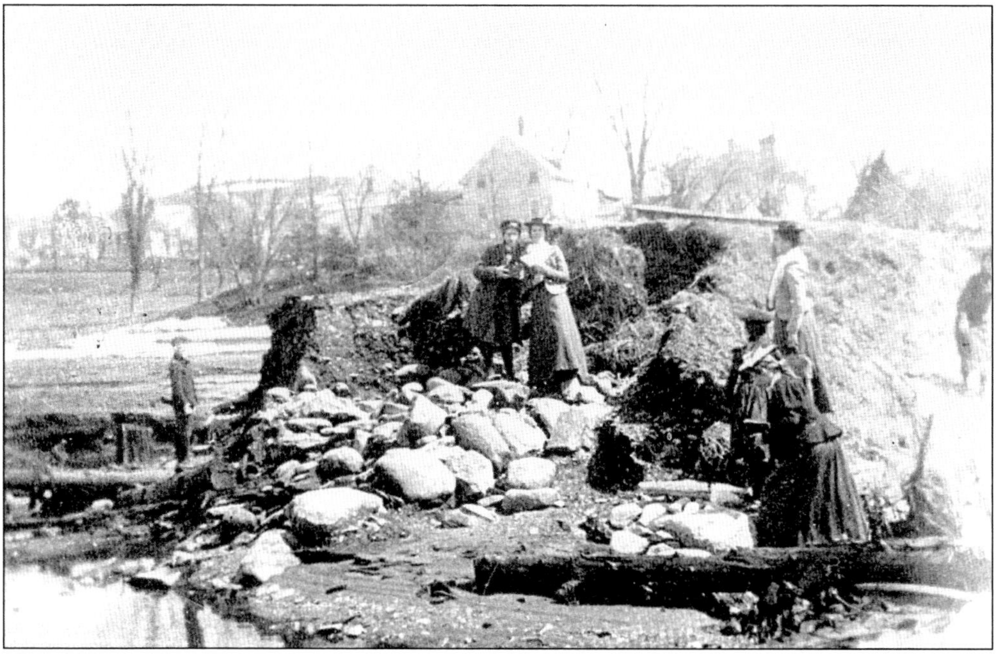

The Brick Mill Dam Washout Draws School Detention. On the night of April 17, 1900, the millpond dam at the Wassookeag Woolen Mill gave way. Enticing 60-degree spring weather melted a long winter's heavy snow and ice, and on April 17, 1900, the millpond dam collapsed near present-day Dexter Shoe on Water Street. Students cut class at Spring Street High School to investigate the dam bursting and got detention for a week. Shown in the photograph are, from left to right, Willis Haines, Grace Moore, Myrtie Folsom, and Marion Small Haseltine (with her camera).

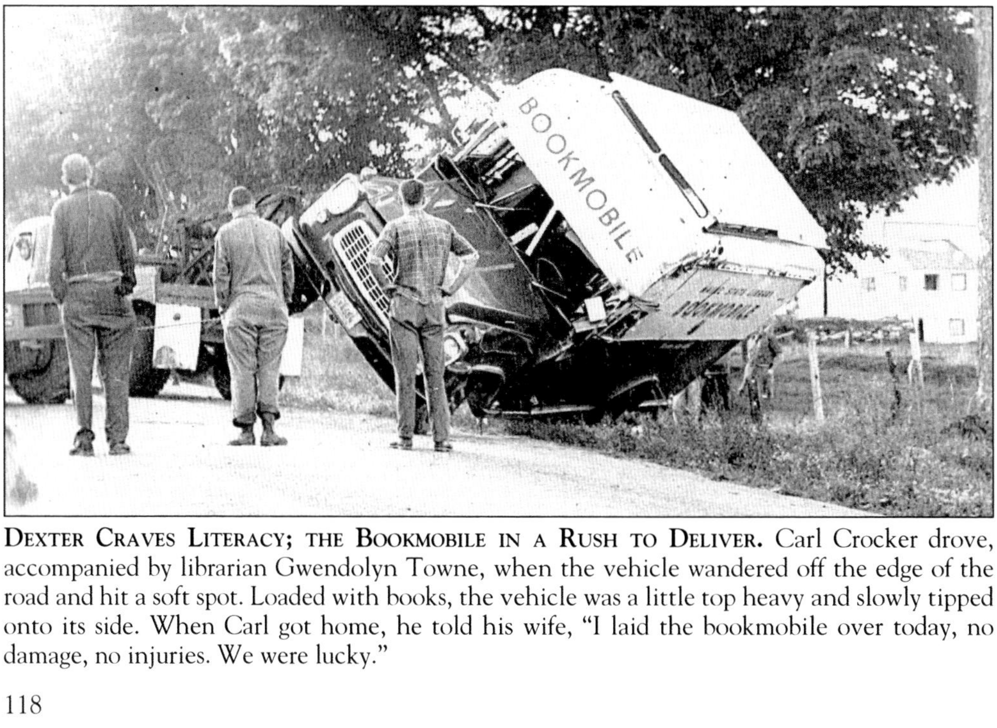

Dexter Craves Literacy; the Bookmobile in a Rush to Deliver. Carl Crocker drove, accompanied by librarian Gwendolyn Towne, when the vehicle wandered off the edge of the road and hit a soft spot. Loaded with books, the vehicle was a little top heavy and slowly tipped onto its side. When Carl got home, he told his wife, "I laid the bookmobile over today, no damage, no injuries. We were lucky."

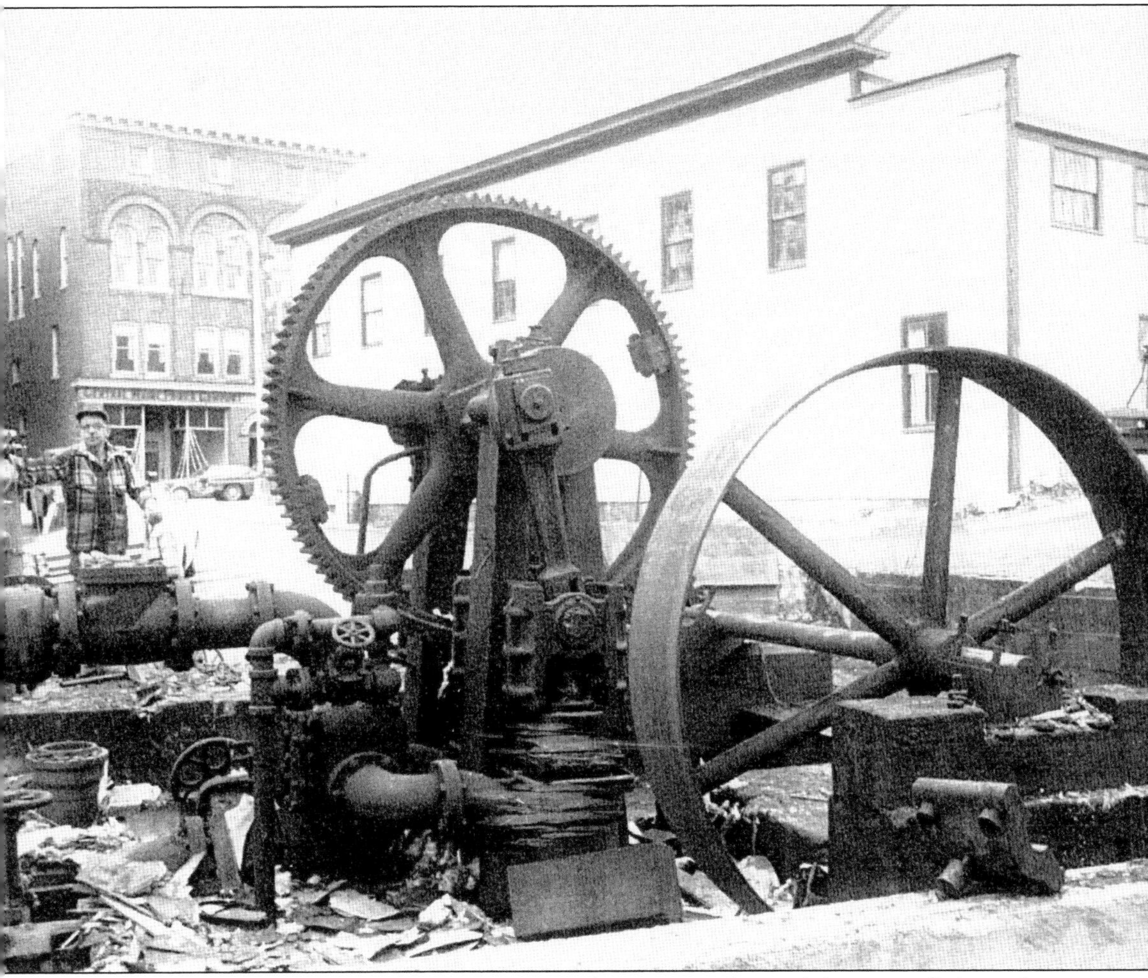

WATERPOWER PUMPS TOWN WATER AT NIGHT. The pump in front of the gristmill (now the Dexter Historical Society Museum) ran by waterpower. It pumped the water from the lake to the reservoir on Upper Main Street. In later years, it ran only at night and an electric motor worked during the day. At the time Clair Wilkins ceased operations of the gristmill *c.* 1965, it was one of the few remaining water-powered mills in central Maine. In the photograph, Leo Murphy works on dismantling the pump.

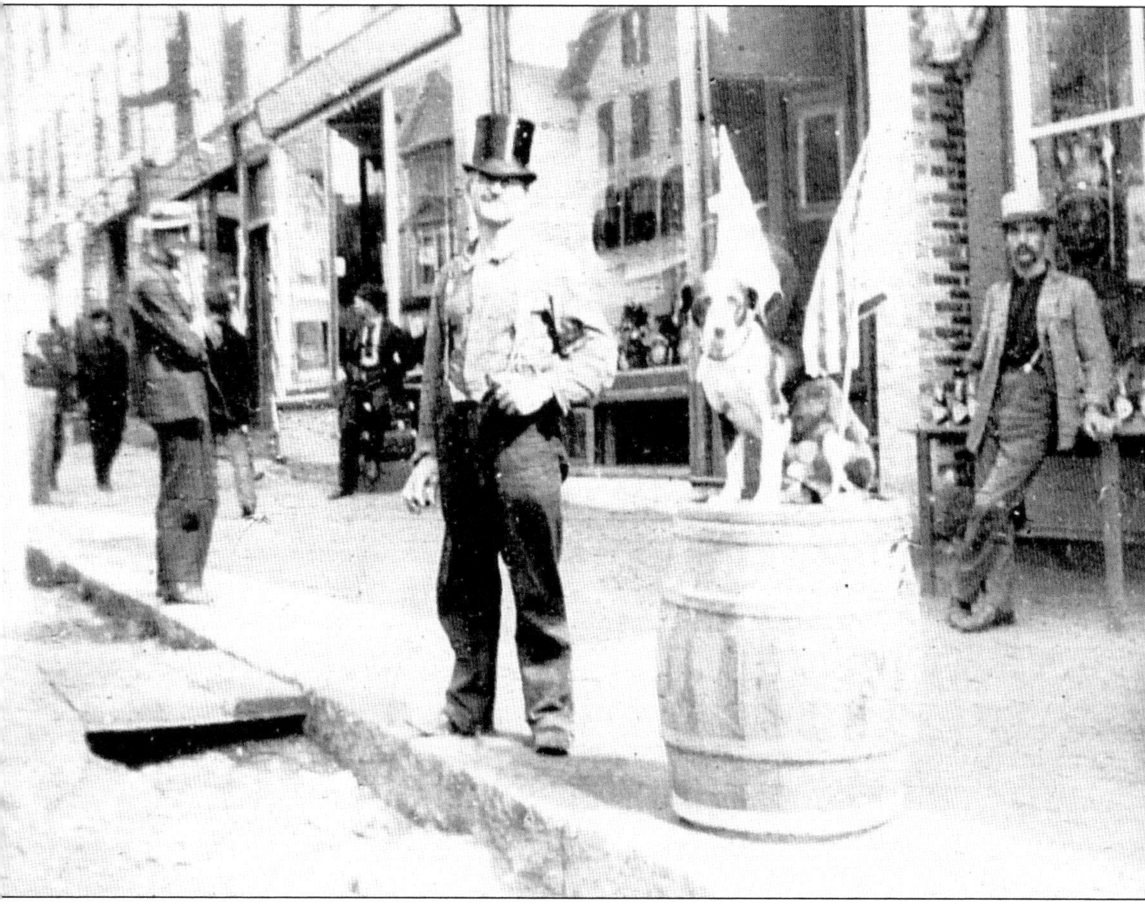

MAIN STREET ALWAYS HAD ITS CHARACTERS. " 'Town characters' . . . With grins Their friends and neighbors hail them, Remark their eccentricities And eagerly retell them. Quaint quirks of gait or speech, Odd dress or comic features Exhibit our originals As rare, outlandish creatures. 'Town characters' . . . We stare, We snicker when we see them, Forgetting, as the years speed by, How soon, perhaps we'll Be them!" (Harold Willard Gleason.)

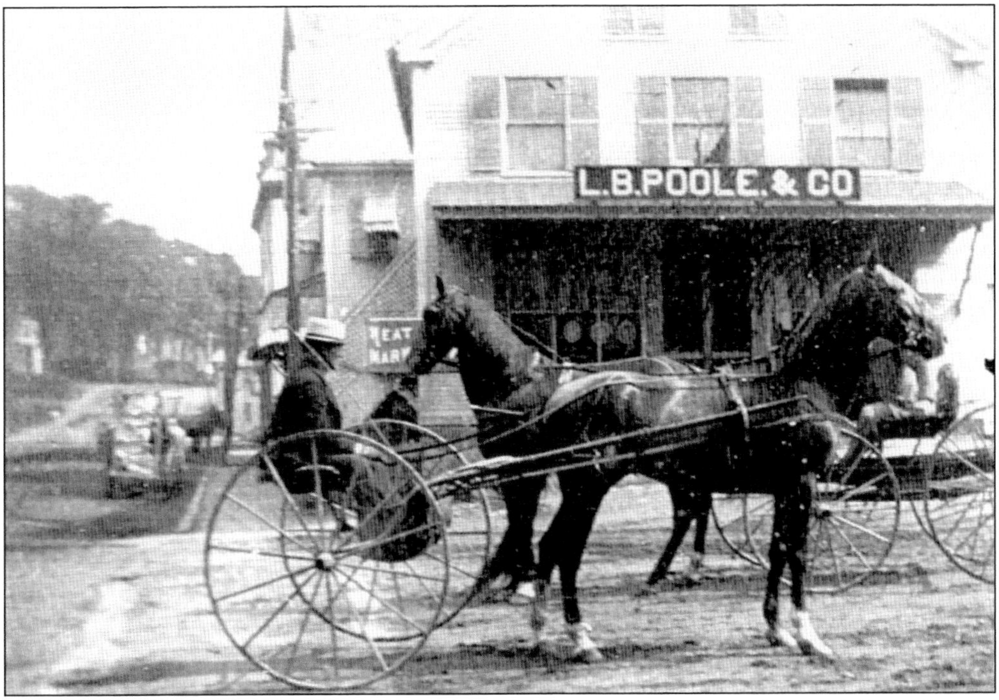

TRAFFIC ON MAIN STREET 100 YEARS AGO. Situated on the corner of Main and Grove Streets (current location of the Dexter Police Department), a well-dressed gentleman drives his sulky past L.B. Poole's clothing store.

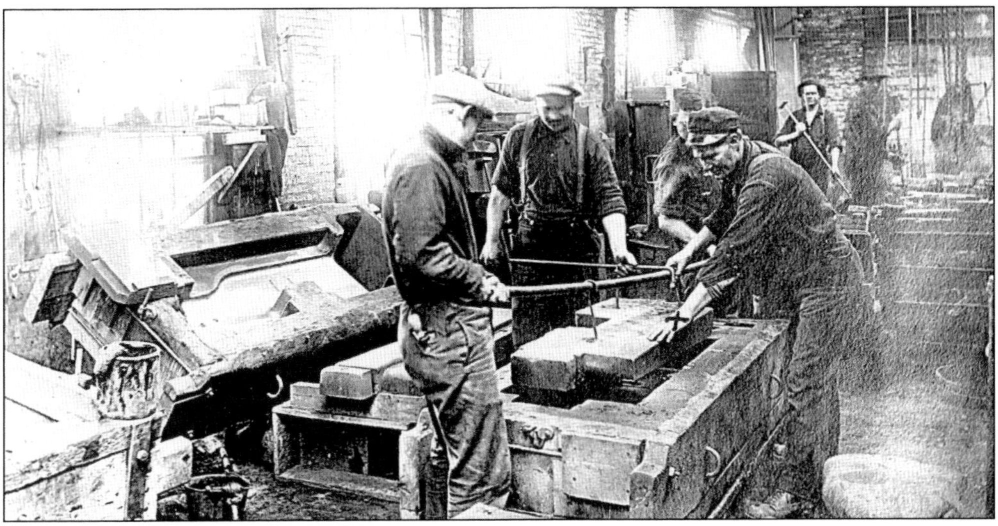

A DEXTER FIREARM IMPLICATED IN THE NOTORIOUS SACCO-VANZETTI CASE. Elbridge Atwater, shown in the center of the photograph, worked in the foundry at Fay and Scott. He had spent some time previously in Norwood, Massachusetts, and while there sold a .38 H&R revolver to Ricardo Orciani, who sold it to Luigi Falzini, who then sold it to Bartolomeo Vanzetti. Vanzetti denied that it was the gun belonging to the guard Alex Berardelli, who was killed during a $15,000 payroll robbery in 1920. Nicola Sacco and Vanzetti were tried, convicted, and ultimately executed for the crime after six years of appeals and worldwide notoriety.

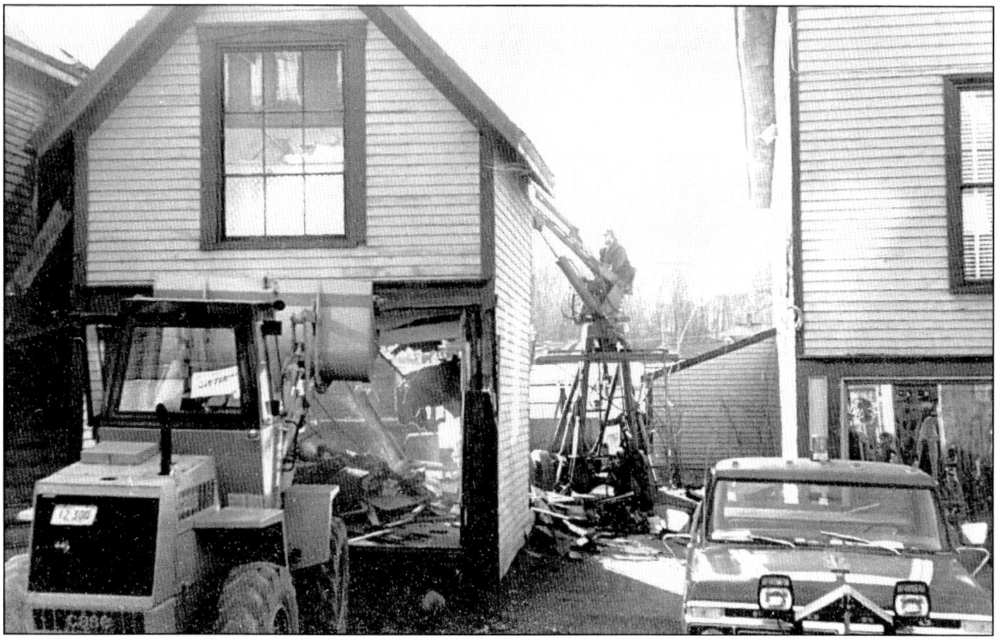

The Ellms Construction Company Taking Down a Main Street Landmark. Built in 1851, this little building on Main Street housed a variety of businesses. It was a jeweler, a milliner, and a barbershop at different times before the 20th century. The loader is seen in front and Chuck Ellms in the rear, demolishing the building *c.* 1980.

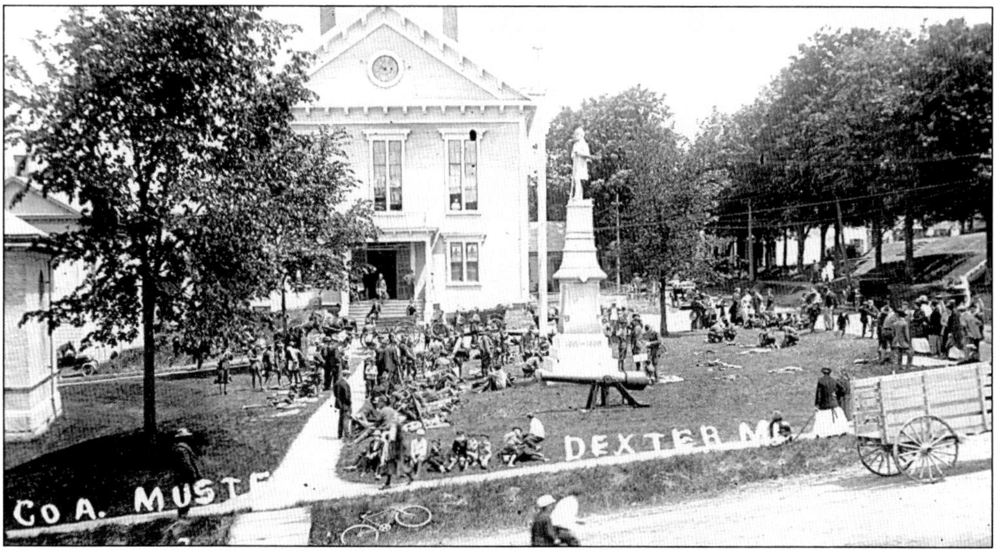

Company A Muster at the Town Hall. "Follow Company A from Dexter down to Kennebunk, where they guarded bridges, up to Camp Keyes in Augusta, for drilling and training, to Camp Bartlett in Westfield, on board the Celtic via New York, Halifax to Liverpool, England, 10 days in camp at Bordon, by train to Southampton, crossing the English Channel on a captured German boat, the arrival in LeHavre France, sightseeing, training in Liffol le Grande, lumbering in the Vosges mountain, building a hospital at Bazoilles, training with the French at Noncourt. Off for the front." (Frank E. Jock, a corporal in Company A, Dexter.)

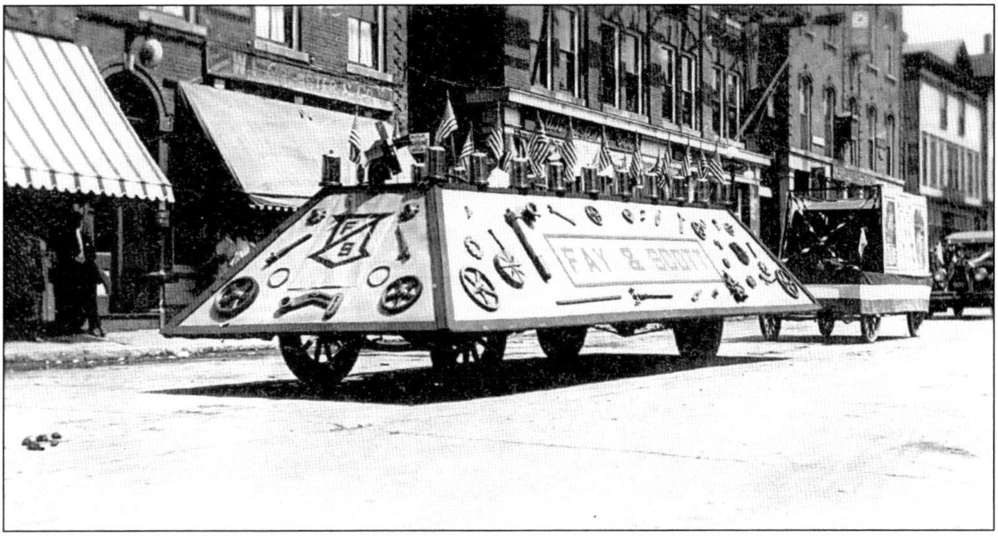

THE FAY AND SCOTT FLOAT IN THE 1925 PARADE. In 1881, N.H. Fay and Walter Scott started a business as general machinists in a building off Main Street. In 1884, they moved to the lower part of town and erected a machine shop and foundry. At one time, they sent their product to all parts of the world.

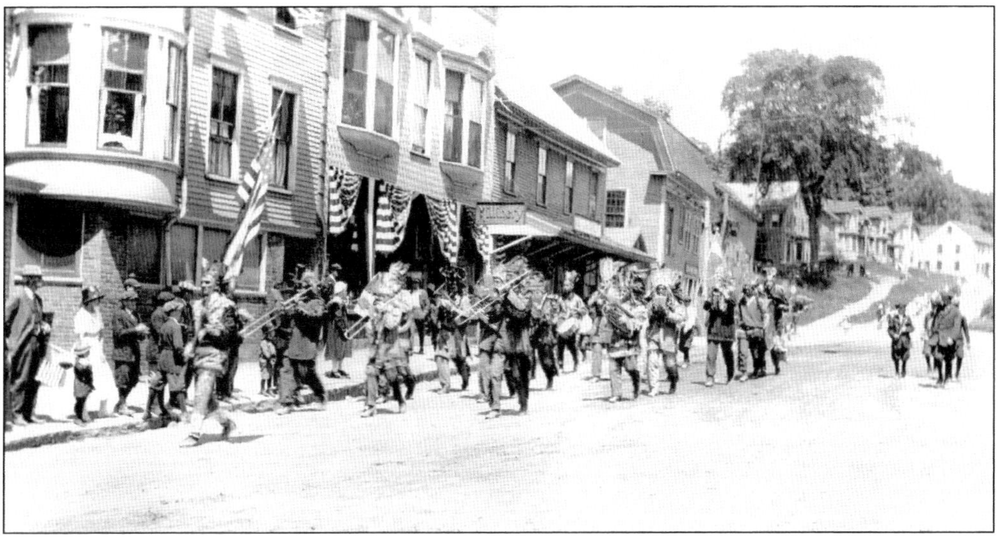

THE INDIAN BAND MARCHES AT THE 1919 "WAR TO END ALL WARS" PARADE. Company A of Dexter was welcomed home after World War I. Dexter lost 10 of the 277 men assigned to defeat the Germans. June 12, 1919, was occasion to celebrate by having a parade on Dexter's Main Street.

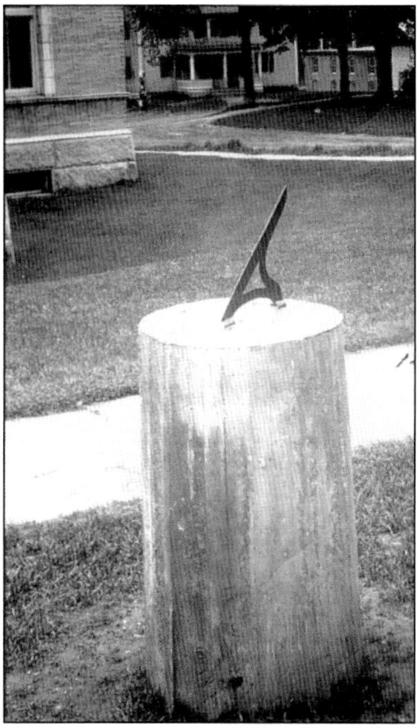

Dexter's Sundial Comes Full Cycle. The sundial on display today in the Dexter Historical Society Museum is not more than 200 feet from its original location. It was "set up by Moses B. Bliss, Esquire, the inventor, from Eau Clair, Wisconsin in 1855 just behind the grist-mill. A lighted candle was nailed to the grist-mill as a record from which to calculate the correct meridian, and complete the adjustment." (From the *Gem and Gazette*, September 1, 1885.) The sundial became lost, and *c.* 1900, when Sam Page saw it in Fogg's Market covering a pork barrel, he purchased it. After Sam's death, Dr. Murphy obtained it from his widow, had it restored, and set it up on the library lawn. It disappeared again sometime in the 1970s only to show up hanging on a nail in Wilson's Welding Shop. Charlie Wilson told me he found it dumped down back of his shop attached to a concrete block. He cut it off the concrete and hung it in his shop. I saw it hanging there and immediately recognized it. It was soon sent to Augusta to be restored again and is now on display on a potato barrel at the gristmill museum.

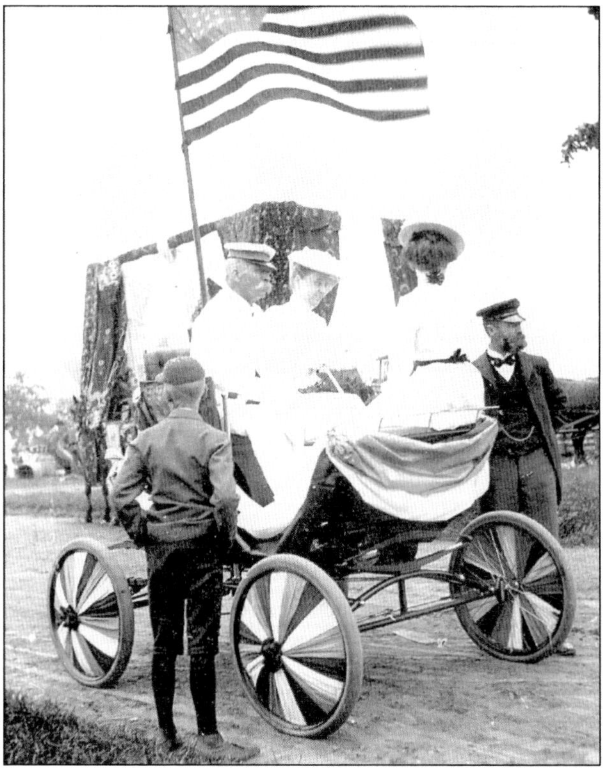

Sam Ireland's Early Locomobile. This automobile, pictured in the 1901 centennial parade, was the second one owned in Dexter. N.H. Fay had the honor of owning the first, a steamer. But the first auto to ever arrive in Dexter was a "St. Louis" driven by Dr. Thomas K. Springall from Malden, Massachusetts, who took three days to make the trip and used 100 gallons of gas in 250 miles. In the 1901 parade, the three autos were put at the very end of the parade so as not to scare the horses, but in 2001, the horses were put at the end of the parade so no one would have to walk through any "deposits" the horses left behind.

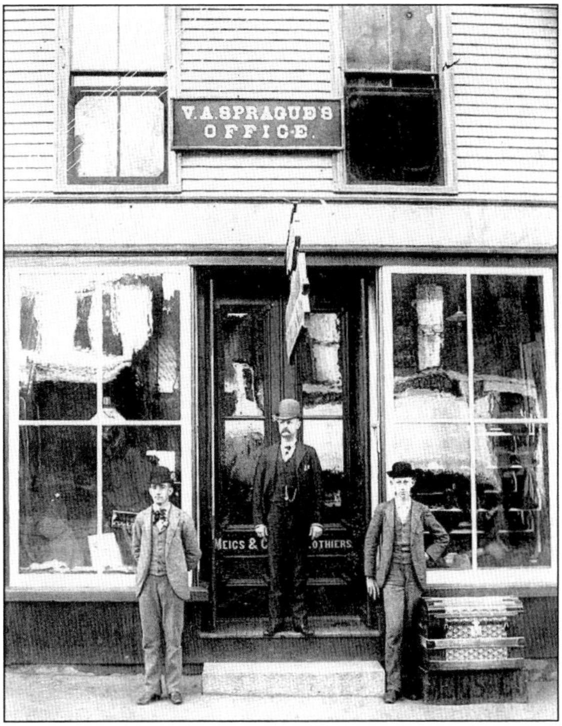

DEXTER CLOTHING HOUSE OWNER MEIGS POSING WITH THE HIRED HELP. This clothing business was established in Dexter in 1875 and had stores in Springfield, Massachusetts, and Bridgeport and New Haven, Connecticut. On the left is Gus Poulin, an enterprising Dexter citizen who invented a hat rack shown in the store window to the right. Gus learned the trade here and eventually had his own store. He was a merchant on the Main Street for most of his life. The sign above is for lawyer Volney Sprague, the son of the early Dexter blacksmith Elijah Sprague. Volney was our local historian and in 1882 wrote a history of Dexter.

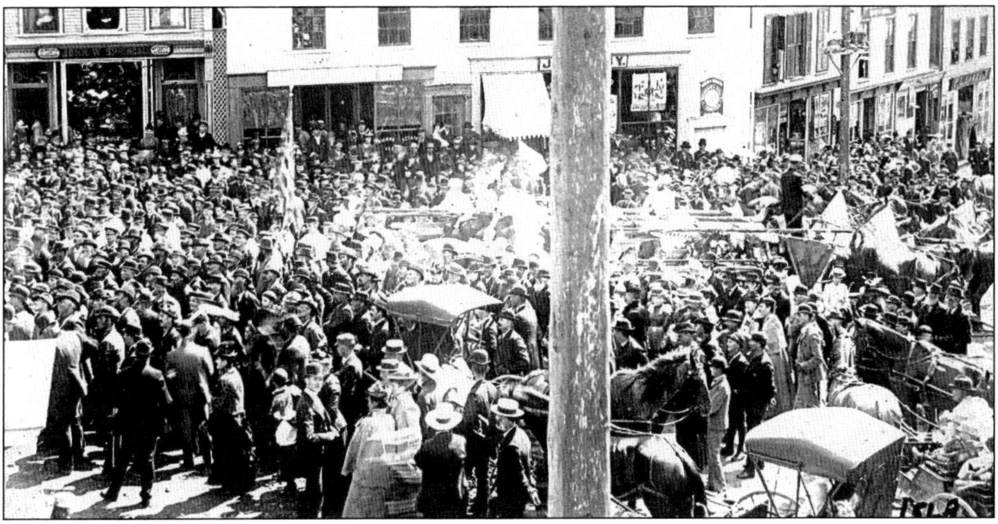

CROWDS FILL MAIN STREET FOR A CELEBRATION. Dexter people like their celebrations, and the one pictured was no exception. Crowds throng to Main Street even today whenever there is an excuse to celebrate. But there are also dark times on Main Street. The store to the far right was owned by P.L. Lowell. Erma Bentley said, "We called him 'Peil' Lowell, and he would shutter and shake like he had the St.Vitus' Dance." On October 31, 1899, when his family was asleep that night, something happened; no one knows for sure. In the morning he was nowhere to be found. Then his coat was found on the bulkhead of the dam on Mill Street. "Dexter people were greatly shocked to learn of the death by drowning in the mill pond of P.L. Lowell. The act was clearly suicidal, being attributed to the ill health and extremely nervous condition in which he had been for some time past." (From the *Eastern Gazette*.)

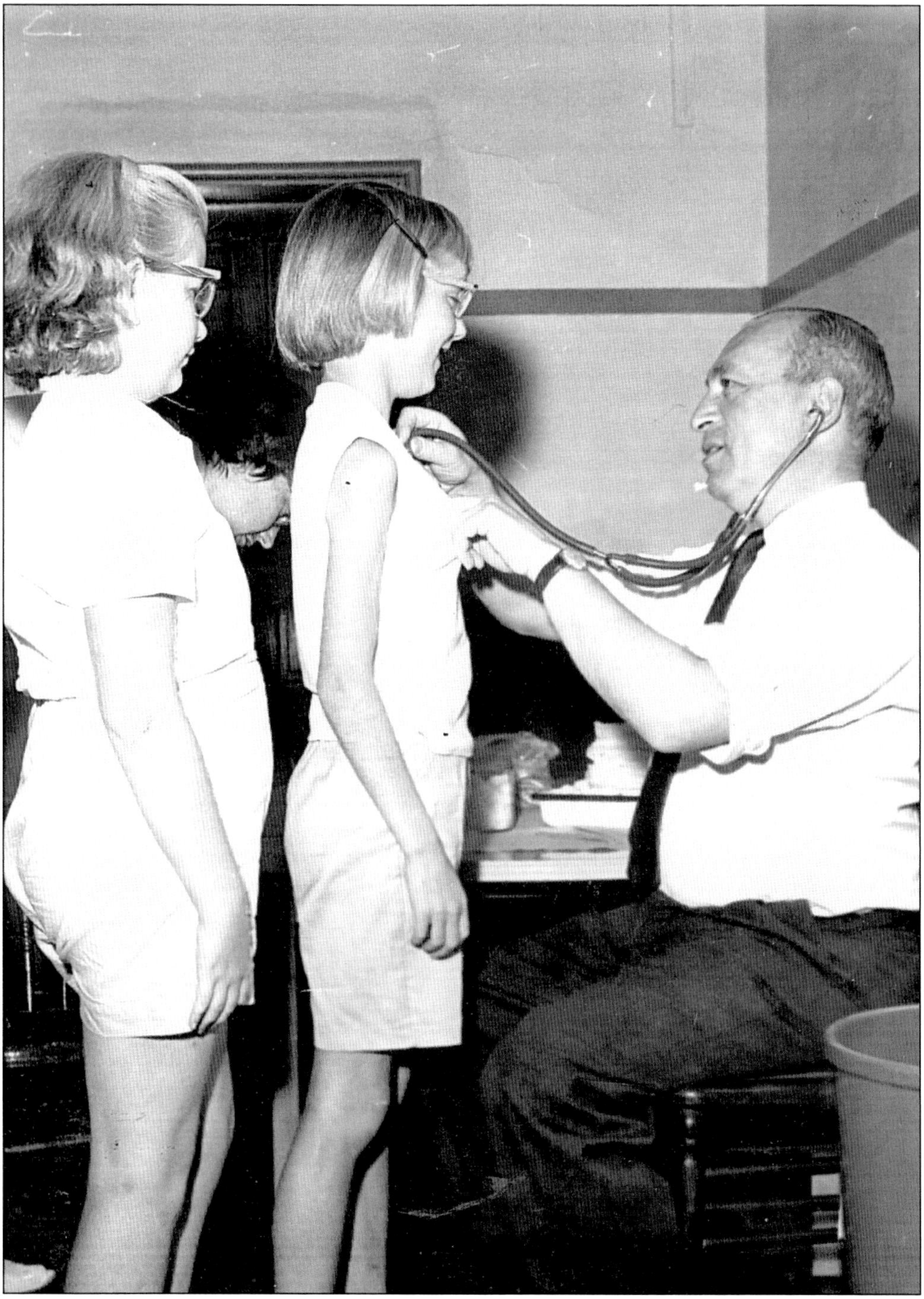

Dr. Shurman Examines the Girl Scouts. Dr. Hans Shurman performed all the school and scout physicals in town. He took his time and personalized each exam. "How's your mom doing," he would ask. He was always interested in what the young people were learning. When injured or sick schoolchildren were brought to his office, Shurman would take them in first, even if the waiting room was full.

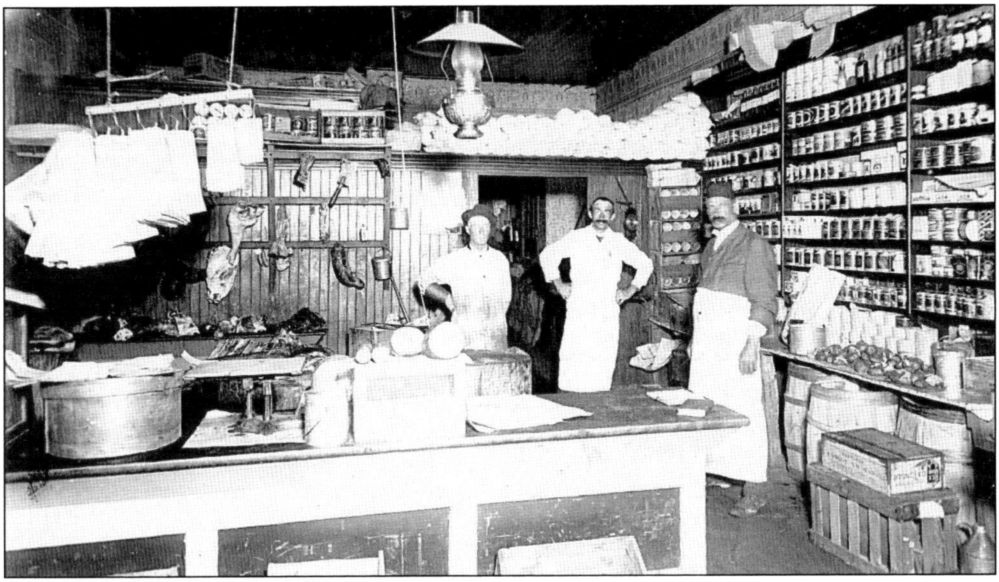

The Local Meat Market Federally Approved? In 1884, when Allen Merrill was 62 years old, he bought the building pictured (the present post office site) and "enlarged it for his dwelling while retaining the basement store," called the People's Market. He later rented the store to several different proprietors, including R.L. Killman. Merrill had tried various business schemes. One was to buy local dried apples at rock-bottom prices from unsuspecting people and mark them up very high and resell them. He recalled one lady that was not fooled; she said "she would rather sit up nights to eat them before she would sell at his price." (From the *Eastern Gazette*, October 9, 1944.)

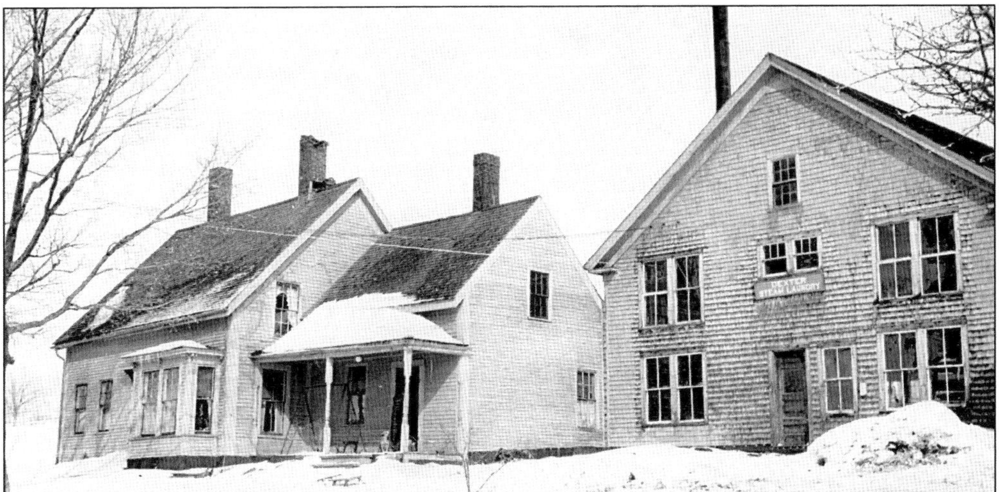

An Attempted Murder Steams up the Laundry. When Fred Wintle was a boy growing up in this house in the 1950s, he was convinced it was haunted. "At the bottom of the stairs, just inside the front entrance he could feel the hairs on the back of his neck bristle." Many years later, he found out why. On February 10, 1930, Merle Cooley shot and wounded Carroll Mace, the owner of the house and the attached Dexter Steam Laundry, on that spot. After his arrest, while still upset because he believed his wife was involved with Mace, Cooley said he was glad he had not killed him.

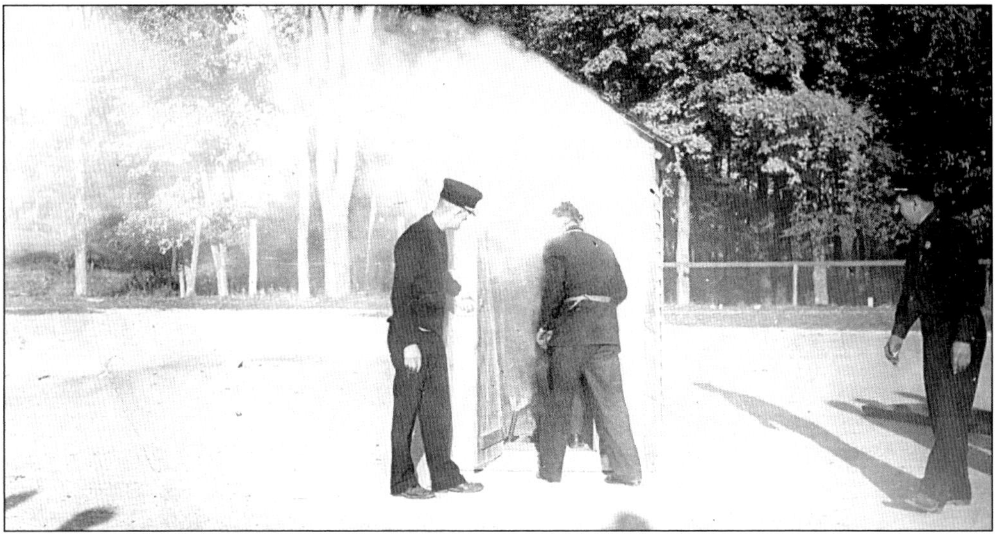

ERNIE ROBINSON EXPERIMENTS WITH A GAS MASK. After World War II, the army donated surplus gas masks to the Dexter Fire Department. The department had no masks of any kind previously, and Ernie volunteered to try one out. The fire squad set up a building at Crosby Park on the ball field and set off a smoke bomb in it. Ernie said the gas masks worked but were not very good. Before they were used, a fireman used to tie a wet bandanna over his face for protection. Ernie spent 42 years as a fireman for Dexter, retiring in 1983. He remembers about 20 people dying in local fires during that time. In the Watson barn fire in 1963, he and Francis Diadone were on their stomachs inside a shed keeping a wall wet to keep the fire from spreading to the house. It worked. These firemen are our local heroes. Pictured, from left to right, are Preston Richardson, Ernie, and Pat Poulin.

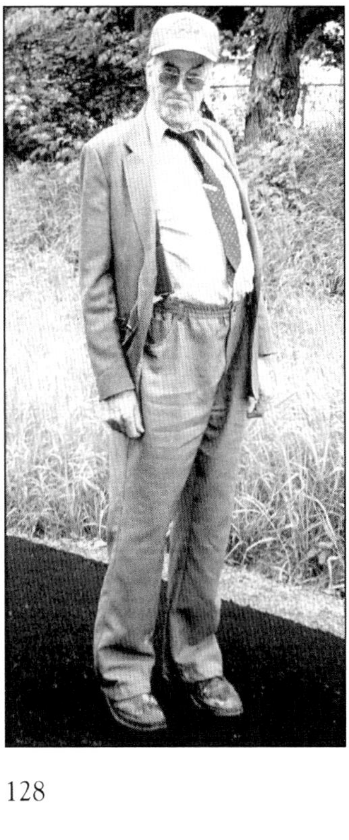

TOM FLANDERS, A MAN ABOUT TOWN. Always a familiar face walking about town, Tom used to leave his job at the Abbott Woolen Mill after second shift around midnight and walk by Kelton's Restaurant on his way home. It was Saturday night about 45 years ago, and we had been to Goodwin's Dance Hall. We always came to Kelton's after the dance to hang around. One night a bunch of us were blocking the sidewalk and would not let Tom pass. Soon after, Dexter had an ordinance that no more than four people could congregate on a sidewalk in Dexter. I wonder if that ordinance is still in existence.